The BIBLE creative

BY DENNIS C. BENSON

THE GOSPEL OF JOHN

group BOOKS

Box 481 • Loveland, CO 80539

THE BIBLE CREATIVE: THE GOSPEL OF JOHN

Copyright ©1983 by Dennis C. Benson

Library of Congress Catalog No. 83-80945

ISBN 0936-664-12-6

All rights reserved. No part of this book may be reproduced in any manner whatsoever without written permission, from the publisher, except in the case of brief quotations embodied in critical articles and reviews. For information write Permissions, Group Books, P.O. Box 481, Loveland, CO 80539.

CREDITS

Edited by Lee Sparks
Designed by Laurel Watson

The scripture quotations in this publication are from the Revised Standard Version of the Bible, copyrighted 1946, 1952 ©1971, 1973 by the Division of Christian Education of the National Council of the Churches of Christ in the U.S.A., and used by permission.

Contents

Not a Word More—Not a Word Less:
Introducing **The Bible Creative** series 5
Introducing the Gospel of John 16
Chapter 1 20
Chapter 2 42
Chapter 3 54
Chapter 4 70
Chapter 5 82
Chapter 6 96
Chapter 7 110
Chapter 8 124
Chapter 9 142
Chapter 10 154
Chapter 11 168
Chapter 12 182
Chapter 13 196
Chapter 14 208
Chapter 15 218
Chapter 16 230
Chapter 17 242
Chapter 18 254
Chapter 19 268
Chapter 20 282
Chapter 21 294
Glossary 306
The Holy Spirit at Work:
Contributors to **The Bible Creative** 310

Dedication

To Marilyn Benson—friend and lover

Not a Word More—Not a Word Less: Introducing The Bible Creative Series

The Word of God stands on its own feet. The Word does not need crutches. Nor does it need to be extracted or expanded. The Bible as it stands is the primary source of our faith, inspiration and life; it is the historical witness to God's redemptive action in the interest of his people.

Why then are biblical study lessons and preaching often so boring? Isn't it surprisingly common for communicators and teachers of the Bible to imagine a vast chasm separating the ancient biblical texts from contemporary human needs? Unfortunately, many times that chasm is not bridged: The hearers of words on the Word are often unmoved, uninspired and unchanged.

Each of us has suffered through more than a few limp sermons and stale learning experiences. And some of us have come away from these experiences with the resolve to "make the Bible relevant to today." A flood of resources has tried to satisfy a superhuman quest for making the Bible modern and relevant for the contemporary person.

The Bible Creative shuns this temptation. We draw from a very different well. Our task is not to "make" the Bible relevant. Our task is to help *ourselves* become more and more relevant to scripture—not scripture to us. We seek to understand the Bible by standing on its own ground in our roles as teachers, speakers and preachers.

What The Bible Creative Is Not

The Bible Creative is not dependent on group dynamics. There are many study books and aids that approach the Bible from particular group process methods. These materials are very helpful to those whose first desire is to unify a group of individuals. While **The Bible Creative** utilizes such approaches at several points, our methods are dictated primarily by the text itself.

The Bible Creative does not focus on literary criticism methods. Some of the more helpful resources for biblical study are those that discover the fresh meanings and implications of the Bible's words, structures and language idioms. While we acknowledge this important study, the biblical text as received remains our primary guide for teaching, speaking and preaching.

The Bible Creative is not rooted in cultural art forms. A few resources for biblical communication provide examples of fine art, poetry, drama and other creative forms. Such collections are helpful to a point. Our task, however, focuses on how *you* can create your own art forms for communicating the gospel.

The Bible Creative is not devoted primarily to historical-critical exegesis. There is a full and rich legacy of commentaries on the Bible. Our work does not duplicate such classic material. Indeed, we encourage you to use your traditional commentaries as a companion to our work here.

The Bible Creative is not a collection of simplistic Bible study gimmicks. We do not search for clever tricks to communicate the gospel. Rather, we allow the text to suggest how it should be communicated. This series is not a "quick fix" for a troubled educational or preaching situation. There is no shortcut to careful study, preparation and presentation. This series does not do your work for you. But it does offer a bench mark for igniting your imagination and teaching.

The Bible Creative is not a "Lone Ranger" endeavor. I have enlisted talents and ideas from scores of faithful brothers and sisters representing a rich diversity of interests in the faith community. This worldwide community of people is not burrowed away from the world. They actively work with, suffer with and rejoice with other people. This series is a child of this community's diverse interests: group dynamics, literature, fine arts, drama, Bible scholarship and theology, education, etc. **The Bible Creative** is both by and for those craving to share how the Word might become flesh in our teaching, speaking and preaching.

What The Bible Creative Is:
The Wine and the Wineskin

We've mentioned a few things **The Bible Creative** is not. So what is it? We are convinced that teachers, speakers and preachers of the Bible need not search far to find creative ways to communicate the gospel. Indeed, the Bible shows not only its content but also suggests ways to present its content. The content suggests the form of proclamation! The "wineskin" of the gospel is as important as the "wine" to us.

Our goal in this series is to help you communicate the Word in ways the Word suggests. Research and interpretation are part of the task. Yet the teaching and preaching ideas offered here are both for you to use and to generate your own creative thoughts, ideas, programs and sermons. **The Bible Creative** is a map to point a few ways to help the text find its way from printed paper to the received Word of God in the people.

The simplicity and beauty of this approach are that the more deeply we dig into the text, the more ideas for teaching and preaching emerge. This simple approach will transform your view of scripture as well as the way you present it.

Perhaps all of this seems "too simple to be true." When one faces the challenge of something new or different, it is easy to dismiss it. It is even more tempting to disregard ideas that call for unfamiliar or uncomfortable tasks. **The Bible Creative** will set new options for you. Please resist initial reactions that an idea is silly or unworkable. Remember that these ideas come from people who are living the Word with the community of faith. They themselves have risked these kinds of things in their own teaching and preaching.

And consider that Jesus met all kinds of needs in all kinds of ways. He was an amazing teacher and preacher. He appealed not only to the intellect but also to the spirit and the senses. The fact that God became flesh and dwelt among us is the most amazing example of wholistic unity of form and content in human history! Jesus was both the wine and the wineskin.

How can we timidly present the gospel after such a model? When we stand before God in final judgment, he will understand how we might have risked in presenting the Word and failed. But how will we explain to him why we made the gospel boring?

The Genesis of The Bible Creative

"You disappoint me, Dennis," Charlie Shedd told me as he shook his head. He and his wife, Martha, were treating me to breakfast while honestly confronting my failure to tackle my Bible resource idea. Two years earlier I had shared my plans with him. "You have to do it now!" Charlie told me. He even contacted publishers for me. Yet I was afraid to undertake this project. Would it be accepted seriously? Would it make a difference in the lives of people?

I had struggled with those questions for years. In the mid-1960s Roger Boekenhauer and I were pastors of mission churches in bordering communities. In our first meetings together we complained about the denomination's incredibly poor planning in placing two churches at the end of a highway that was never completed! But our mutual friendship and faith soon led us to confess that we were not celebrating the Christ of hope with our litany of despair.

We formed a pastoral covenant and agreed to co-lead a Bible study for the people from the two congregations. We halted our young pastors' helter-skelter schedules (non-stop calling on prospective members, teaching, preaching, hospital calls, etc.) for one day each week. Roger and I spent the whole day as a retreat for study, prayer and preparation. We struggled with the teaching methods for our joint Bible study. How could we best engender in our people a sense of awe, understanding and love for the Bible so that their lives would be changed? Eventually we ended our search where it began—the Bible itself! Our method for that Bible study became the prototype of **The Bible Creative**: The biblical material determines the method of communicating the message!

The discovery changed our lives as we looked to the scriptures for both the content *and* the form of our teaching and preaching. Our ministries were more joyful and simple. The discovery also exposed some of the flaws in our ministerial training. If we're biblical preachers why should we transform the Bible week after week into sermons with three points and a few illustrations? Should a parable, for example, be treated the same as a historical narrative? Was God saying something to us about the content by preserving the message in a particular form?

The Bible Creative Is From and For the Faith Community

The generating force for **The Bible Creative** is the faith community. Our contributors are all active in the church. Their ideas and clues for teaching and preaching from the text were mixed and matched with my own to create the resource you're holding. These ideas are intended to bring life into your faith community.

We also realize that the Word has come to use from a given people in a given context. The gospel today was also gospel to the faith community throughout a vast history. We read and believe the witness of another time and an earlier "tribe." The intersection of the ancient texts with the contemporary believer produces a moment of mystical and practical power. We must interpret the texts in a way that authentically bridges the past, present and future in the history of salvation. Such bridge building is at the very heart of discipleship.

We consider the faith community the "air we breathe" in our roles as teachers, speakers and preachers. It is in this environment that our ideas are planted, nourished and harvested.

I also kept nine areas of research in mind as I worked through these ideas. Since these areas are the *context* from which I worked, they may not be readily apparent in the ideas unless they in some way directly aid the task at hand:

1. Establish the text. The ancient texts have thousands of variant readings. No original document of our Bible exists. We only have copies of copies of copies. Yet one is still able to determine the most likely reading of the text.

2. The context of particular passages. Very few biblical passages stand alone. We must think about what comes before and after the passage, the purpose of the book, similar ideas in other parts of the Bible, etc.

3. The study of words. What do some of the words in their original language add to our task?

4. Other ancient writings. What extra-biblical materials contemporary to the Bible might add to understanding? For example, gnostic and Qumran writings indicate some of the problems confronted by the writer in the Gospel of John.

5. The Apostolic Fathers. Their writings, written shortly after the time of our New Testament, often refer to biblical books and give an idea how they were interpreted in the early church.

6. The apologists. As Christianity grew to a major world force, these writers explained and defended the faith to a curious yet unbelieving Roman world.

7. The classic church fathers. After the church replaced the Roman Empire as the dominant institution in the civilized world, these writers defined and clarified the faith. Their use of the Bible in settling internal disputes is particularly interesting.

8. The Reformers. Martin Luther and John Calvin have been particularly useful. Their "rediscovery" of a personal God in the scriptures is most helpful for our modern-day interpretation of the Bible.

9. Modern thinkers. Karl Barth (who may be to theology what Einstein was to physics) was particularly helpful in his fine biblical discussions.

While we have respect for the wealth of scholarship available to us all, **The Bible Creative** is firstly committed to helping local teachers and preachers (both professional and volunteer lay people) develop ideas for instilling in their people a lifestyle inspired by God's Word.

The Format of The Bible Creative

It is easy to find your way around in **The Bible Creative**. Each chapter in each volume corresponds to a chapter in a book of the Bible. And each chapter is composed of four parts: the biblical text, "Creative Commentary on the Scripture," "Creative Bible Study Ideas" and "Creative Speaking and Preaching Ideas."

Creative Commentary on the Scripture: The task of **The Bible Creative** is not to duplicate any commentary on the Bible. Our primary task is to be a catalyst for creative Bible study, speaking and preaching in local churches. Therefore our notes on the text are very sparse in relation to the creative ideas and clues. Study of the text, however, is the necessary starting point for creative ideas.

We have intentionally kept commentary on the text to a minimum. We have passed along only those clues from the text that might trigger creative ideas for experiential Bible study, speaking and preaching.

One of the hardest tasks of putting together **The Bible Creative** was sorting through the wealth of research on the biblical text's historical setting and critical issues. Serious biblical study is one of the more exciting areas offered to the faith community. It is a shame that most Christians never have an opportunity (or interest?) to immerse themselves in the rich legacy of biblical scholarship. Yet it is so helpful in communicating the Bible with fresh and authentic ideas. So we urge you to use and enjoy a good standard commentary as a companion to **The Bible Creative**. I have listed a few of my personal favorites under "Commentaries" in the glossary.

Creative Bible Study Ideas: The undergirding of a person's faith is his or her learning experience in the Christian community. To neglect one's Christian education is to assemble carelessly a weak, jumbled and incomplete foundation of faith.

The Christian faith is historical. We are the people of God not only in the present but also related to the past and future. Christian education is the key to transferring the historical faith to others.

Many religious teachers have felt great anxiety in their calling. We fear that the "substance" of the faith is somehow not received in our students. These fears are justified when we face adults and young people who do not even know half of the Ten Commandments, much less who or whose they are in the faith.

The "Creative Bible Study Ideas" section of **The Bible Creative** presents a substantially different approach to learning/teaching. We are wholistic in our methods. We offer ideas for learning for all aspects of human personality. Our ideas aim for students' intellect, emotions, spirit and behavior. Our goal is not to merely pass the content of the Bible on to our students. We also emphasize helping the students *experience* the emotions and spirit of the story. And we don't stop the Bible study at the end of the session. Where possible, we offer ideas for learning by *doing* something authentic for God and his world. Our methods, suggested by the biblical text, help students learn by thinking, feeling and doing.

Our contributors to this section come from a variety of teaching situations. Their students cut across age groups, interest and faith development. Yet these ideas are workable for you in your situation. You are the key to transferring them to your students' needs. God has given you plenty of creative abilities to do just that. And we've defined terms that may be unfamiliar in a glossary. But we must leave it to you to pull together fragments of ideas and mold them into a new creation.

A good part of successful teaching is knowing the "pulse" of your students. Search out their needs. Best of all, draw them in your circle for planning and teaching. It is no secret that the one teaching a class learns far more than the students. So allow your people to learn by sharing the spotlight with them.

Another hint to good teaching: Recognize your students' abilities. We assume in **The Bible Creative** that the Holy Spirit has delivered your students to you. Their path to you may have been poorly paved. But at least they are there. Trust them. Believe in them. Sometimes they will appear uninterested in the faith and even less interested in changing the situation. I have experienced such painful moments. But I've also experienced golden moments when students see the light and it all comes together powerfully.

How does one move from a traditional approach to the studies offered in **The Bible Creative**? I can't blame people who feel shocked when something is forced on them like a terrorist raid. Remember: Pull no unexpected surprises. You may need to organize a new study group for a multi-week course as an "experimental" setting for experiential learning. Recruit a class with a clear understanding that these sessions will be taught differently. You might even publicize the course something like this: "Danger: Creative encounter with the Bible. Expect the unexpected."

Once you've assembled your group, join in a covenant that recognizes the class as a community of faith. Make another covenant for expectations of the students: attendance, participation, costs, etc.

Finally, give the gospel straight. I believe we have been far too timid about presenting the gospel's cost of discipleship. To embrace Christ is to embrace peace. Yet we also embrace the pain and suffering of the world in order to bring it to Christ. The methods in **The Bible Creative** are intended to inspire the students to embrace Christ and, in turn, the world. Join us in this fascinating and wondrous journey.

Creative Speaking and Preaching Ideas: The full meaning of "gospel" in Greek is both the message and the medium. The Good News of Christ *must* be proclaimed. The word "gospel" is yet another example of the Bible's intricate connection of form and content. The implication is clear: How we preach is nearly as important as what we preach.

The sermon, homily or message is probably the most common characteristic among Christian churches throughout the world, cutting through all cultural and denominational barriers. And speaking-preaching has always held a special place among the gifts in the church.

The preacher is a person to be envied and consoled. What a wonderful calling! How special it is to share the life-changing story of Jesus' life, death and resurrection! Yet preaching also is a heavy burden. It is so easy for the preacher to cloud the pure and simple proclamation. The preacher faces constant tensions: What is Christ and what is cultural religion? Should I risk my job to preach on touchy issues?

The heaviest burden on preachers is simply the danger of boredom. There is a fatigue factor at play when a single person prepares and delivers 50 or more sermons a year. The task tends to become the same over and over. We want to reduce it, to tame it, to a manageable size. Three points and illustrations can a sermon make. At that point the act of gospel has deteriorated into an old wineskin.

The faith community simply will not tolerate "old wineskin" sermons indefinitely. Our culture is rapidly changing. We live in an age of mass media and computers. Yet our preaching reflects the models developed over 100 years ago. Our preaching and speaking models must speak to this age lest they become dinosaurs waiting for the weather to change.

The "Creative Speaking and Preaching Ideas" sections in **The Bible Creative** offer new wineskins for sermons, talks, homilies, etc. As with the "Creative Bible Study Ideas" section, we look to the biblical text for clues on what to preach and how to preach it.

Our preaching section is far different than the dozens of books with illustrations for sermons. It is different from the commentaries for preachers. (Most of these are similar to television commentators after a presidential speech—they tell what was said, and then throw in some context, explanations and less-than-subtle biased opinions.)

We challenge preachers to break out of the mold. Loosen that white-knuckled grip on the pulpit! Jesus became flesh in order that we might know salvation and *how* to share it!

He used all kinds of media: story, dialogue, drama, miracles, objects. We are challenging preachers to enjoy the variety of speaking-preaching methods inspired by the biblical texts.

The faith community craves contemporary preaching. It is one of the few acts of worship in which most worshipers enjoy innovation. Music, liturgy and sacraments are far more resistant to change than the preaching-speaking moment. So challenge yourself to seek the undiscovered "new worlds" of preaching. God be with you as you listen to the Bible for new wineskins for creative speaking and preaching.

The Last Word Before the Feast

I hope that the rich spirit of **The Bible Creative** has caught hold of you. There is something very special happening when kindred spirits gather to proclaim the Word to our fearful and broken world. The Holy Spirit provides a kinship that spans all time and space. The brothers and sisters in the faith who came before us are here cheering as we struggle in a common task.

My respect and appreciation for those who communicate the gospel are enormous. I have been criticized because my attitude and work assumes that people in local churches are creative, courageous and risking. Critics have called me naive. Yet I seem to find the kind of people I expect: The people of God are the most creative and resourceful people on Earth!

No last word is complete without a few words about evaluation. Marilyn, my wife and co-worker, likes to help evaluate my work by asking a simple question: "So what? What difference will it make?" We ask you to evaluate the process and result of this series with that simple question. We pray that this series will help you bear the gospel to your people in a given moment, in a given place and in a unique context.

If you follow the way of **The Bible Creative**, there will be moments of butterflies and failure. But there will also be fantastic successes. Regardless of how these ideas work, we believe your life and ministry will be substantially changed. You'll free your imagination with new and exciting understandings of scripture and methods for communicating them.

We are asking you to join in a task that does not lend itself to easy evaluation. Feedback to your efforts may be confusing. People may like what we are doing and still we have failed. People may be outraged with our teaching and preaching but we have been faithful to our calling. I remember my first teaching assignment. I was a college student trying to pour the Bible into the hearts of uninterested high school kids in Sunday school. I tried just about anything. After class one Sunday, Jim stopped and put his arm on my shoulder. The tall jock was not known to enjoy Sunday school. He looked me in the eye and gave me his ultimate compliment: "Benson, baby, you make it painless Christianity." I was thankful for the feedback but also a bit uncomfortable. The gospel is not painless! Yet Jim apparently was encountering God through the Bible in a significant way.

So go easy on yourself when you ask, in the dark of the evening, whether your efforts to communicate the gospel in new wineskins worked or not. If you approach the receivers of the gospel with respect and integrity, they will respond to you in kind. Most of all, be prepared intellectually, emotionally and spiritually for your teaching and preaching experiences. And if it still doesn't work, so be it. Perhaps the most Christlike response to your efforts will be something like this: "I didn't get much out of what we did this morning, but I appreciate what you're trying to do. Keep at it."

We encourage you to allow God to use you in new and creative ways as you seek to proclaim the gospel. We are delighted that you are joining us in this courageous journey. We dedicate this series to the glory of God and the proclamation of the Word. May God continue to bless us with courage as we creatively risk for others.

Dennis C. Benson
Pittsburgh, Pennsylvania

Introducing the Gospel of John

The old man stomps one foot at a time and slowly rubs his freezing hands together as he tries to shake off the blanket of cold wrapped around him. The city streets stir with thousands of pedestrians going here and there. The light changes and a mass of people start across the intersection. The old man's worn face suddenly brightens. He draws a fist full of tracts from his coat pocket and eagerly approaches the first person to cross the street. "Get your passport to salvation," he says to a surprised woman. She looks puzzled as he hands her a reprint of the Gospel of John. "This book saved me from my sinful life and led me to follow the Lord Jesus." She turns abruptly and goes on her way, throwing the fourth Gospel into the street.

This brief scene offers a history of the fourth Gospel. The Gospel of John has been revered, rejected, reviled and deeply respected by generations of Christians. John seems to have drawn and repelled people from the very first. There were those who squirmed at John's tone differences from the other three Gospels. Others tried to discredit John by assigning it a late composition date or pointing at the strange company it once kept. Some of the enthusiasts in the early church who embraced the book were among the first heretics. Gnostics (those who claimed special personal knowledge about God) were often linked to this Gospel. Fortunately, the power of the Gospel of John was eventually accepted by the church and recognized for its place in God's Word.

The centrality of Jesus in John has inspired millions of people to follow Christ. Most of the materials used to reach those outside of the faith come from passages in the fourth Gospel. A majority of the Christian songs written in our time are drawn from ideas and images in this book. And John 3:16 still stands as the favorite summary of the Christian faith.

The period of the early church provides very limited documentation about the original text of John. We have copies of copies of copies of the canonical (chosen) books of the New Testament. There are scant writings from the church and the secular community of the first centuries. Time and systematic "cleansing" of undesirable materials by the winners in dogmatic disputes have left us with very little information about the history of our texts.

The book's author has long been a topic of debate and speculation. Was there a John as author about whom we have no knowledge? The disciple of Jesus? A school of writers? The mysterious "beloved" disciple? It does seem clear that we cannot be sure. The language of the book would suggest that the author had Hebrew as his background language and was probably writing from Syria. The Gospel of John was probably written between the later years of the first century and the early years of the second century. And, incidentally, the oldest known manuscript of the New Testament is a small papyrus scrap containing a few words from the Gospel of John.

The order of the book has also been the subject of much study by those who read the text carefully as a literary document. When put under the lens of careful reasoning, it seems that the Gospel's flow of events are logistically incorrect. There are abrupt transitions where Jesus is placed in locations where the story would not logically suggest. Rudolf Bultmann (a German Bible scholar) and others have suggested that the state of the book as we now have it is not the original form. They assume that the book somehow has come to us in a rearranged form. There is also the difficulty of chapter 8. This powerful story does not appear in any of the early manuscripts.

These concerns are important and provide some of the most interesting areas of biblical study. Those who point out these problems, however, are not able to provide very convincing alternatives to the Gospel of John's form as it stands. The centrality of the message is clear and vital. The interpreter and communicator of the fourth Gospel need not focus on these particular problems. While we seriously acknowledge the textual and transmissive issues concerning John, we accept, for our task, the Gospel as it stands.

We are listening to what the passages say to us. It is important to be aware of the questions raised in the course of our encounter with the Word, but that is not our primary task. We look to the Word for teaching, speaking and preaching. Our guiding question is: How does the text suggest that we communicate its message with our people in a given time and place?

The Gospel of John is presented in an interesting communication structure. It is hard to develop a definitive outline of the book. There have been a number of interesting proposals. It can be seen as a book of signs or miracles provoked by Jesus on his road to the fulfillment of his ministry. We are then given manifestations of his glory, his farewell discourse and his passion. The book ends with a postscript (chapter 21).

The Gospel of John has a dramatic appeal to it that invites us to explore and create experiential ideas for creative study, speaking and preaching. Why should we limit ourselves to unimaginative presentations when the very nature of God's outreach to us comes through a most wondrous and dramatic mode of communication?

The Gospel of John is an exciting challenge for those who embark upon the experiential or "new wineskin" approach to teaching and preaching the Bible. It is both particular and speculative in its presentation of Jesus. John's rich use of images (e.g., light/darkness, life/death, new/old) pulls us out of our limiting vision of God's call. These themes bump up against powerful particular stories of times and people who meet the Word become flesh. This tension between the smell of sweat and the glory of heavenly light is a wonderful gift.

Jesus Christ of the Gospel of John calls us to grasp fully and faithfully both his divinity and humanity. For the communicator of the faith, this is an extremely important reminder. Classic struggles over this problem in the church have resulted in heresy. Whenever only one aspect of Christ becomes the exclusive center of our lives, we tend to distort the fullness of divine revelation. The correction to this temptation is the community of faith. We must rejoice when we are truly in communion with brothers and sisters who are permitted to share their unique vision of faith. By receiving the experience of faith from others, we are able to see the fullness of Christ before us. We hope that you come to your task as a teacher, speaker or preacher who has others to help you.

You as teacher, speaker or preacher bear a great responsibility to communicate the power of the gospel. You may be secretly wondering why the students stay away from your class or fail to respond to discussion. Perhaps you know in moments of honesty that the people in the pews are falling asleep or failing to feel the impact of the gospel in your preaching. We offer these creative ideas not only to awaken the people of God but also to draw them into an authentic relationship to God's Word. We are confident that the ideas inspired by the Gospel of John for the communication of the faith are authentic and helpful. But we have only begun the creative process. We invite you to change, combine, challenge and transform our beginning points to fit your task and your inspiration. Welcome to a new vision for the Gospel of John.

CHAPTER 1

THE WORD BECOMES FLESH

In the beginning was the Word, and the Word was with God, and the Word was God. ²He was in the beginning with God; ³all things were made through him, and without him was not anything made that was made. ⁴In him was life,ᵃ and the life was the light of men. ⁵The light shines in the darkness, and the darkness has not overcome it.

6 There was a man sent from God, whose name was John. ⁷He came for testimony, to bear witness to the light, that all might believe through him. ⁸He was not the light, but came to bear witness to the light.

9 The true light that enlightens every man was coming into the world. ¹⁰He was in the world, and the world was made through him, yet the world knew him not. ¹¹He came to his own home, and his own people received him not. ¹²But to all who received him, who believed in his name, he gave power to become children of God; ¹³who were born, not of blood nor of the will of the flesh nor of the will of man, but of God.

14 And the Word became flesh and dwelt among us, full of grace and truth; we have beheld his glory, glory as of the only Son from the Father. ¹⁵(John bore witness to him, and cried, "This was he of whom I said, 'He who comes after me ranks before me, for he was before me.'") ¹⁶And from his fulness have we all received, grace upon grace. ¹⁷For the law was given through Moses; grace and truth came through Jesus Christ. ¹⁸No one has ever seen God; the only Son,ᵇ who is in the bosom of the Father, he has made him known.

THE TESTIMONY OF JOHN THE BAPTIST

19 And this is the testimony of John, when the Jews sent priests and Levites from Jerusalem to ask him, "Who are you?" ²⁰He confessed, he did not deny, but confessed, "I am not the Christ." ²¹And they asked him, "What then? Are you Eli'jah?" He said, "I am not." "Are you the prophet?" And he answered, "No." ²²They said to him then, "Who are you? Let us have an answer for those who sent us. What do you say about yourself?" ²³He said, "I am the voice of one crying in the wilderness, 'Make straight the way of the Lord,' as the prophet Isaiah said."

24 Now they had been sent from the Pharisees. ²⁵They asked him, "Then why are you baptizing, if you are neither the Christ, nor Eli'jah, nor the prophet?" ²⁶John answered them, "I baptize with water; but among you stands one whom you do not know, ²⁷even he who comes after me, the thong of whose sandal I am not worthy to untie." ²⁸This took place in Bethany beyond the Jordan, where John was baptizing.

29 The next day he saw Jesus coming toward him, and said, "Behold, the Lamb of God, who takes away the sin of the world! ³⁰This is he of whom I said, 'After me comes a man who ranks before me, for he was before me.' ³¹I myself did not know

---

a Or *was not anything made. That which has been made was life in him*

b Other ancient authorities read *God*

him; but for this I came baptizing with water, that he might be revealed to Israel." ³²And John bore witness, "I saw the Spirit descend as a dove from heaven, and it remained on him. ³³I myself did not know him; but he who sent me to baptize with water said to me, 'He on whom you see the Spirit descend and remain, this is he who baptizes with the Holy Spirit.' ³⁴And I have seen and have borne witness that this is the Son of God."

"COME AND SEE": JESUS' FIRST DISCIPLES

35 The next day again John was standing with two of his disciples; ³⁶and he looked at Jesus as he walked, and said, "Behold, the Lamb of God!" ³⁷The two disciples heard him say this, and they followed Jesus. ³⁸Jesus turned, and saw them following, and said to them, "What do you seek?" And they said to him, "Rabbi" (which means Teacher), "where are you staying?" ³⁹He said to them, "Come and see." They came and saw where he was staying; and they stayed with him that day, for it was about the tenth hour. ⁴⁰One of the two who heard John speak, and followed him, was Andrew, Simon Peter's brother. ⁴¹He first found his brother Simon, and said to him, "We have found the Messiah" (which means Christ). ⁴²He brought him to Jesus. Jesus looked at him, and said, "So you are Simon the son of John? You shall be called Cephas" (which means Peter').

PHILIP AND NATHANAEL: "CAN ANYTHING GOOD COME OUT OF NAZARETH?"

43 The next day Jesus decided to go to Galilee. And he found Philip and said to him, "Follow me." ⁴⁴Now Philip was from Beth-sa'ida, the city of Andrew and Peter. ⁴⁵Philip found Nathan'a-el, and said to him, "We have found him of whom Moses in the law and also the prophets wrote, Jesus of Nazareth, the son of Joseph." ⁴⁶Nathan'a-el said to him, "Can anything good come out of Nazareth?" Philip said to him, "Come and see." ⁴⁷Jesus saw Nathan'a-el coming to him, and said of him, "Behold, an Israelite indeed, in whom is no guile!" ⁴⁸Nathan'a-el said to him, "How do you know me?" Jesus answered him, "Before Philip called you, when you were under the fig tree, I saw you." ⁴⁹Nathan'a-el answered him, "Rabbi, you are the Son of God! You are the King of Israel!" ⁵⁰Jesus answered him, "Because I said to you, I saw you under the fig tree, do you believe? You shall see greater things than these." ⁵¹And he said to him, "Truly, truly, I say to you, you will see heaven opened, and the angels of God ascending and descending upon the Son of man."

---

c From the word for rock in Aramaic and Greek respectively

CHAPTER 1

Creative Commentary on the Scripture

VERSES 1-5: Verses 1-18 are referred to as the "prologue" of the Gospel of John. Verses 1-5 provide a poetic opening for the Gospel. The rest of the chapter is prose. "In the beginning" indicates the time frame of creation and salvation. The prepositions carry the story of the Word becoming flesh. Who is the speaker of this passage? Some interpreters might consider these verses as material for intellectual debate. The Bible, however, is more than thought and organized theory. This prologue is not an invitation for argument. It is another channel for God to share his will for us. There is little room for speculation; God offers only obedience or disobedience.

One of the more important and demanding concepts in the prologue is the use of "logos" ("Word"). There are several influential streams of tradition that explain the use of logos as the term expressing God's communication with creation. Many scholars note the Hebrew impact of Genesis' account of creation is readily apparent here: "In the beginning ... God said." The role of wisdom (such as in Proverbs 8:22-36) can be felt here: God is one with creation. Logos conveys the action of thinking. (The *-ology* suffix on English words is a legacy of ancient logos.) Jesus is the logos. He is inseparable from the creator God and yet is the dynamic extension of this sole source of life. Note here the unity of form and content.

Logos also was a popular term among many schools of Greek thought. The term "gnostic" links together a wide range of religious groups living at the time of the early church. The nature of this wing of theology is hard to describe carefully. The major documentation from these groups comes to us from the arguments against them by the Christian theologians. The few preserved documents written by gnostic groups come from a time well after the period in which the groups actually flourished. But it does appear that these groups believed that concepts like logos were actually entities of deity. The logos figure was a divine personage apart from the God who created the heaven and earth. Therefore God could not become a genuine human being in gnostic thought. The logos of the gnostic was separate from the ugly taint of the flesh.

Logos, while a powerful concept on its own, takes on a more full meaning in its context in John. The sentence, the paragraph, the message unit and the complete work are really the basis for definition of key terms. It is clear that the author of this Gospel defines logos in a particular manner as we progress from creator God to life, light and finally (in verse 17) to Jesus Christ. The author shades the word with many meanings. He seems to relish in using language in such a way that the reader is forced to see beyond one meaning. Dr. Dale Goldsmith suggests an intriguing idea that the Hebrew "word" and Greek "word" may represent "hot" and "cool" meanings. He is referring to Marshall McLuhan's thesis that different media evoke different kinds of understanding. Does a "hot" Hebrew application of logos evoke a "radio-like" response from the audience while the "cool" Greek definition offers a "television-like" response?

The Gospel writer offers more than a message about life after death. Life after birth is as important. The prologue is a promise of abundant life open to the soft pain of love and vulnerability.

VERSES 6-18: Personality is introduced with John the Baptist. John the Baptist is the last of the prophets from the Old Testament. A textual variant reading of verse 13 makes the birth verb singular. This suggests some interest in the birth of Christ. The verbs in these verses (as in most of the fourth Gospel) seem to suggest a God of action and life.

VERSES 19-34: The mode of revealing the Baptist's witness is dialogue. The concept of a voice crying indicates the Baptist's prophetic role announcing the coming of the Messiah. The lamb and the dove are used as symbols for the ministry of Jesus. How is Jesus like these two images? How are these figures used elsewhere in the Bible? See Exodus 12, Isaiah 53:7 (for lamb) and Genesis 8:8-12, Matthew 10:16,

Psalm 74:19 (for dove).

Baptism is the important context for the presentation of Christ and his disciples. Yet it is amazing that God chooses to start "bottom up" in announcing the coming attractions. Instead of starting with kings or a board of directors, he sends forth a weird and angry man living in the wilderness. God works sometimes in surprising, unpredictable and unexpected ways. Here is John with no credentials, no place in society, no authority over others, and yet God's power is at work! His humility concerning the sandal of Jesus provides a foreshadowing of the footwashing by Jesus at the Last Supper.

VERSES 35-42: Jesus invites the curious to "come and see" (physical response to spiritual quest). Under his hospitality (table experience?), Andrew and another recognize the Christ. Finally, there is the naming of the one who becomes Christ's disciple. Notice Peter's name change, a special theological sign, e.g., Jacob's change to Israel.

VERSES 43-51: Philip is impressed by simple signs from Jesus. Jesus promises more sensual signs. (Loosely translated, verses 50-51 can say, "You ain't seen nothin' yet.") The question of Jesus' place of origin (verse 46) suggests the lack of elitism in God's work. He surprises us by giving us good things in unexpected packages. Philip repeats Andrew's act of evangelism by bringing Nathanael to Jesus.

Creative Bible Study Ideas

A FIVE-SESSION OUTLINE BASED ON 1:1-5

The prologue in the Gospel of John "recycles" the Genesis' creation (Genesis 1:1-31) in order to set the stage for the new creation, Jesus. This five-session outline explores God's incredible creative acts in the first five verses of John and how they relate to our lives.

SESSION ONE: Verse 1

1. Pass out pads and crayons.
2. Play lively classical music (e.g., Dvorak) as background music for this session.
3. Read, as a litany, Genesis 1:1-31 with John 1:1 inserted after each occurrence of "... it was good" phrases.
4. Ask the students during the litany to doodle, draw or

26 THE BIBLE CREATIVE

write on the pads with the crayons. Encourage them to pick up the joy of the divine act of creation in their doodles or drawings.

5. Move into dyads (pairs).

6. Have your people share their doodles and the feelings experienced during the reading of Genesis and verse 1.

7. Gather in a large circle.

8. Ask each partner in the dyads to show the doodles of his or her partner. He or she should also share the positive insights discovered about the other person in the dyad.

9. Post the doodles in the meeting room.

10. Ask each person to bring in one artifact that demonstrates humanity's poor stewardship of God's creation. These can be things like beer cans, a jar of polluted river water, pictures of soil erosion, a toy gun, etc.

SESSION TWO: Verse 2

1. Review the prior session's creations. Repeat the reading of session one (the integrated litany of Genesis 1:1-31 with John). Include verses 1-2 this time. Then repeat the doodling process. This time, ask each person to share his or her own creative doodles with the group.

2. Ask the students to go around the circle and quickly share one word or phrase describing the wonder of the original creation.

3. Assign each person a passage from John describing the trials of Jesus during his ministry, e.g., 2:13-22, 10:22-39, 11:45-53, 19:1-16. Or, perhaps better, ask the students to search through the Gospels for these examples.

4. Form dyads and discuss these moments of pain and difficulty.

5. Gather the group and discuss the contrasts between the time when the Word (Jesus) was with God and when he dwells among us now. List the creation's goodness on the left of a large newsprint sheet or blackboard. List the new creation's (Jesus') difficulties in the midst of fallen humanity.

6. Pass out a page of a recent local newspaper to each person or have them share the items they collected during the past week.

7. Ask for volunteers to share how humanity is violating (or respecting the goodness of) God's creation through the examples in the newspaper or in the artifacts.

8. Ask each person to talk to one other person about the

threat against the goodness of creation in our daily life. As members of the body of the new creation, what are some things we can do to respond appropriately to God?

SESSION THREE: Verse 3

1. Read the Genesis 1:1-31 litany. This time, add only verse 3 after each of the creative acts ("it was good").

2. Pass out pieces of clay (or Play-Doh).

3. Ask each person to let his or her hands fashion something new and fresh as if he or she were back to the time when nothing was made without the Word. You might use the music from the first session during this time.

4. Ask them to form dyads and share their clay creations. How is God reflected in these humble shapes?

5. Share the reflections on the clay creations as a total group.

6. Place all the clay together and create a single community structure while the litany (see #1) is read again.

7. Share the creation and the story of this event in worship as a part of the service. Perhaps there are some local responses to the destruction of creation which the congregation can support (recycling, ecological renewal, etc.). Be specific when you are before the congregation in worship.

SESSION FOUR: Verse 4

The author of this Gospel is celebrating the gift of Jesus Christ to the world. In this session we are suggesting an experiential means of crawling into the text which draws upon the Christmas story of Luke 1—2 and Matthew 1—2. Invite a parent in the congregation to bring a young baby to the session. If this is absolutely impossible, you might bring a baby blanket.

1. Gather the class in a circle of chairs.

2. Read Luke 2:1-19 with John 1:4 repeated between the verses.

3. Pass the child around the circle if it is a small class or use the baby blanket. It is important that each person either see the baby or touch the blanket.

4. Ask each person to share how this child or personal memories of a special baby reveal some things about the truth of this passage. What is the light of this verse?

5. What kinds of darkness will this child encounter as the bearer of our legacy? How does God speak to this situation?

6. Review the vows taken by the congregation in the liturgy of baptism or dedication. What is our responsibility to this child and his or her family? If your church has no liturgy of this kind, discuss the responsibilities of a faith community toward the children in the church.

7. Close with a prayer circle of thanksgiving for God's gifts and a time of rededication of discipleship in a ministry of light to others. You might conclude with a serious discussion on the kinds of support your congregation provides for the children and parents. Are children and youth really included in the life of the community? You might want to make some recommendation for your board concerning the ministry in this important area.

SESSION FIVE: Verse 5

1. Pass out single pages from a local newspaper. Read verses 1-5. Repeat verse 5.

2. Ask each person to find a sentence in the paper which suggests that the "darkness" (despair, sin, etc.) might seem to be gaining strength.

3. Lead a "living" litany by reading verse 5 between the statements selected by the students as you go around the circle.

4. These items will touch upon the pain and suffering of brothers and sisters in our world. Ask your people to deal with the gap between the hope of the passage and the real despair of the world. How do we keep from becoming "pie-in-the-sky" Christians (those who, when overwhelmed by the world's apparent hopelessness, become obsessed with heaven and the second coming of Christ)? What does it *mean* to be faithful to the Good News?

5. Focus on how this study group can start action which will make changes in the hopelessness of contemporary society. Take the items used in the living litany (see #3) and work on them in triads. Focus on genuinely workable ideas.

6. Share these ideas with the whole group.

7. Have the clusters translate their ideas into short sentences of affirmation which mention the problem. For example: "We see lonely people in our community. We will befriend them and let them know the Good News."

8. How can these recommendations become reality? Work

on some ways your class can make some changes in your community. You might want to write a joint letter or approach your board at the church.

9. Close by using a living litany of hope based on verse 5. After individual members share a problem in the community, the whole class responds by saying verse 5 aloud in unison.

SESSION BASED ON 1:1-5

1. Create a "clock" of creation according to John 1:1-5.
2. Have each person or cluster of persons (if it is a large group) take one of the five verses.
3. Ask these living verses to create a human clock by placing themselves on its imaginary face. The imaginary clock is on the floor.
4. Have them sit on these spots and discuss in pairs or groups the questions raised by such a clock. Where is the beginning? Was God before time? What kind of time do the passages suggest?
5. Share these ideas with the whole group. The leader might want to put the ideas on a "clock" designed from newsprint.
6. Now have your students place themselves on a salvation "clock" that reflects where they are at this time. This can be an individual or small-group task. You can help this process along by having them place chairs around an imaginary clock face.
7. Close by sharing how they feel that the Good News of this passage will move them along this clock of salvation. Do they help each other? Are they open to change? What's one thing they can do to increase in discipleship?
8. Ask each person to write his or her name on a slip of paper. Collect the slips. Redistribute the slips. Each person should have a name of someone else. Keep these secret. Ask the group if they will pray for that person at a set time during the day in the coming week. The experience of someone else praying for you each day at a set time is quite moving. Share these experiences both as the giver and receiver of prayers.

SESSION BASED ON 1:1-5

This outline is based on the use of the prepositions in the first five verses of the prologue.

1. Read the passage. Ask the students to call out the prepositions in verses 1-5.

2. List the prepositions used in these verses on newsprint or on the blackboard. (Some examples of prepositons used in 1:1-5: *In* the beginning . . ., . . . the Word was *with* God . . ., all things were made *through* him.)

3. Give each student either a preposition or noun from the prepositional phrases in the verse. You may have prepared for this by writing them out on paper before the session.

4. Create pairs of students and have them talk about how the two words they have relate to each other and reveal something special about the content.

5. Ask them to take a couple minutes to think of a way to act out or mime the relationship between their words for the whole group.

6. Share these scenes.

7. Read the passage again and discuss new insights into the meaning of it.

8. Gather the teams in a circle that follows the order of the five verses.

9. Have the students say their prepositional phrases as a "chain" reading. The leader or others can say the verbs and other parts of the sentences at the appropriate points. This can be the closing circle. Ask each student to look for examples in the media, school or home that illustrate a prepositional phrase studied in this session. This can be shared at the next class meeting.

AN EIGHT-SESSION OUTLINE BASED ON 1:6-51

This course focuses on discipleship and the nature of Jesus. While each session is built around certain verses, the whole passage is really the thrust of the course.

SESSION ONE: Verses 6-8

1. Pass out paper and pencil to each student. Ask them to list groups they belong to and to describe their role in each one (family, school, work, community, team, etc.). They are not to consider the faith part of their lives at this point.

2. After a few minutes ask your people to share their lists with the group. In what ways are they the center of the groups and in what ways are they outside the limelight? How do they consider themselves unique or separate from the stereotyped perceptions of their groups? For example,

how might I be different than the jock image of the football team?

3. Cluster your people into small groups. Have each group pick two conflicting groups, e.g., Democrats and Republicans. They are then to prepare a positive one-minute presentation on both groups. Perhaps a sales format can be used. A late-night television advertising-spot format will make the sharing fun and enthusiastic.

4. Share the sales pitches.

5. Reflect together on how much the pitches were genuine and how much they were simply slick-packaged.

6. Read verses 6-8. Then read a description of John the Baptist in Matthew 3:1-6.

7. We have seen how John the Baptist witnessed. How should we represent Christ in our discipleship today? What is the nature of this light in the darkness of our time? Was he a winner by today's standards? Pursue this discussion for a few minutes. Then write verse 6 on the board or newsprint but leave the word "John" out.

8. Ask your students to use their pads and reflect on how each one can reflect the light of the Son. Each person writes verse 6 on the paper, filling in his or her name at the verse's end. Then ask each one to adapt verse 7 to explain how he or she will bear witness to the light.

9. As a parting act, invite each person to read his or her rewritten passage of commitment to personal witness. Ask them to live out this statement during the coming week.

SESSION TWO: Verses 9-13

1. Darken the room. You might need to shift the class to another setting for this session. Place a lighted candle in the center of your study circle.

2. Read the passage (verses 9-13).

3. Pass the candle around the circle and share how the light of the Son adds something special to the faces of those present. As it is held by a person, ask others how this person is changed in this special "true" light of the gospel flame.

4. Put out the flame.

5. Sit in the darkness for a few seconds.

6. Ask your people to share how people of the world might refuse to see the light of Christ. Let folks speak out as they wish. Suggest that they share a story about a direct

refusal they know from their experience.
7. Light the candle again after this sharing.
8. Read verses 12-13.
9. Pass around a baby blanket which has a touch of baby-powder smell to it. As each person handles the blanket, he or she reflects on what it means to be a "child" of God. In what way has this kind of birth touched your life or the lives of others you know? Ask each person to change some small part of his or her life during this week to reflect freshly the reality of the new birth.

SESSION THREE: Verse 14
1. Read the verse.
2. Ask your people in the circle to look at their hands.
3. Share some expressions used to describe the roles played by hands ("press the flesh," etc.).
4. Ask each person to share how his or her hands in some way symbolize the kind of discipleship demanded by the "Word became flesh" (service, personal qualities, etc.).
5. Form the students into dyads.
6. Take turns looking at the palms of each partner and reflecting how grace and truth are in some way symbolized by his or her hands. These are imaginative tasks. Encourage your students to be led by the Word in their sharing.
7. Rejoin the group. Ask each person to share his or her reflections with the total group.
8. Hold hands and close with prayers of thanksgiving for the gift of the Word becoming flesh. Ask for commitments of particular actions which will touch other people in special ways during the coming week. "I will become the hands of Christ this week as I . . ."

SESSION FOUR: Verses 15-18
1. Share the experience of "touching" others as the hands of Jesus during the past week.
2. Share newspaper reports or other print items about the success of the electric evangelists and other ministries outside those of your church family. You might utilize a picture of a cult leader or some other religious figure.
3. Ask the people in your group to share their feelings about these "competitive" religious movements.
4. Focus on a reflection of the positive qualities of these splinter groups. What would attract a person to such faiths?

If you were a publicist for such a leader or group, what weaknesses in the existing faith (your church) could you exploit? Make a list of these.

5. Explore why there is little room for feelings of competition or threat by reading and discussing verse 16.

6. Close by having each person fold his or her arms in a self-embrace as you read verse 18 ("... the only Son, who is in the bosom of the Father ...").

7. Ask each person to make a commitment to witness in a fresh way to others during the coming week. How can Christ be known without using the traditional words of faith?

SESSION FIVE: Verses 19-28

1. Record the sounds of a baby crying or some other voices crying out a concern (cheerleaders, etc.).

2. Ask your people to close their eyes and imagine your local community. Take them on an imaginary tour of your town. Then describe a major town in your state. Continue with a description of some place in another culture. Focus on the needs and cries of people in this guided fantasy. Play the tape while you talk.

3. Ask them to open their eyes and share the "cries" of the people in our world.

4. Write these contributions down on newsprint as they are suggested, large enough for all to see.

5. Write verse 23 on the newsprint.

6. Share in what ways the "way of the Lord" touches on the "cries" of the people in our day.

7. Spend some time sharing the frustration that arises when we try to bear the message of the Lord in the midst of the world's cries. Compare these frustrations to the humble strength that John the Baptist exhibits ("the thong of whose sandal I am not worthy to untie").

8. Give each person a short piece of leather, symbolic of the sandal thong.

9. Commission each person to undertake the ministry of John the Baptist during the coming week. Ask each student to bring the piece of leather back to the next session.

SESSION SIX: Verses 29-34

1. Share the experiences of the past week. You might ask each person to display the leather thong and tell his or her story.

2. Find a piece of wool which is free from dye and looks close to its natural state.

3. Pass it around the study circle while you read the passage (verses 29-34).

4. Talk about the qualities of the sheep (goes to slaughter without resistance, meek, etc.). Explore the motif of sacrifice for others with each person when he or she is holding the wool.

5. Ask your people to suggest how our discipleship should take on the Lamb of God aspects of Jesus.

6. Pass a bowl of water around the group.

7. Ask each person to anoint the hands of the person next to him or her with the blessing, "May the Holy Spirit descend on your life and remain with you as you touch the cries of others."

8. Follow along and dry the person's hands with a towel.

9. Send the students out to undertake a ministry of discipleship during the next week. In the closing prayer circle, ask each person to focus on a particular person in our school, home or work who needs special care. Commission the students to carry the leather thong into a week of special ministry.

SESSION SEVEN: Verses 35-42

1. Arrange to have a stranger come to your group separately from you. Ask that he not speak to anyone. He should have a pad of paper and pen. You will be focusing on hospitality as a context for hearing the gospel.

2. Read the passage (verses 35-42).

3. Have everyone go around the circle and offer a brief introduction of himself or herself to the group. When you come to the stranger, he merely writes a note to the class ("I come to see").

4. Encourage the class to engage the stranger as he struggles with the decision to become a disciple. The stranger now talks. He wants to know what it means to be a disciple and whether or not he should become one. Ask each student to tell his or her own faith story to the stranger.

5. Let the session unfold as the class desires.

6. Form a prayer circle with the eyes of all closed. The stranger leaves during this time.

7. Discuss the feelings the students had during this time.

Did their discussion work or not? Why? How did they feel about trying to convince others to become disciples?

8. Ask your students to make a commitment to do discipleship work during the next week. This task is a bit different from the ones suggested for the other sessions. This week you will ask your students to talk directly with another person about discipleship. Hopefully your people have discovered in this session that the story of one's faith is one of the best ways to share the faith with another.

SESSION EIGHT: Verses 43-51

This session will explore the role of signs as motivation for discipleship. Blessed are those who don't see, but still believe. If you are teaching these courses in a series, you will want to begin by having your people share the results of their action from the last session (personal discipleship).

1. Bring in a book of horoscopes which can be purchased at newsstands, drugstores, garage sales, flea markets, etc. Or cut them out of a newspaper or magazine.

2. Give each person a page of horoscope.

3. Ask the students to share the kinds of things predicted in the material.

4. Have them explore why people are so impressed by these kinds of signs about the future.

5. Read the story of Nathanael's wonder at the notice Jesus took in him.

6. Let your students share the kinds of signs or wonders they look to in their lives.

7. Give your people a few minutes, working in triads, to develop some of the signs promised by Christ that they are awaiting.

8. Ask your students to focus on one of the signs seen in Christ that means the most to them. Suggest that they find a confirmation of this sign in some aspect of their lives during the coming week.

SESSION BASED ON 1:19-34

The model discipleship we find in the person of John the Baptist suggests a spectrum of priorities that differ from those held by many Christians in our time. It might be interesting to thrust your group into the world of radical obedience to the will of God by leading a learning experience drawn from John's message as it touches today's concerns.

Ask the group to divide into two working units. Put the students in different rooms. One unit is given the assignment to put together a stewardship or giving campaign to support the ministry of the local church. Try to make it as real as possible. Encourage them to use the latest and best in fund-raising techniques. If you have time, have them outline the steps of the program, write the theme of a sermon, organize the calling procedure and even develop a theme.

The other group is to undertake the same task. However, they must do it as John the Baptist might undertake such a stewardship campaign. Encourage them to work out the details for the whole program.

Gather the whole class and share the results. Compare the approaches. What sets of values have been expressed in the two systems? Read the passage as part of this process. Deal with questions about the practical aspects of living with the radical obedience of John the Baptist. Does God demand less of us? How can your session lead to some change in your faith community? Make some recommendation which can be passed to a church committee for consideration. Perhaps members of the class might want to accept the responsibility for pursuing the conclusions. Authentic biblical study should lead to life-changing acts.

Creative Speaking and Preaching Ideas

A CLUE FROM 1:1-5

The poetic form of the first five verses suggests that we present the text for worship in a form consistent with this quality. Congregations generally have members highly skilled in musical gifts. Suggest that these verses be set to music. Perhaps a group of liturgical dancers could interpret this important message of salvation. Mime is another poetic art form which is easy to develop and highly effective in presenting powerful biblical themes.

The text can be woven into the Genesis 1 account of creation to present the full meaning of the passage. Verse 1:1 can also be presented as a repeated refrain with the reading of the Advent stories in Matthew and Luke at a Christmas worship experience.

The author's style of linking the thoughts through the connecting flow of language suggests that we might use a fresh approach to present the passage. The scripture reading might be done in a "lining out" style. This country or frontier practice assures that the congregation focuses on the passage. The leader reads a line and then it is repeated by the worshipers. This technique works very well with the prologue.

The incarnational message (God in human form) of the prologue also suggests that we might receive the Word by doing it! A few basic gestures can be developed. The reader encourages the congregation to follow the motions (mostly with hands) as the passage is read. Use the "sign" language of the deaf to communicate the passage.

The repetitive nature of the prologue encourages us to repeat the text several times as it is presented in the service. You might work through it two or three times using the different approaches which have been suggested. For example, you might call to worship with verse 1, read verse 2 before a hymn, verse 3 as an introduction to stewardship, a sermon on verse 4 and the benediction as verse 5.

When using this text in an evening or a dark environment, you will want to draw upon the important motifs of light and darkness that dominate the first five verses. The use of a candle can be most helpful in presenting the content of this message. For instance, you have a moment in the service when unlit candles are in a circle around a central lit candle. Ask worshipers to come up one at a time with a prayer request (for a person or a cause) and state this aloud while lifting one of the unlit candles to the source candle.

A CLUE FROM 1:6-34

Verses 6-34 provide a dramatic unfolding of the nature of Jesus' impending ministry. It begs to be presented in a dramatic sermon form. The passage can be developed as a one-person-sermon drama by the preacher taking the role of John the Baptist. You can actually become this person. Some preachers have found local little theater groups very helpful in providing makeup and costumes for this purpose. The flow of the sermon can follow the flow of the text as the preacher talks directly to the congregation. The entry to the sermon time can be made from the narthex of the church.

A CLUE FROM 1:19-34

If the biblical presentation of John (study the story of

John the Baptist in the other Gospels) is appealing, you might become this character and build upon the dialogical character of verses 19-34. Hold a press conference. (See the glossary for detailed instructions on how to set up a news conference.) Encourage questions from the congregation concerning his ministry and his relationship to the coming of Christ. You might alert a couple members before the service and ask them to be ready with questions. If your congregation is not prepared for this style, include slips of paper with the bulletin and have the liturgist or co-leader request questions for the guest preacher. Ask them to place the questions with the offering in the plate. Bring the stack of questions to "John the Baptist" at the sermon time.

A CLUE FROM 1:19-51

Verses 19-51 present the story of discipleship as a situation in which others witness to the coming of Jesus. This setting suggests that you might try to present the message as if the congregation is participating in a trial. The characters in the passage (John the Baptist, priests, Andrew, etc.) are involved in a search for truth. Perhaps the congregation could be asked to play the part of a jury. A series of witnesses are called to present the amazing claim (prologue) concerning Jesus. Several people could present the position of the characters in the passage. The sermon can close with an appeal to the jury to make its decision concerning Jesus.

A CLUE FROM 1:9-13

This would be an excellent passage for a baptism or dedication service. The Gospel is presenting the concept of birth and rebirth on more than one level of understanding. It is always tempting for the people of God to take care of baptisms as efficiently as possible. Yet, we may be missing the grace of time for significant Christian rites of passage. There should be time for the celebration of God's action in our lives as a worshiping people!

Try to consider the focus of baptism or dedication as an event for a single family or person at a given service. This event is a means of grace for everyone present. It provides the people of God with a chance to experience the incredible Good News of this message. We are often tempted to bunch as many baptisms together as possible on a particular Sunday. It is better to give this important moment the special energy it deserves.

Place the parents in chairs at the front of the service center. Draw the congregation into the experience of this moment of celebrating the gift of becoming children of God. Pick up the baby and carry him or her down the aisle into the congregation. Do your sermon with the child in your arms. You will have to be brief and informal. Pray for the parents. Let them and the congregation feel the grace of God as they look forward to all sharing in the raising of the child.

Close by passing small safety pins to all of the worshipers. Ask them to accept this as a symbol of their reaffirmation that they are children of God through Jesus Christ. You may encourage them to wear the pins as a reminder and witness to the fact that Jesus has created a family of God that embraces the young and old.

If you are celebrating adult baptism, you can make this a special event by enabling the person confessing faith to witness to the work of God in his or her life.

A CLUE FROM 1:29-34

The first chapter of John mentions an animal (lamb) and a bird (dove). These creatures are used to provide a deeper understanding of Jesus' ministry. You may want to act on these clues. The use of a lamb has been utilized by a number of preachers. This works particularly well in an Advent setting. One pastor held the Christmas Eve service in an old barn where animals surrounded a manger. (Bringing a live animal into a church can present problems. However, it has been done.)

The dove might be a more useful clue. There are people in every community who own pigeons and other birds. One pastor took the congregation into the parking lot and released a pigeon as a symbol of the spirit moving in their community.

A CLUE FROM 1:9-13

In conjunction with one of these preaching models you might enable the children in the congregation to participate in the celebration of these glorious promises. If you are using this passage at Christmas or Pentecost, give each of the children a sparkler with the warning to be careful. Perhaps an adult can help them. Light them from a Christ candle and hold them up as an act of celebration while the congregation sings "Joy to the World" or some other festive hymn.

A CLUE FROM 1:19-23

Ask people in the congregation to close their eyes and imagine a wilderness. Lead them on a journey through the wilderness. Suggest that they feel, smell, visualize, touch and listen to the desert. Let them imagine the particulars of these sensual clues.

Tell them that they are also experiencing twists on the path through the wilderness. Suggest that these difficulties in the road are caused by sin and other human problems. Ask them to silently think about their own sins, failings and other "twists" in the road. After they have wandered in the wilderness for several minutes, ask them to open their eyes. Have some helpers distribute balls of tangled yarn. Distribute a few balls to each pew. Then read the scripture passage. Ask them to think of each thread as a problem on the twisted road of their guided wilderness wandering. As they straighten out the yarn encourage them to talk with others in the pew about the particulars they have focused on in their guided imaginary journey.

After they have done this, ask the people to share some ways we have distorted the way of the Lord. Have someone list these at the front of the worship center on newsprint or a blackboard. Talk briefly on how making our paths straight for the Lord benefits our lives. Stretch out the strands of untangled yarn. Ask each person to place his or her hands on some part of the yarn and have the congregation sing "Blest Be the Tie That Binds."

A CLUE FROM 1:24-34

Use small glass cups if your tradition utilizes this form of communion distribution. Have them filled with water and distribute them to the worshipers. Ask each person to reflect on the water they are holding. Suggest that they look at it by holding it up to the light. Focus their thinking on how water is used (water power, cleaning, etc.).

Ask the congregation to think back on their own baptism. What happened in that moment? What does the miracle of this act say about God's nature? These thoughts can be shared by people in the congregation. Invite them to drink the water as an act of rededication. You may want to remind them of the "living water" theme from the fourth Gospel.

A CLUE FROM 1:35-51

After you read the text, ask the congregation to sing the popular rhyme "Mary Had a Little Lamb." You will probably notice a marked uneasiness in the pews. Ask the worshipers to share how this illustrates and conflicts with the uneasiness to follow Christ's teachings. If singing a song is hard, how much harder is it to be a Christian? If they are hesitant to speak out, you might ask them to write responses on cards stored in the pew racks. When is following a virtue and when is it a weakness? In verse 39, Jesus invites his disciples to "come and see." What keeps us from doing this? Collect the cards and read responses. Or you can have the cards redistributed to the worshipers. Each person can then look at another person's card and share his or her response to the question on it.

CHAPTER 2

JESUS CREATES WINE FROM WATER

On the third day there was a marriage at Cana in Galilee, and the mother of Jesus was there; ²Jesus also was invited to the marriage, with his disciples. ³When the wine gave out, the mother of Jesus said to him, "They have no wine." ⁴And Jesus said to her, "O woman, what have you to do with me? My hour has not yet come." ⁵His mother said to the servants, "Do whatever he tells you." ⁶Now six stone jars were standing there, for the Jewish rites of purification, each holding twenty or thirty gallons. ⁷Jesus said to them, "Fill the jars with water." And they filled them up to the brim. ⁸He said to them, "Now draw some out, and take it to the steward of the feast." So they took it. ⁹When the steward of the feast tasted the water now become wine, and did not know where it came from (though the servants who had drawn the water knew), the steward of the feast called the bridegroom ¹⁰and said to him, "Every man serves the good wine first; and when men have drunk freely, then the poor wine; but you have kept the good wine until now." ¹¹This, the first of his signs, Jesus did at Cana in Galilee, and manifested his glory; and his disciples believed in him.

12 After this he went down to Caper′na-um, with his mother and his brothers and his disciples; and there they stayed for a few days.

JESUS CLEARS THE TEMPLE

13 The Passover of the Jews was at hand, and Jesus went up to Jerusalem. ¹⁴In the temple he found those who were selling oxen and sheep and pigeons, and the money-changers at their business. ¹⁵And making a whip of cords, he drove them all, with the sheep and oxen, out of the temple; and he poured out the coins of the money-changers and overturned their tables. ¹⁶And he told those who sold the pigeons, "Take these things away; you shall not make my Father's house a house of trade." ¹⁷His disciples remembered that it was written, "Zeal for thy house will consume me." ¹⁸The Jews then said to him, "What sign have you to show us for doing this?" ¹⁹Jesus answered them, "Destroy this temple, and in three days I will raise it up." ²⁰The Jews then said, "It has taken forty-six years to build this temple, and will you raise it up in three days?" ²¹But he spoke of the temple of his body. ²²When therefore he was raised from the dead, his disciples remembered that he had said this; and they believed the scripture and the word which Jesus had spoken.

23 Now when he was in Jerusalem at the Passover feast, many believed in his name when they saw the signs which he did; ²⁴but Jesus did not trust himself to them, ²⁵because he knew all men and needed no one to bear witness of man; for he himself knew what was in man.

CHAPTER 2

Creative Commentary on the Scripture

Chapter 2 offers two incidents concerning the nature of Jesus' ministry. The theological promise of the prologue is expressed here through two experiences, the wedding at Cana and the clearing of the temple.

VERSES 1-12: The setting is one of hospitality (a wedding). Therefore, this first act of Jesus' ministry has the same kind of community texture as his last act on the shore with his disciples (fish fry in chapter 21). Does this say something to us about the role of hospitality as the experiential setting for the faith? Family and disciples are related to the story. Jesus has an interesting response to his mother's request. Is he claiming his independence or is he giving her the freedom to be her own person? "Woman" was a polite address. Jesus simply asks her how the lack of wine is his concern. Jars, water and wine are common forms that illustrate the sensual aspects of the passage. Yet Jesus uses these common objects to manifest the first public sign of his glory. Verse 11 says the disciples "believed in him," continuing the events of chapter 1. Perhaps this indicates discipleship is not instant. Rather it is a lifelong growth experience.

There is an epiphany (or exposure) element to this story: It takes place in order that others might experience the glory of God in the Son. The "sign" of this experience is meant to point to something more significant than the act itself.

There is disjointed or misdirected quality to the flow of this amazing event. The people in the story don't seem to understand fully what is going on here. Perhaps this repetitive motif (people missing the significance of what is happening) in the fourth Gospel is an important contribution to our faith.

There is what clown minister Floyd Shaffer calls a "transrational" quality to the text. The writer helps us understand the transition between the intellectual and the emotional. The text is telling us that something very real and important is happening. We understand it and don't understand it. Faith is the celebration or life feast that holds us in the tension between these two conflicting states. The Cana wedding is an excellent example for making this point today.

VERSES 13-22: Another important story unfolds about the natural tension of Jesus' ministry. This action tale presents a strong emotional response in Jesus toward merchants and those changing Roman money into Jewish money in the temple area. A few ancient texts try to moderate the assertive reaction of Jesus by adding that the "whip of cords" was an instrument only "like" a whip. These texts reflect the uneasiness among some Christians toward an angry Jesus. But we must affirm that Jesus indeed was moved to anger by the unrighteousness of those in the story.

Jesus is seen in another disjointed dialogue with opponents. They don't seem to understand the parallel between the temple and his ministry. It is as though Jesus invites his listeners to enter into his message in order that they might find the answers to the questions themselves. What does this kind of participatory communication say to preachers and teachers of our day? Verse 22 suggests that this style of proclamation led to the disciples' understanding the gospel after they had experienced more of Christ. It is within the biblical tradition, then, that today's disciples should follow Christ without the luxury of knowing all the answers.

VERSES 23-25: This terse presentation is most helpful in illustrating the limits of human understanding and the power of temptation. Jesus knows our fallibility and does not trust his ministry to those who are satisfied with simple thrills. It is only in the context of a history of salvation (death, resurrection and personal sacrifice) that the fullness of his glory will be understood. This insight into the understanding of Jesus suggests an interesting exploration into human nature. How do we view clearly the reality of sin within each person without being overwhelmed by hopelessness? These verses amplify the hope in Christ by pointing out the ultimate fallibility in humanity.

This chapter and the material which follows profile the ministry of Jesus against the background of religious seasons. The interface between the natural and supernatural, the mystical and the practical gives us a special encouragement in our preaching/teaching work as creative communicators. The cognitive and the experiential are inseparably interlocked in authentic Christian growth and celebration.

Creative Bible Study Ideas

SESSION BASED ON 2:1-12

The focus of this session is to explore the nature of adult-youth relationships by crawling into this passage.

1. Gather the group in a circle of chairs.
2. Play a tape recording of crowd sounds as background. This can be taped on a cassette recorder at some other social gathering.
3. Give each person a piece of paper and a pen.
4. Ask students to close their eyes and remember a party or some other social gathering they attended with parents. Can they remember an embarrassing moment between themselves and their parents?
5. After a few minutes, suggest that each person write down the feelings that went through him or her while reliving that moment.
6. Form pairs and share these feelings and stories.
7. Share some of the feelings and stories with the whole group.
8. Now read the story of the wedding at Cana. Then read verses 1-5 again.
9. Choose someone from the group to role play the situation described in the passage. This can be done something like this: Place two chairs in the circle. Ask the volunteer to be Mary as she talks to Jesus about providing the wine.
10. After a few minutes have the person change chairs and take the role of Jesus talking to Mary.
11. Have the other people in the group talk about the interaction in this biblical situation. Why did Jesus seem to feel the way he did? How did Mary feel? Does the work of Jesus put aside family considerations? In what ways does this story apply to our situation as we try to assume our place as adults?
12. Close with a prayer circle focusing on the gifts of love and patience in being sons and daughters.

46   THE BIBLE CREATIVE

13. You might ask each student to isolate one aspect of his or her relationship with parents. During the next week, commission each person to work at improving this part of the relationship. Share the results at the next session.

SESSION BASED ON 2:1-12

1. Place six jars or clay pots in the center of your circle.

2. Read the passage to the group.

3. As the verses are read have someone act out the scene by pouring water into the jars.

4. Give a jar to every second or third person (depending on the size of the group).

5. Ask them to talk about how they would respond if they had been there when the water turned to wine. How does it feel to have only water and not to have seen such a sign?

6. Ask each person to drink from a jar (use paper cups if this will cause a problem) as a final act of celebration. You might use this act as a closing moment. Perhaps you will want the persons in the group to focus on a part of their lives that needs change. Have the students write a response to this request. Ask them to draw upon the promise of Christ to make the needed change. A word of blessing might be added: "May God perform a miracle within you as you drink this water."

7. Results can be shared at the next class. Don't be afraid to promise that the message you teach continues to change the lives of the faithful.

SESSION BASED ON 2:1-12

You can enable a class of children to enter into this text by announcing a party for the next session. Whey they arrive, the room should be very bare. In one corner place an old box. Put in the box all the things needed for a party (streamers, uninflated balloons, mix for punch, cups, snacks, games, etc.).

Start the class as you usually do. Pretend as if there will be no party. Allow several people to drop by and ask about the party. Then read the passage and talk about what God was saying to the people at the Cana party. Does this passage say something about the importance of celebration? Does he give the spirit for the party to believers?

Discover the box. Encourage the children to make the party themselves. A few minutes before ending the party, stop the celebration and reflect on what has happened with this party that is similar to the Cana party. What about the guests? Perhaps the party needed strangers. Could you have a better party with someone else here? Have them think of someone not present (older person, etc.). If possible, have them go and bring the person to this party.

SESSION BASED ON 2:1-12

The appearance of miracles plays an important role in the flow of this Gospel. Yet many people are uncomfortable with this aspect of the Christian story. You might look at this text as a time for your students to explore their feelings about signs and miracles.

Divide the group into two parts. Ask one group to pass around a clay jar you brought to class. Their task is to look back in their lives or the lives of those around them and list on newsprint some miracles they have seen or heard about. The other group is requested to list on newsprint some specific ways Gods acts today.

Share these lists and discuss how we know if the Holy Spirit is working. How are we channels for the work of God? Send them forth to be vehicles or signs of the goodness of God. Help them focus on particular areas where they could cause change. Have them share the results of their witness at the next session.

SESSION BASED ON 2:13-17

1. Before the session place a file of pennies (several hundred) and a whip made of cords or pieces of rope in the middle of the classroom table.
2. Play a tape-recorded message from a religious station that features only the concluding pitch for money. Ask a young person to do this recording for you before this session.
3. Read verses 13-17.
4. Pass out the pennies to each person.
5. Ask them about the relationship between the use of money within the Christian community and what Jesus taught in this passage. What about church suppers, lawn sales and other fund-raising events? What are some examples of profit motive in the church? outside the church?

6. Working in groups of two or three, give your people pieces of paper that describe a cash gift to your congregation. The amount is $500,000. Each group must decide how the money will be spent. There are many ways you can invest it for a steady income and there are places to give the funds away.

7. Gather the teams and share the conclusions reached. Then attempt to work out a proposal satisfactory to the whole group. Chances are that this will be impossible. By now the group should be ready to list guidelines for using money. Ask them to share some and list them on newsprint. Then pray for God's guidance in personal and congregational stewardship.

SESSION BASED ON 2:13-17

This creative exercise illustrates a part of Jesus' often-overlooked emotion: anger.

1. Gather a number of pictures showing Jesus in different poses and settings. These can be found among your Sunday school materials or in a church supply closet.

2. Ask your students to share their reactions as a group to the personality revealed in these pictures.

3. Read verses 13-17. Introduce a "whip" made from a roll of newspapers.

4. Ask them to imagine a situation or event which makes them mad. Suggest that the humanity of Christ included anger. The passage is saying that unrighteousness or injustice can produce a strong emotional feeling in Christians.

5. Go around the circle and ask each person to stand in the middle and grab the newspaper whip. You have placed a sawhorse in the center.

6. The task is to encourage each volunteer to take a turn giving a short talk on the area which makes him or her mad. With each word the person must hit the sawhorse with the paper "whip." In just a few seconds the person will really be speaking with conviction and feeling.

7. After the speech, talk as a group about the feelings of letting out the anger. What was the issue behind this righteous indignation?

8. Change direction on the conversation. How do we keep perspective and not let our feelings get carried away? How do we reconcile the peace-loving Jesus and the angry enforcer of righteousness? What is proper "zeal" as compared

to improper "zealous" behavior?

9. Gather the scraps from the broken paper "whip" into a pile.

10. Close with a prayer circle around the remains of your expressions of zeal.

SESSION BASED ON 2:18-22

1. Present the story of Jesus in the temple (verses 13-17) as a mime. Assign several parts to those who arrive early for class. You can use persons to play the roles of Jesus, moneychangers and bystanders.

2. Let the whole class become disciples. What does this sign or action point to?

3. Let the person who played Jesus stretch out on the floor. The whole group surrounds "Jesus" and together lifts the person off the ground.

4. Read verses 18-22 while the person is held aloft.

5. After the person playing Jesus is placed back on the floor, share any thoughts about the action of Jesus. Does discipleship always lead to martyrdom? Share these ideas by writing them on a person's outline cut out of a sheet of newsprint or butcher paper.

6. Focus on the major parts of the body (arms, legs, hands) as you dream about opportunities in daily life for being the body of Christ in the world. For example, we can write in the hand of the paper: "Let us offer a warm hand of welcome to new people in the group."

SESSION BASED ON 2:23-25

1. Play a tape of hysterical applause as the members of the class come into the room. You can make such a tape with your cassette recorder at a local sports event or borrow a sound-effects record from the local public library.

2. Use pages from a world records book (e.g., Guiness') or newspaper accounts of sports accomplishments. Hand out a copy or piece of the printed page to each student. For more fun, ask each person to take on the role of the sports figure and tell the group why she or he deserves applause. For example: "I'm Muhammed Ali, the greatest. I deserve a standing ovation because I'm the greatest boxer in the whole world." The group gives a standing ovation.

3. Have them share how it feels to get the glory of the world for doing something special. What things have happened in their lives that gave them this kind of recognition? What is it like when the cheering is over? Turn off the applause tape.

4. Read the passage. How does Jesus regard the world's response to his sign?

5. What kind of recognition is lasting? Close the session with reflections on this question. Hold hands and pass a word of affirmation around the circle. Or give each other a standing ovation for simply being who you are in Christ.

Creative Speaking and Preaching Ideas

A CLUE FROM 2:1-11

A pastor was being installed in a new pastoral position. He found in this passage the perfect means to draw the congregation into their joint ministry. After noting the sign or miracle that took place at the beginning of Jesus' public ministry, the new pastor invited the people to the communion service (love feast) that featured bread and small cups filled with water. He invited them to partake of the Lord's Table and prayed that the Holy Spirit would perform a miracle and transform their lives as they entered together into a new ministry. The water was a reminder of Jesus' transforming power within us.

A CLUE FROM 2:1-11

There are several different kinds of understandings represented by the people in this story. This is a good passage to bring people into the message of the text. There are at least four different viewpoints seen in the story: Jesus, his mother, his disciples and the other guests.

Bring six jars into the sanctuary and place them out of sight until the speaking moment. Carefully place them on the communion table as you tell the story or have someone else read it. Explain that this sign or miracle marked the beginning of Jesus' ministry. It was understood in different ways. Invite the congregation to look at this holy moment through the eyes of those in the story.

Walk over to one side of the room and point out several rows of people for the role of Mary. Ask them to enter into her mind and heart. Present the scene and ask them to feel the mixture of feelings concerning the ministry of their son.

JOHN 2—SPEAKING & PREACHING   51

If you are comfortable, you might have a dialogue with the group taking the role of Mary.

Next, move to another group of people in the congregation and ask them to crawl into the biblical presentation of the people at the wedding who don't understand what is happening. Go to the third group, representing the disciples. Finally, create a group standing in the sandals of Jesus.

You might want to start passing a clay jar among the people in the particular group you're addressing. End the experiential sermon by placing all the jars on the communion table, fill them with water and ask God in your prayer that the people change and grow in faith as they experience the miracle of Jesus' ministry among the congregation.

A CLUE FROM 2:13-22

Money is one of the most important symbols of faithfulness in the church today. Unfortunately, many people feel that the only way they can express their disapproval or their faith is through the withholding and giving of funds. Angry Christians sometimes withdraw their financial support if an expression of mission is not in keeping with their interests. Others are most comfortable when they can give generously to the work of the church. How does one place the positive and negative roles of money in the life of the person of faith? When is an appeal to support a Christian cause an act of faithfulness and when is it misplaced energy?

This passage offers an excellent opportunity to struggle with this very sensitive issue. The people running the bingo games or the missions bazaar will not look kindly on any discussion of fund raising. The internal struggle of this passage invites you and your people to crawl into the message of Jesus at this point. Let the Holy Spirit lead your people to the answers placed before them.

This is a very dramatic story. Jesus is obviously angry over the tainting of worship. He is filled with zeal concerning the glorification of God the creator. In fact, his life and ministry is closely related to the sanctuary of God.

You might pick up the symbols of the passage and encourage your people to focus on them. Find a thick piece of rope. Unbraid it and give out strands to a few people who you've chosen as judges. Give them the position of righteous indignation. They bear the perspective of Jesus in the temple.

Now present prepared vignettes (the youth group should enjoy a chance to act) which present an obvious abuse of money. One of the vignettes might be the distribution of pennies to the members of the congregation. The people distributing the money might carry on a sales pitch of a person selling peanuts at a baseball game or a sales pitch of a person selling vegetable peelers. The people with the strands chase them away. In between vignettes, offer a few words about the use of money and then introduce the next vignette.

Close the sermon with all actors in the various vignettes gathered around a simple cross. In a closing prayer, ask for good judgment and wise use of money.

A CLUE FROM 2:23-25

These verses cut through our pretense of righteousness. Jesus loves us and calls us to be perfect. Yet he does not suggest that we are free of sin. Our trust always must rest with God, not the good intentions of sinful people. Fame and glory are fleeing factors.

This passage challenges the view of many faithful people. They often want to believe that they have risen above sin. The Gospel of John reminds us that the very fact of our sinfulness enriches the meaning of God's love and grace. He loves us *because* of our needs and failures.

Carry in the Sunday newspaper as you enter for the service. Place it on the communion table. At the sermon time, tear it into strips and pass them out to the congregation. Ask the people to look over the scraps of paper. Read the passage and ask them to note items that in some way support or deny the thrust of the passage (the basic sinfulness of all people).

If this is a new kind of preaching format for your congregation, you may mention beforehand to a couple people that you will be using the newspaper this way and that you would appreciate their response.

A CLUE FROM 2:13-25

What parameters do we put around worship that keep us from praising God? You might focus your sermon around the nature of worship. Focus on the order of the service you are using. Take the congregation through the service from the opening. Ask the congregation to view how you worship from the perspective of Jesus. It may be helpful to hold a whip or a bundle of ropes and begin the process after you have read the passage.

Starting with the setting before the prelude, move through the service quickly. Ask the people to share things that Jesus would notice. In order to keep this worship sermon from becoming a complaint session, ask that they raise questions Jesus might ask. These can be written on cards and handed in or you can invite people to speak out.

This should be a fast-moving process. Have the organist play just a couple notes of each hymn to start the music discussion. Push to define what it is that Jesus demands of those who worship him. Are we stumbling blocks to worship by our behavior, dress, etc.?

You might use the whip to drive out (symbolically) the practices that defile the holiness of God's place. This type of presentation will accomplish several important goals: education about worship, feedback on service, making the point that we are all responsible for the purity and authenticity of praising God's name.

You might utilize the church bulletin in this dramatic "cleansing" of the temple. Why not distribute blank bulletins to the worshipers as they enter the building? The service could "construct" the pure worship service.

You might enact the cleansing of the service as the opening and build the service freshly around the centrality of Jesus (John 3:16). This active sermon would embrace the whole worship service. This model may seem iconoclastic to those from a rich liturgical tradition. But it can still be a helpful approach if you want to deepen the understanding of your church's historical ways of worship. It is amazing how many people take their heritage for granted. Sometimes the shedding of meaningless things in our lives enables us to restore the important things. Jesus permitted the people in the temple to return to the basics by whipping away the unimportant. Why shouldn't our church?

CHAPTER 3

NICODEMUS COMES TO JESUS BY NIGHT

Now there was a man of the Pharisees, named Nicode′mus, a ruler of the Jews. ²This man came to Jesus[d] by night and said to him, "Rabbi, we know that you are a teacher come from God; for no one can do these signs that you do, unless God is with him." ³Jesus answered him, "Truly, truly, I say to you, unless one is born anew,[e] he cannot see the kingdom of God." ⁴Nicode′mus said to him, "How can a man be born when he is old? Can he enter a second time into his mother's womb and be born?" ⁵Jesus answered, "Truly, truly, I say to you, unless one is born of water and the Spirit, he cannot enter the kingdom of God. ⁶That which is born of the flesh is flesh, and that which is born of the Spirit is spirit.[f] ⁷Do not marvel that I said to you, 'You must be born anew.'[e] ⁸The wind[f] blows where it wills, and you hear the sound of it, but you do not know whence it comes or whither it goes; so it is with every one who is born of the Spirit." ⁹Nicode′mus said to him, "How can this be?" ¹⁰Jesus answered him, "Are you a teacher of Israel, and yet you do not understand this? ¹¹Truly, truly, I say to you, we speak of what we know, and bear witness to what we have seen; but you do not receive our testimony. ¹²If I have told you earthly things and you do not believe, how can you believe if I tell you heavenly things? ¹³No one has ascended into heaven but he who descended from heaven, the Son of man.[g] ¹⁴And as Moses lifted up the serpent in the wilderness, so must the Son of man be lifted up, ¹⁵that whoever believes in him may have eternal life."[h]

16 For God so loved the world that he gave his only Son, that whoever believes in him should not perish but have eternal life. ¹⁷For God sent the Son into the world, not to condemn the world, but that the world might be saved through him. ¹⁸He who believes in him is not condemned; he who does not believe is condemned already, because he has not believed in the name of the only Son of God. ¹⁹And this is the judgment, that the light has come into the world, and men loved darkness rather than light, because their deeds were evil. ²⁰For every one who does evil hates the light, and does not come to the light, lest his deeds should be exposed. ²¹But he who does what is true comes to the light, that it may be clearly seen that his deeds have been wrought in God.

JOHN THE BAPTIST: "HE MUST INCREASE, BUT I MUST DECREASE"

22 After this Jesus and his disciples went into the land of Judea; there he remained with them and baptized. ²³John also was baptizing at Ae′non near Salim, because there was much water there; and people came and were baptized. ²⁴For John had not yet been put in prison.

---

d Greek *him*
e Or *from above*
f The same Greek word means both *wind* and *spirit*
g Other ancient authorities add *who is in heaven*
h Some interpreters hold that the quotation continues through verse 21

25 Now a discussion arose between John's disciples and a Jew over purifying. ²⁶And they came to John, and said to him, "Rabbi, he who was with you beyond the Jordan, to whom you bore witness, here he is, baptizing, and all are going to him." ²⁷John answered, "No one can receive anything except what is given him from heaven. ²⁸You yourselves bear me witness, that I said, I am not the Christ, but I have been sent before him. ²⁹He who has the bride is the bridegroom; the friend of the bridegroom, who stands and hears him, rejoices greatly at the bridegroom's voice; therefore this joy of mine is now full. ³⁰He must increase, but I must decrease."*i*

31 He who comes from above is above all; he who is of the earth belongs to the earth, and of the earth he speaks; he who comes from heaven is above all. ³²He bears witness to what he has seen and heard, yet no one receives his testimony; ³³he who receives his testimony sets his seal to this, that God is true. ³⁴For he whom God has sent utters the words of God, for it is not by measure that he gives the Spirit; ³⁵the Father loves the Son, and has given all things into his hand. ³⁶He who believes in the Son has eternal life; he who does not obey the Son shall not see life, but the wrath of God rests upon him.

---

i Some interpreters hold that the quotation continues through verse 36

CHAPTER 3

Creative Commentary on the Scripture

VERSES 1-10: Jesus and Nicodemus talk. We have another person introduced into the texture of the Gospel of John. Particulars are given about him. Nicodemus is presented as one coming "by night" (John's light/darkness theme). The signs or miracles witnessed by the people in the previous chapter have carried this religious leader to Jesus. The encounter concerning the new birth is another double-meaning dialogue. Nicodemus simply does not understand the deeper journey of teaching that Jesus sets before him. Several words cut one way in Jesus' mind and another in Nicodemus' ("from above" or "again"; "spirit" or "wind").

It is helpful to look at this encounter as gently humorous. Jesus is smiling at the irony of a highly respected, learned man confounded by the gospel's simplicity. The text suggests that humor is a close relative to the deep emotions involved in growth and change. So why is rebirth such "deadly serious business" for Christians when childlike gifts await discovery and celebration? Perhaps this text suggests that we are unwittingly walking blindly in the shoes of Nicodemus with our "grave" faith. Jesus calls the listener to feel and respond on the simplest and most profound levels.

VERSES 10-15: In verse 11, John draws upon the role of the senses concerning the witness to salvation ("what we see"). The fact that Nicodemus does not comprehend the message of the Word become flesh suggests that he cannot understand the spiritual teachings of Jesus.

The image of the womb is much like that of a cave. It is sometimes hard for a person to emerge from the safety and protection of the known into the realm of the unknown. Jesus is acting like a midwife or guide. He is beckoning for Nicodemus and all of us to embrace a new environment of existence. We cannot return to the womb or the cave. Yet there is the temptation to yearn for it. This is why the text seems to call believers of every generation to shun the comfortable and risk walking with Christ in an uncertain journey.

The fourth Gospel pictures Jesus as the one lifted up in spiritual power through the sacrifice of the cross. In fact, this act of the Son alludes to the serpent that Moses lifted up in the wilderness. This is an image of healing and life. In addition, the imagery of the serpent as a means of evil in Genesis is replaced with the healing of sin through Christ on the cross.

VERSES 16-21: This text presents the most famous summary of the Christian faith: 3:16. The language indicates that God's supreme act has been fulfilled now and forever. God's love extends to the whole created order (cosmos).

VERSES 22-30: John the Baptist returns to clarify his secondary role in relationship to Jesus. The image of the friend of the bridegroom describes this role.

VERSES 31-36: The writer stresses once again the importance of origin in terms of our spiritual quality. Jesus has a different source of power than does John the Baptist. The concluding statement expands upon verse 16 by adding that judgment awaits those who turn away from the promise of eternal life. It is significant that the present tense is used by John. Eternal life is the gift to the believer right now. Jesus also notes that there are negative consequences when one lives outside of true obedience.

Creative Bible Study Ideas

SESSION BASED ON 3:1-15

In this important dialogue passage Nicodemus simply does not seem to understand what Jesus is teaching. This clue can help us plan a learning experience to draw our students into the text.

You might want to build your session on the problem of understanding. Put your students in a situation where they must explain to Nicodemus what Jesus is teaching. Have someone take the role of the Pharisee. Another person can present the person of Jesus in this encounter. The two characters move through this exchange by reading a paraphrase worked out by you and some of the students or they can ad-lib the exchange.

Now the rest of the students can carry on a press conference or tutoring session with this puzzled man of old. You will be amazed to see how your students can teach others! The person playing the role of Nicodemus can ask the other students for help in understanding what Jesus teaches. You'll need to carefully help the discussion along to cover the main teachings of the passage.

You can offer a variation on this design by saying that the visitor doesn't understand English. The students will have to communicate the themes of the passage by using mime or charades!

Ask the students to explore a popular publication during the next week (newsmagazine, sports publication, etc.) and make a collage presenting this passage from the images in these periodicals. Or, provide these at your session and have the students create them there. These paraphrases can be shared at this or the next session or it would even be better if they could be shared with other classes in the educational program of the church.

SESSION BASED ON 3:16

Martin Luther called this verse "the little Gospel." Each word is packed with Good News! With younger students you might build upon the poetic quality of the text by teaching it with music. For instance, a group of third graders might crawl into this message by creating a song based on it. Use a pentatonic scale like C,D,E,G,A and mix the sounds with the verse. You have a fresh and original experience of the passage! They learn the words as an extension of their own vocal rhythms. Then let the children share their new song with adults through a "tour" of the other classes. Invite the children to lead the congregation in the singing of their biblical song during the morning worship experience.

Even if you are unsure about your musical ability, don't reject the use of this powerful medium. There are many musicians who can complement your teaching role. Feel free to draw upon these people when a passage suggests special approaches.

SESSION BASED ON 3:16-21

1. Gather the group in a circle.
2. Pass out to each person a transparent glass marble, the kind with streaks of color in it.
3. Read the passage in a "lining out" style. One person volunteers to read the text line-by-line. After he or she reads a line, the group repeats what was just read aloud.
4. Ask the students to imagine that the marble in their hands is Earth as seen from God's perspective. You might play a selection of classical music while they think about the cosmos.
5. Ask each person to close his or her hand on the marble, completely covering it as he or she reflects on the people in the world who are lost in darkness.
6. Share the kinds of examples that come to mind about the people caught in darkness and condemnation.
7. Ask everyone to hold the marble between two fingers in the light (from ceiling light or special bulb in center of circle).
8. Ask them to share how the light of Christ (the gift of eternal life) transforms the darkness of the world.
9. You might focus on special examples of people locked in evil. Can they be touched? What is our role in this transformation by God?
10. Ask each person to carry the marble during the next week and reflect on it at lunch time. Perhaps they can offer a special prayer for someone trapped in sin. You might even suggest that the students give their marble to a person facing great difficulty. They can tell the recipient that the marble is a reminder of their prayers and that all of creation rests in the loving hands of God.

SESSION BASED ON 3:1-22

1. Ask each student, one at a time, if he or she is a Christian.
2. Encourage them to share what is meant by this claim. You should want them to understand that Christian growth is an ongoing process that impacts their lifestyle and thinking. Ask a few students to share how they are different people since becoming a Christian.
3. Illustrate the growth process with a morality play (an art form from the Middle Ages). The theme will be: "Being Born Again in Christ." You can encourage them to use mu-

sic, mime, etc. Work in units of three or four if you have a large number of students. Use a bedsheet to divide the before-change life and after-change life. The "old" person enters one side and mimes (place a light behind the sheet to highlight shadows) the unredeemed life. The reborn person then exits to the other side of the sheet and mimes the results of the change. For example, a slouching, slow, sad person walks behind the sheet. He or she straightens, lifts up hands, maybe even jumps up and down. Then the person exits to the other side of the sheet in good posture and beams a peaceful expression. Leave the process in the hands of the students.

4. Share the short plays.

5. Debrief the new insights the participants have about transformation through the new birth.

6. Arrange to have these plays or the best one or two shared as a part of worship for the whole congregation.

SESSION BASED ON 3:22-30

Do you ever wonder if God calls us for our weaknesses and not for our strengths? This would mean that we permit others to supplement our deficiencies and thereby enable them to serve in a special way. Being second-best is also a calling from God. This passage opens up these intriguing ideas. John the Baptist exposes the ultimate flaws in our success-at-all-costs culture. The story of John the Baptist suggests a special opportunity for your students to explore the New Testament view of success: obedience to the will of God.

1. Purchase a cardboard cutout of a super-hero(ine): Superman, etc. They can be found in the toy departments of most stores. These paper forms are usually human-size and can be displayed easily.

2. Write out a little narration introducing the super-hero. You might even record the narrated introduction on cassette tape with bombastic music in the background. Really ham it up.

3. Place the cutout before the group and play the narration that has been recorded on a cassette machine. Or, you might play the narration, then open a closet door where your super-hero cutout is waiting. If you're in a hurry, "live" narration will do.

4. Ask the members of the group to name the qualities

that make this comic-book character such a winner.

5. Introduce another character. This one is much different from the super-hero. You have simply copied the form of the super-hero(ine) shape onto a piece of paper or cardboard. Tell them that this is Herman or Lucy. He or she is the sibling of the comic character. This person has none of the characteristics of the star. In fact, Herman and Lucy might be considered normal, perhaps even dull.

6. Discuss how it might feel to be the brother or sister of such a star. What kinds of comparisons are made? Have you had any such experiences in your life?

7. Read the passage (verses 22-30).

8. Discuss the situation of John being compared to Jesus. Why does John the Baptist seem to accept a "second-place" situation joyously? Don't let anyone get away with the idea that because he is in the Bible he isn't tempted like we are.

9. Read verse 30.

10. Pass around newspaper stories about people struggling for equal opportunities, people obviously being manipulated by others or people stuck in a dead-end situation.

11. Ask the students how they might support these people in the various struggles. Would you be willing to lose some of your rights to help them? What does the Gospel of John say about this? Is it possible to be "second-place" to the ones Jesus called the "least of these"?

12. Close with a circle of affirmation. You might ask each person to say this to the person on the right, one at a time: "You are a child of God and I rejoice with you that nothing can rob us of the love of Christ."

This session is a natural for youth. But don't dismiss the ideas created by this passage if you teach adults. In fact, the childlike idiom of comic-book characters may be the best way to get around any defensive walls to the success syndrome of the adult. You might want the youth to share the learnings of this session with the rest of the church. Perhaps they could teach an adult class by using the same design!

SESSION BASED ON 3:36

The flip side of the promise in this verse is the judgment. This verse makes this truth quite clear. We are tempted either to beat people with the judgment of God or ignore it.

The Gospel of John in this passage seems to say that we can do neither.

Modify the design offered in the speaking and preaching section on this verse. It will work well for a creative Bible study.

Creative Speaking and Preaching Ideas

A CLUE FROM 3:1-15

The dialogue form of this passage suggests that the story can be presented utilizing either readers' theater or drama. The former technique creates a "script" out of the text. Two or more people can then read the passage. This is an excellent way of getting into the interior dynamics of the message. It is amazing how many lay people are powerful readers of the Word. They are often more natural in their presentation than clergy.

It might be wise to utilize several readers to provide the litany between your terse comments about the text. As the dialogue unfolds, you can flesh out the message with sermon scraps that punctuate and clarify the vital message in these verses. Jesus is using a highly dramatic and provocative presentation for this discussion of eternal life. Allow your preaching to show Jesus' provocative creativity.

A CLUE FROM 3:1-15

Another dramatic form suggested by this text is that of the preacher crawling into the role of Nicodemus. Don't be shy about entering fully into a biblical personality. It takes a little more risk to go into costume and makeup. Prepare by entering into the spirit and mind of this ancient Pharisee. Help the congregation feel sympathy for this seeker of truth. He has missed the point of Jesus' teaching, but he has at least pursued the questions. Nicodemus' struggle is our struggle. Don't be afraid to let your people feel the unconcluded quest of Nicodemus. He has not wrapped up the answers to his questions in a neat package.

Another way to close is to ask the congregation to explain what Jesus was trying to teach Nicodemus. The character can have dialogue with the worshipers. Let the people have a part in proclaiming the gospel. Trust the Holy Spirit working through your people.

A CLUE FROM 3:1-15

The text has a great deal to say about the role and meaning of baptism. Why not celebrate a baptism in the context of a creative sermon on the Jesus/Nicodemus encounter? Ask an adult or young person who seeks baptism to present a dialogical sermon on the text. He or she could represent Jesus as you take the role of Nicodemus. After the sermon, tell the congregation that your helper has understood the meaning and joy of baptism. Then proceed with the act of baptism.

A CLUE FROM 3:1-15

Interesting sermon clues can be found in the sensual aspects of this passage. Peek through these windows to the message. Perhaps a cassette recording of a baby crying could be used as you talk about the "sounds" of rebirth. The sound of wind (or spirit) can be provided by people blowing with their mouths or by another cassette recording of wind.

The reference to Moses in the wilderness in verse 14 relates the Old Testament story of the serpent to Jesus on the cross. Pass out two pipe cleaners to the worshipers as they enter the sanctuary. In the course of the sermon, ask them to bend the pipe cleaners into serpent shapes; then the shape of the cross.

You might ask the whole congregation to follow you with motions as you lead them in this sensual experiencing of the passage. For example, you can go through the mime of rocking a baby as you talk about the two kinds of birth or invite everyone to raise hands as you lift the "serpent" to become the cross.

A CLUE FROM 3:1-21

This is an excellent text for a baptism Sunday. You might use the passage's confused dialogue style to show Nicodemus' confusion. Fashion a dialogue with another person similar to misunderstood dialogues in comedy material. ("Who's on First?" by Abbott and Costello is perfect for this purpose.) The basis of this humor is the misunderstanding of what the words mean. Each participant is expressing something that the other person doesn't understand.

Don't be afraid of humor. There is a feeling in this text that Jesus is actually using humor. He knows the difficulty this scholar of the Jews is having with simple things. You might want to create your dialogue out of the actual text. Present it as a humorous exchange.

It is significant that we move from the gentle humor of Jesus to the deepest part of the proclamation: John 3:16. Is Jesus suggesting that humor is one of the greatest entry points to the new birth? Perhaps we do not all need the-road-to-Damascus experience to find new life.

A CLUE FROM 3:16

The whole gospel is packed into the few words of this verse. The familiar text reaches out and touches all the other aspects of the life, ministry, death and resurrection of Jesus. The message is old and comfortable but it also cuts into our complacency.

You might permit the passage to speak out freshly by asking someone in the congregation or community to "sign" this verse. ("Signing" is used with the deaf.) Learn the gestures for the main nine words and phrases in the verse ("God," "loved," "world," "gave," "only Son," "whoever," "believes," "not perish" and "eternal life"). You might explore these concepts by letting your people express them with their hands. You could even preach a nine-week series around the themes in this single verse. Each week another "sign" can be added.

This simple idea can be utilized in such a way that neither leader nor people are threatened by the experience. You might utilize the litany or responsive-preaching style. Each time you mention the word of this week's theme, the congregation is encouraged to make the sign for the term.

A CLUE FROM 3:17-21

These verses deal with sin and salvation. Judgment for sin is something either taken too seriously or not seriously enough by the faith community. It seems that many church people do not want to think about sin. The confessional or forgiveness experience in worship seems very weak. This text invites an exploration into this important aspect of theology and life.

The images of "light" and "darkness" are important biblical ways of describing good and evil. This clue suggests that we use the visual sense to probe the theological struggle between evil and good.

This passage would take on particular meaning if it were the text for a sermon given at an evening service. The surrounding darkness would provide the perfect context for the message. In the beginning, God created order and light in the midst of chaos and darkness. The absence of faith/light brings evil/darkness and judgment. We are told in these verses that those who love the darkness hate the light. There is a suggested quality of distance in such a concept: To be close is to embrace, to separate from something is to hate it.

You might take these clues and begin the sermon experience by passing out kitchen matches and something rough to light them (e.g., a small piece of sandpaper). Encourage your people to reflect on the potential in this piece of wood tipped with chemical. Paraphrase the Son/light coming into the world to bring light/life and salvation/wholeness to creation. Then ask each person to light the match. Let it burn for a few seconds. Describe the winds of sin that endanger the light. Have everyone blow out the match.

Ask them to smell the lingering smoke and the darkness of the room after losing the light. Talk about the temptation to walk in the darkness/sin by separating from the needs and lives of others.

You might pass out candles and light the first one and have the first person light the next and so on until all are lit. When the room is flooded with light, share the promise that the light is given by God through Jesus Christ and the darkness can never overcome the light.

Send the people into the world with the commission to keep the light burning in the midst of darkness and despair.

A CLUE FROM 3:22-30

We return to John the Baptist as he defines the nature of his call in relationship to Jesus. We receive the ultimate model of humility. He is willing to be second-best in comparison with Christ. The closing verse is a hard saying for most Christians and leaders of Christians.

Preaching a sermon titled "The Importance of Being Second" would not be welcomed in most competition-oriented cultural settings. Yet this passage beckons the believer into the experience of Christian humility.

Collect stories from sports magazines and newspaper sports sections on losing teams and athletes. It will be quite easy to make such a collection or ask several young people to assist you. You will be amazed how interest in preaching will quicken once you begin utilizing the experiential approach. Make them partners with you in this task. In a week they will find more than enough articles on losers for each person in worship. Let the helpers distribute the items.

Use the dialogue idiom of the passage and ask for examples of losers from the articles they hold. The first 40 seconds after asking for such sharing is always the hardest. It is so tempting to step in and continue when you don't have an immediate response. Don't give in to the temptation. Someone will speak up.

Field the stories people will have to share. Don't draw conclusions from each example. Just accept them and at the appropriate moment ask if your people have any personal stories about coming in second. What were the feelings at these moments? Accept these moments of sharing.

Remember that you don't have to agree or disagree with what people feel called to share. Accept these contributions. Turn to the passage and note John's willingness to be "decreased" as Jesus is "increased." How does such a viewpoint strike us if this is applied to women's rights, minority opportunities, Third World problems, increased benefits for the aged? Accept the reaction of people in the congregation.

Note that John uses the example of the friend of the bridegroom. What does this image suggest about this message? (The relationship between first and second is inseparable. They could not exist independently.) Close the sermon with a challenge to the congregation to outdo one another in humble acts of love.

A CLUE FROM 3:36

This summary of the chapter balances verse 16: God's punishment rests upon the person who is disobedient to the Son. This person will not see life/light, but experience the judgment of God.

Radical obedience to Jesus Christ is a foreign concept to the faith experience of many within the church. The harsh delineation between those who bear the witness of obedience and those who hate the light is an important theological theme for the people of faith. How can you create a preaching occasion in which they can experience this call? The classic evangelists like Jonathan Edwards could preach in such a way that "grown men" would quake with fear. These preachers from the golden age of preaching created a drama of salvation into which the listener was drawn. He or she could experience the agony of hell and the ecstasy of heaven. But we no longer live in this kind of cultural texture. However, the power of this passage is vital to our understanding of the Christian life at this time.

If you have an old cemetery near by, take some young people with you and make gravestone rubbings. This is a simple process. Tape rice paper across the face of a gravestone. A soft crayon is rubbed across the paper. The indentations in the engraved stone will remain white while the black or dark-colored wax will be solid. You can easily read the inscriptions on the stones. In the old cemeteries, you will find some moving inscriptions concerning life and death. The hope of reward for the faithful will be clearly etched in stone.

You will also want to collect obituaries from newspapers. Be sure to ask some of your people to help in this process. You will find that this co-preparation for worship will excite your people as they contribute to the service in a fresh way.

Staple or print some sample obituaries in the worship bulletin. The cover might even be printed with a gravestone inscription. Have the co-liturgists (helpers) walk up and down the aisles with the gravestone rubbings "worn" like sandwich boards. They might moan softly, "Woe is me, woe is me." Read the passage as they slowly walk down the aisles and around the sides of the worship area.

If the stones are very old and there are no personal family connections with the persons in your church, each helper might be costumed from the head up with a bonnet or hat of the dates from the stone. Have each person become a talking gravestone. Work these monologues out with the participants beforehand. Each short presentation can be a bit different. All should raise the question of obedience to the Son. "I lived in a difficult time. It was hard to know the way of God. The Civil War divided my family. I fought with the Confederates; my cousin with the Union. Was I obedient or was my cousin obedient to Jesus?"

Ask each worshiper to write his or her own obituary statement. Is the punishment of God upon me? Ask people to share their feelings for themselves or those in the talking gravestones. You might collect their statements and pass them out again. Everyone would have a different one. Now you can encourage the sharing of what was written in a less-threatening way.

Close by reading the passage and encouraging obedience to the Son regardless of present-day pressures, worries or fears.

CHAPTER 4

JESUS THE LIVING WATER

Now when the Lord knew that the Pharisees had heard that Jesus was making and baptizing more disciples than John ²(although Jesus himself did not baptize, but only his disciples), ³he left Judea and departed again to Galilee. ⁴He had to pass through Sama'ria. ⁵So he came to a city of Sama'ria, called Sy'char, near the field that Jacob gave to his son Joseph. ⁶Jacob's well was there, and so Jesus, wearied as he was with his journey, sat down beside the well. It was about the sixth hour.

7 There came a woman of Sama'ria to draw water. Jesus said to her, "Give me a drink." ⁸For his disciples had gone away into the city to buy food. ⁹The Samaritan woman said to him, "How is it that you, a Jew, ask a drink of me, a woman of Sama'ria?" For Jews have no dealings with Samaritans. ¹⁰Jesus answered her, "If you knew the gift of God, and who it is that is saying to you, 'Give me a drink,' you would have asked him, and he would have given you living water." ¹¹The woman said to him, "Sir, you have nothing to draw with, and the well is deep; where do you get that living water? ¹²Are you greater than our father Jacob, who gave us the well, and drank from it himself, and his sons, and his cattle?" ¹³Jesus said to her, "Every one who drinks of this water will thirst again, ¹⁴but whoever drinks of the water that I shall give him will never thirst; the water that I shall give him will become in him a spring of water welling up to eternal life." ¹⁵The woman said to him, "Sir, give me this water, that I may not thirst, nor come here to draw."

16 Jesus said to her, "Go, call your husband, and come here." ¹⁷The woman answered him, "I have no husband." Jesus said to her, "You are right in saying, 'I have no husband'; ¹⁸for you have had five husbands, and he whom you now have is not your husband; this you said truly." ¹⁹The woman said to him, "Sir, I perceive that you are a prophet. ²⁰Our fathers worshiped on this mountain; and you say that in Jerusalem is the place where men ought to worship." ²¹Jesus said to her, "Woman, believe me, the hour is coming when neither on this mountain nor in Jerusalem will you worship the Father. ²²You worship what you do not know; we worship what we know, for salvation is from the Jews. ²³But the hour is coming, and now is, when the true worshipers will worship the Father in spirit and truth, for such the Father seeks to worship him. ²⁴God is spirit, and those who worship him must worship in spirit and truth." ²⁵The woman said to him, "I know that Messiah is coming (he who is called Christ); when he comes, he will show us all things." ²⁶Jesus said to her, "I who speak to you am he."

JESUS' FOOD: TO DO THE WILL OF GOD

27 Just then his disciples came. They marveled that he was talking with a woman, but none said, "What do you wish?" or, "Why are you talking with her?" ²⁸So the woman left

her water jar, and went away into the city, and said to the people, ²⁹"Come, see a man who told me all that I ever did. Can this be the Christ?" ³⁰They went out of the city and were coming to him.

31 Meanwhile the disciples besought him, saying, "Rabbi, eat." ³²But he said to them, "I have food to eat of which you do not know." ³³So the disciples said to one another, "Has any one brought him food?" ³⁴Jesus said to them, "My food is to do the will of him who sent me, and to accomplish his work. ³⁵Do you not say, 'There are yet four months, then comes the harvest'? I tell you, lift up your eyes, and see how the fields are already white for harvest. ³⁶He who reaps receives wages, and gathers fruit for eternal life, so that sower and reaper may rejoice together. ³⁷For here the saying holds true, 'One sows and another reaps.' ³⁸I sent you to reap that for which you did not labor; others have labored, and you have entered into their labor."

THE SAMARITANS BELIEVE

39 Many Samaritans from that city believed in him because of the woman's testimony, "He told me all that I ever did." ⁴⁰So when the Samaritans came to him, they asked him to stay with them; and he stayed there two days. ⁴¹And many more believed because of his word. ⁴²They said to the woman, "It is no longer because of your words that we believe, for we have heard for ourselves, and we know that this is indeed the Savior of the world."

JESUS HEALS THE OFFICIAL'S SON

43 After the two days he departed to Galilee. ⁴⁴For Jesus himself testified that a prophet has no honor in his own country. ⁴⁵So when he came to Galilee, the Galileans welcomed him, having seen all that he had done in Jerusalem at the feast, for they too had gone to the feast.

46 So he came again to Cana in Galilee, where he had made the water wine. And at Caper'na-um there was an official whose son was ill. ⁴⁷When he heard that Jesus had come from Judea to Galilee, he went and begged him to come down and heal his son, for he was at the point of death. ⁴⁸Jesus therefore said to him, "Unless you see signs and wonders you will not believe." ⁴⁹The official said to him, "Sir, come down before my child dies." ⁵⁰Jesus said to him, "Go; your son will live." The man believed the word that Jesus spoke to him and went his way. ⁵¹As he was going down, his servants met him and told him that his son was living. ⁵²So he asked them the hour when he began to mend, and they said to him, "Yesterday at the seventh hour the fever left him." ⁵³The father knew that was the hour when Jesus had said to him, "Your son will live"; and he himself believed, and all his household. ⁵⁴This was now the second sign that Jesus did when he had come from Judea to Galilee.

CHAPTER 4

Creative Commentary on the Scripture

This chapter brings us stories rich with the special fourth Gospel qualities. Real persons in need emerge from the text. We care for them. They are instruments of grace whose actions and encounters with Jesus carry special meanings for the faithful of every age.

VERSES 1-26: This story is rich in experiential clues for teachers and preachers. The familiar style of disconnected dialogue (see chapter 3 commentary) plays an important role with the Samaritan woman. We should be alert for clues concerning Jesus' attitude toward women. A very affirming position is suggested. Human themes of thirst, love, racial acceptance, as well as the prophetic role of Jesus are vividly presented here.

It is significant that portions of John in general and this chapter in particular are often quoted in worship contexts. For example, verses 23-24 are frequently used to open church services. There is a liturgical character to the text which suggests that we experience it in worship.

VERSES 27-30: This material continues the preceding story. The disciples' reactions are helpful indicators of the radical nature of Jesus' ministry.

VERSES 31-38: This transitional passage gives the disciples some "travel directions" for their discipleship which they will understand later. You can almost hear Jesus whispering to us, "Surely, these words are not without meaning."

VERSES 39-42: The Gospel writer makes it clear that the crowds touched by Jesus were moved because of his teaching and not just by the sparkle of the woman's report. The personal encounter or experience with Jesus moves people to embrace him as the savior of the world.

VERSES 43-54: Jesus provides another sign to glorify the Father. The role of faith plays an important role in the restoration of the official's son. Many others are touched by this single act of inspiring the faith of one person. The time frame of the story is important to validate the action by Jesus. He heals the boy by the power of his word.

Creative Bible Study Ideas

This chapter is a delight for those seeking teaching opportunities that draw students into the Bible material. The author gives us two important stories with key theological concepts.

This is perfect material for the utilization of media forms that give students a chance to get inside the story. Our suggestions may be beyond your immediate experience. However, we are often limited by only doing things we have used previously. There are always people in your community who will be glad to supplement your communication skills. We have found that when we ask others to contribute their gifts to ministry, they then are ready to receive our teaching and preaching.

SESSION BASED ON 4:1-26

This dramatic story has often been presented as a drama. The dialogue is striking. As we have suggested in the preaching section, this material begs to take on dramatic flesh. Members of your class take the roles of Jesus, the woman, disciples and townspeople. Perhaps you can even cast the whole class as one of the groups involved in the story. A disciple might turn to the class and ask about this action by Jesus: "Why has he spent time with this Samaritan woman?"

The passage suggests that a story is being told that must be shared with others. The videotape machine, which is now a common piece of equipment in most congregations and communities, can provide such an opportunity. Individuals in your church will have one of the video units. Public libraries, public schools and even auto dealers now have machines on loan. Gather your students around this passage and ask them to produce a video piece (short or long) on this passage. The process of creating this material will force the students to get a good grasp on the content. Be sure to arrange opportunities for the students to share what they have created. One church had the junior highers produce short biblical videos each week. They would then go to other classes and show the video material weekly.

Puppetry is also a helpful medium for communicating a passage like this. Your students can create the puppets, write the script and record the sound track. They can then share this biblical story with other groups in the church and community.

Another exciting medium inspired by the passage is clown ministry. This popular form permits the person of faith to have a creative outlet that is also firmly grounded in theology. The white face of the mime/clown can easily communicate the characters and situation.

SESSION BASED ON 4:1-26

One of the clues emerging from this passage is the role of artifacts in the story. The well, the jar and the water play important roles in communicating the message.

The jar is the medium the woman used to respond to the needs of Jesus. It was the means for drawing the water from the well. At the end of the conversation, she rushes off filled with a sense of the living water and forgets her jar (verse 28). It would be interesting to present the session from the perspective of the jar. As the group gathers, create a circle. Place a large, worn clay jar in the center of the circle. The focus will be the story told by the jar.

You might record the story on cassette tape before the session and play it as if the jar were talking. Younger children will enjoy this technique. A few of them might work with you on this before the session. The jar story can be presented as a sympathetic view of the mistress. The woman's character can be unfolded gently. If you want to add a bit of fun to the process, you can create an echo sound by recording in a closed space or holding a large box over the head of the narrator and microphone.

At the end of the story, turn off the tape and tell the students that we don't know much about the woman's later life from the biblical story. Yet we know that Jesus touched her life. Pass the jar around the circle and ask each person to continue its story based on what he or she thinks the gospel would do to change her life. If the students are unaccustomed to this kind of involvement based on their own thoughts, you might start with each person adding one word to describe her feelings after she returned to the village. You may first focus on the Samaritan woman's view of herself. You may make several more rounds with the jar with other areas of her life: her lifestyle, the way others now viewed her, etc.

You may close the session with a circle prayer of thanksgiving that we all are jars or vessels of God's grace.

SESSION BASED ON 4:43-54

Parents feel the pinch of responsibility when they consider their role in parenting. It is particularly hard for a mother and father to confront the pain and danger of a child. This section of the chapter invites a class of adults to enter an important aspect of Jesus' teaching. You will be able to make the emotional connection point between your students and the text quite easily and deeply.

You might begin by projecting one slide on a screen or wall of the classroom. Don't darken it totally. Just take the most direct light off of the image. The students should be able to see the picture, but faintly. Choose a slide of a small baby wrapped in a blanket. You can pull one out of your own family collection or just talk to someone in the church who does a lot of photography. Every family seems to have such photos.

Ask the students to focus on the slide and think about a baby they have known and loved. Guide them through a reflection on the dependency of such a small life. Then read verses 43-54 from the Gospel of John.

Have the group cluster in units of three and share their feelings as if they were in the shoes of the official at the moment he was driven to beg the help of Jesus. After three or four minutes, break in and ask them to continue the discussion by sharing any moment when they as parents were frightened by one of their children's illnesses.

Gather the groups together and share the reflections and stories that emerged in the small clusters. You might read the passage once again before this sharing.

After everyone has had a chance to share the feeling of crisis, have the whole group talk about how their faith in some way played a role in facing these moments of worry.

How were others touched by your struggle? In what ways did God work through others?

If you do not choose to use a slide, you might simply bring in a baby blanket and pass it around the circle. This physical reminder of the helplessness of a baby will aid the students in their quest to enter into the text.

There are also certain actions suggested by this text. Child abuse, children in the hospital, educational needs, unemployed family situations, damaging media programming for children and other local concerns may demand action from your class. Jesus heals a child as a sign of his ministry. Should not your people hear the call to minister to the physical and emotional needs of children and youth? Your class could study the needs in your community by interviewing parents and community service agency directors in the area. These findings can result in recommendations for action by your church.

Creative Speaking and Preaching Ideas

A CLUE FROM 4:1-15, 27-30, 39-42

The Samaritan woman came out to Jacob's well to draw water. We also go again and again to our own well. We reach deeply down into our past, our history, our triumphs. There is a symbolic sense in which we fill our buckets and with great labor draw them up. We are drawing up our dreams, hopes and wishes for the future. These utopias become means of avoiding the truths about ourselves which we do not want to face.

Once we make this kind of connection between the story and our own survival we can design a means so that the people of God at worship can walk with the woman. Distribute or have affixed to the bulletins slips of paper. Ask the worshipers to write down single words or phrases that describe the "heavy" things which have made the quest for refreshment so hard to pull from our "wishing well." On the reverse side, ask them to list the hopeful things they wish to drink (economic, social, political, etc.).

Collect these notes and place them in a symbolic well at the altar area of the sanctuary. You can make this from a few flat rocks piled in a circle, or you might use a jar. Drop the sheets into the well. Commit them to the well with a blessing: "Lord God, accept the hopes and burdens of these disciples. Give us the living waters."

You might have water in the jar. Pour out the water in small cups. As you do this, talk about the living water that Christ promises (from the text). You can take five or six minutes to share the wonder of Jesus' gift to the Samaritan woman.

Now invite all those who are thirsty for the living water to come forward and receive from the well. This will be particularly striking for those congregations not accustomed to coming forward to receive the Lord's Supper. You are not serving the sacrament. You are simply putting them into the passage and letting them sensually experience what Jesus is teaching to the woman. Don't worry if only a few come forward. You might select a hymn that speaks about the living water as background for this act of renewal.

You might ask several worshipers to aid you in the ministry of the well. Be sure that each person is handed a cup with a blessing. "Whoever drinks of the water that I shall give will never thirst; the water that I shall give will become in you a spring of water welling up to eternal life" (paraphrase of verse 14).

You might carry this experiential sermon one step further by asking the congregation to write once again. This time ask them to write down the "living waters" they have received: persons, events, acts, places, etc. Gather these and read a few as a final prayer of thanksgiving.

A CLUE FROM 4:16-26

We find Jesus talking with a woman about her romantic life. He is more comfortable talking about matters of the heart than she is. She quickly tries to get "religious" with him once she discovers that he sees through her heart. Spirit and truth are known in the intimate relationship of worship. He moves the discussion to her immediate relationship with the person behind the theological ("Messiah") category: "I who speak to you am he."

You might utilize a heart-shaped candy box for your sermon. Fill it with intimate messages (on small slips of paper). You can model them on the kinds of sayings found in "fortune cookies" or sayings from the wisdom literature (Psalms, Proverbs, Ecclesiastes, etc.). Get a group of people to help you with this task.

Pass the box around and ask each person to take a sweet from the heart. Explain that these notes cannot possibly apply to the people receiving them. Yet there might be an application if we think of others in our lives. How does the saying touch the heart of our human condition with some truth? Ask for people to share.

After worshipers have shared, ask them to help make connections between daily problems and spiritual truth. Jesus did this as he talked with the Samaritan woman. In fact, her scandalous life became the springboard for countless others to encounter Christ with their own "closet" problems.

This sermon might also fit in well with a seasonal celebration like Valentine's Day.

A CLUE FROM 4:16-26

This passage is a paradigm for pastoral counseling. The person of faith goes to the core of the human spirit, identifies the problem, and then brings the parishioner to see it, understand it, confess it and have it healed. Jesus has dissected the woman's life and offered the real source of her hope and potential.

You might build upon this process by drawing your people into a sermon experience in which you take the role of a pathologist doing a postmortem of the Samaritan woman. But don't let on the identity of the person until later. You might have a table at the front of the worship center. Perhaps you can borrow a mannequin used to model clothing in store windows. Use the microphone as if you were describing the person from what you see. Mention items found on the body (engagement ring, pictures of children, etc.), bruises from stones ("She must have been stoned by a crowd") and perhaps even a bent back from carrying water for years. The purpose is to discover the personality of the imagined woman from the evidence at hand.

After performing the postmortem, tell your people that the evidence indicates the woman on the table was the one at the well. Point out that you found both good and bad personality characteristics. Jesus also knows *exactly* what's in our hearts. The woman was neither a super-goody person nor a bad one. But Jesus accepted her. And John clearly shows her as an instrument of God's revelation through Christ. That's the gospel: God dissects our hearts, minds and spirits. He knows both the good and bad in us and turns us around for manifestations of his work.

This format will provide a biblical setting for helping your people find Jesus Christ in their own treks to the well.

A CLUE FROM 4:31-38

The setting for this clue is drawn from the theme of harvesting. There is a sense of evangelism and outreach in the message of the text. The preparation for the sermon is done in the week *before* the service. At the end of the worship experience of the week before, pass out apples to each person in the congregation. It is best if you can polish them and wrap them in foil. The young people can be helpful with this task.

At the close of the service, give an apple to each person with the encouragement to give it to a person he or she does not know. Encourage your people to explain to the strangers that the apple is a gift freely offered because of the love given to us by God.

The people are encouraged to return next week prepared to share the story of what happened when they gave the gifts to others. Your people will provide the sermon for the following week by telling their stories!

Accept their stories of what happened in their ministry of sharing and sowing. Now focus on how their experiences relate to the words of Jesus (John 4:36).

You will be amazed how a sermon experience like this will cut across age groups. Children as well as older people can take part in this sermon. This model enables your people to sow seeds among those who do not know the faith, as well as reap the fruits in the sermon experience.

A CLUE FROM 4:48

Many believers are treated to worship that talks to their minds about the great acts of God, but they leave without the experience of miracles and signs. This "flat" worship is contrasted to the magic of the electronic church. The sermons are always wonderful (the miracle of tape editing), the music perfect and the inspiration assured. It is understandable that people seek the signs and miracles in the house church or store-front revival center downtown or on the television. People are longing for healings, resurrections, conversions for dry spirits. In this passage Jesus speaks to this human condition.

Have the young people work with you in the preparation of this sermon. First, make blindfolds for each worshiper. These can be cut out of paper or old pieces of cloth. At the service, invite your people to put on the blindfolds. They are entering a world without light, without anything in the field of vision. There is bareness. The lack of sight will encourage your people to rely on their sense of hearing in an acute way.

In the darkness, there is really a miracle and sign of God's love and work. It is possible to listen carefully and hear evidence of others in the body of Christ. You might suggest that people put their hands on the back of the pews and touch each other. This is a sign of God's grace!

It is also possible to blindfold only yourself. You can preach from the perspective of sharing your journey into darkness. You might stumble to the communion table to describe the signs of God's care as you touch bread and cup, Bible and cross. The congregation can experience Jesus' blessing of those who must believe without seeing miraculous signs.

Remove your blindfold or have the worshipers take theirs off. Ask them to focus on something in the room that is a sign of God's gift to us. You might ask them to share what they see now that their sight is restored. Accept their insights without comment.

A CLUE FROM 4:43-54

This text suggests that it be presented in dramatic form. It will make a fine mime. This can be organized by writing in such a way that it becomes a script. Perhaps the choir or a chorus of young people can do the reading while another group presents the story as a mime.

The story can also be told with expansion. One helpful technique enables you to draw several volunteers from the congregation. You "line out" or guide them as they act out the story. It works extremely well. You might stop them at certain points and ask how they feel as the characters at that place in the story. The congregation can play the part of the "household."

If you feel overwhelmed by such dramatic presentations, don't forget that there are people skilled in drama and mime in most congregations or in the community. They are resources for you! Use them!

CHAPTER 5

THE HEALING AT THE POOL

After this there was a feast of the Jews, and Jesus went up to Jerusalem. 2 Now there is in Jerusalem by the Sheep Gate a pool, in Hebrew called Beth-za'tha,*j* which has five porticoes. 3 In these lay a multitude of invalids, blind, lame, paralyzed.*k* 5 One man was there, who had been ill for thirty-eight years. 6 When Jesus saw him and knew that he had been lying there a long time, he said to him, "Do you want to be healed?" 7 The sick man answered him, "Sir, I have no man to put me into the pool when the water is troubled, and while I am going another steps down before me." 8 Jesus said to him, "Rise, take up your pallet, and walk." 9 And at once the man was healed, and he took up his pallet and walked.

Now that day was the sabbath. 10 So the Jews said to the man who was cured, "It is the sabbath, it is not lawful for you to carry your pallet." 11 But he answered them, "The man who healed me said to me, 'Take up your pallet, and walk.'" 12 They asked him, "Who is the man who said to you, 'Take up your pallet, and walk'?" 13 Now the man who had been healed did not know who it was, for Jesus had withdrawn, as there was a crowd in the place. 14 Afterward, Jesus found him in the temple, and said to him, "See, you are well! Sin no more, that nothing worse befall you." 15 The man went away and told the Jews that it was Jesus who had healed him. 16 And this was why the Jews persecuted Jesus, because he did this on the sabbath. 17 But Jesus answered them, "My Father is working still, and I am working." 18 This was why the Jews sought all the more to kill him, because he not only broke the sabbath but also called God his own Father, making himself equal with God.

"THE DEAD WILL HEAR THE VOICE OF THE SON OF GOD"

19 Jesus said to them, "Truly, truly, I say to you, the Son can do nothing of his own accord, but only what he sees the Father doing; for whatever he does, that the Son does likewise. 20 For the Father loves the Son, and shows him all that he himself is doing; and greater works than these will he show him, that you may marvel. 21 For as the Father raises the dead and gives them life, so also the Son gives life to whom he will. 22 The Father judges no one, but has given all judgment to the Son, 23 that all may honor the Son, even as they honor the Father. He who does not honor the Son does not honor the Father who sent him. 24 Truly, truly, I say to you, he who hears my word and believes him who sent me, has eternal life; he does not come into judgment, but has passed from death to life.

25 "Truly, truly, I say to you, the hour is coming, and now is, when the dead will hear the voice of the Son of God, and those who hear will live. 26 For as the Father has life in

---

j Other ancient authorities read *Bethesda*, others *Bethsaida*
k Other ancient authorities insert, wholly or in part, *waiting for the moving of the water;* ⁴*for an angel of the Lord went down at certain seasons into the pool, and troubled the water; whoever stepped in first after the troubling of the water was healed of whatever disease he had*

himself, so he has granted the Son also to have life in himself, 27and has given him authority to execute judgment, because he is the Son of man. 28Do not marvel at this; for the hour is coming when all who are in the tombs will hear his voice 29and come forth, those who have done good, to the resurrection of life, and those who have done evil, to the resurrection of judgment."

"I SEEK THE WILL OF HIM WHO SENT ME"

30 "I can do nothing on my own authority; as I hear, I judge; and my judgment is just, because I seek not my own will but the will of him who sent me. 31If I bear witness to myself, my testimony is not true; 32there is another who bears witness to me, and I know that the testimony which he bears to me is true. 33You sent to John, and he has borne witness to the truth. 34Not that the testimony which I receive is from man; but I say this that you may be saved. 35He was a burning and shining lamp, and you were willing to rejoice for a while in his light. 36But the testimony which I have is greater than that of John; for the works which the Father has granted me to accomplish, these very works which I am doing, bear me witness that the Father has sent me. 37And the Father who sent me has himself borne witness to me. His voice you have never heard, his form you have never seen; 38and you do not have his word abiding in you, for you do not believe him whom he has sent. 39You search the scriptures, because you think that in them you have eternal life; and it is they that bear witness to me; 40yet you refuse to come to me that you may have life. 41I do not receive glory from men. 42But I know that you have not the love of God within you. 43I have come in my Father's name, and you do not receive me; if another comes in his own name, him you will receive. 44How can you believe, who receive glory from one another and do not seek the glory that comes from the only God? 45Do not think that I shall accuse you to the Father; it is Moses who accuses you, on whom you set your hope. 46If you believed Moses, you would believe me, for he wrote of me. 47But if you do not believe his writings, how will you believe my words?"

CHAPTER 5

Creative Commentary on the Scripture

VERSE 2: Note the careful detail John gives us of the physical surroundings. This suggests that the author wants the readers to experience a story with details and a sense of reality. The setting is reported against the backdrop of a "sign" of Jesus as the Son of God.

VERSE 3: "A multitude of invalids" describes the setting of the pool and perhaps today's world. We are given the figurative meaning within the reality report.

VERSE 4: This verse is a good example of the nature of ancient biblical texts. It is not found in most of the earliest and reliable copies of copies that we have. Some texts include it, but note that it is not a sure reading. There is also the presence of words and expressions that are not common to the fourth Gospel. You will note in the Revised Standard Version of the Gospel of John, which we have used in this book, that there are marginal notes that show an alternative or less acceptable reading. Such variants in no way detract from the Good News of this book. In fact, the text is remarkably well-preserved considering the ravages of time. The variety of reading can be a great aid in understanding the meaning of the passage. Scribes often added a word or two to make things clearer or in closer harmony with their understanding of the message. We are given a wonderful peek at how the earlier receivers of the Word heard what has been written.

VERSE 6: "Do you want to be healed?" This seems like a strange question, for who would not want to be healed? The question acknowledges the man's freedom to choose and it recognizes the very real fact that some (many?) people would rather not be healed.

VERSE 7: The man's response to Jesus' question seems

strange also. Not a direct answer. However, through this inquiry, Jesus gives the man a chance to make a choice. Even in Jesus' day, people were competing for medical care! Who is going to get the dialysis machine? Who is going to get the healing that evidently only one can get when several need a "pool" of healing?

VERSE 8: A straightforward command of healing. The man is told to accept the responsibility of acting.

VERSE 9: The word of healing is followed by the action. God's initiating word results in creation, the logos and healing.

VERSE 10: The positive affirmation of the commandment is harshly perverted by legalists into a prohibition.

VERSE 14: What is the connection between sin and illness? And what does the command "sin no more" really mean? Is it possible not to sin?

VERSE 15: The now-healed man evidently didn't realize that he was getting Jesus into trouble.

VERSE 17: The source of Jesus' power is the Father. What is the source of our power? Is what Jesus says also true of us? This verse points to the absolute obedience that is characteristic of Jesus.

VERSE 19: "What he sees the Father doing" offers a curious idea by describing the Father as the object of "seeing."

VERSE 20: What does "marvel" imply? Is there something beyond the mere astonishment or wondering that "marvel" sometimes suggests?

VERSE 24: Why does John fail to use his favorite preposition "in" when talking about belief? Does the omission mean something special here? Eternal life is discussed by using the present tense. The Gospel is saying that eternal life has arrived already!

VERSE 25: Are the "dead" of this verse the same as those who "are in the tombs" (verse 28) or are the "spiritually dead" being described?

VERSE 29: The verse promises judgment. In the common language of Christians today, we speak of the "resurrection" exclusively in terms of the "resurrection of life." What has become of the "resurrection of judgment"? What does it mean?

VERSE 30: Jesus' authority is from God. Jesus' judgment is just because it is God's judgment. Jesus' will is one with God.

VERSE 39: Is this a charge which could be leveled at those who worship the Bible today?

VERSE 40: It is not the scriptures that have life, but Jesus himself.

VERSE 42: What more serious charge could be placed against a person than this? What does this verse say about studying the Bible for selfish reasons?

VERSE 45: It appears that Jesus is saying that his critics are not even reading the scriptures very carefully, for if they were they would see that Moses had already accused them.

Creative Bible Study Ideas

SESSION BASED ON 5:1-9

This session takes very seriously the details of the passage as means for enriching the lives of your students. The session develops by looking carefully at the passage before us. John often seems to encourage us to move from the particular to the figurative.

1. As students enter the room, give each person a plastic bracelet like those issued at a hospital. You might be able to get some of this material from the local hospital or you can construct them from plastic lunch bags. Include a piece of paper in the bracelet upon which words can be written. You might want to create an "admissions" desk in the hall outside the classroom. Set up the chairs as in a waiting room of a hospital or doctor's office.

2. Picking up the idea of the Greek word meaning "those who are weak" (translated "invalids"), either assign or ask them to choose an illness or weakness that demobilizes people in our world (emotional, physical, spiritual). The students can write these maladies on their wristbands.

3. As the students get seated in your "waiting room," have them fill out their admissions forms. You might give them a sheet with several questions on it: What is the most difficult aspect of your weakness? What keeps you from getting better? How can you be helped?

4. You or someone else can now take the role of the healer or doctor as you go around the circle asking the patients to share their problems.

5. After this sharing, ask other patients to react to the things shared by others.

6. Tell them that a wonder drug has been prepared that promises a cure for all of these weaknesses. However, you are also forced to tell them that there is not enough for everyone. You must choose who will be healed. Who is the most deserving to receive it?

7. After working at this problem for a while, close with the gospel news that the source of hope is open to all. Now, how can this group as individuals and collectively do something about the needy in the community? Help them focus on particular people and situations in your area. Let them develop plans for action. They could make a visit, volunteer or urge special action by the church or groups within the church.

8. Go around the group and share the water as you wash their hands.

SESSION BASED ON 5:1-9

The lame man's first response to Jesus is that of making an excuse for his life situation. Jesus quickly upsets this game. You might enable your people to experience the thrust of this encounter by putting together a little game called "Excuuuse Me!" Ask your students to make up their own life situations with excuses as to why they can't extricate themselves from their circumstances. Each person gets a chance to stand before the group and offer excuses for his or her situation.

The other students keep asking: "Why?" The standing student must keep offering excuses until they become more and more absurd. Then read the passage and discuss how Jesus is really addressing our situations as well as that of the lame man. How can the class pass along the gospel of this message to others? Perhaps they could be given some time in worship for a sharing of this Good News. It might be utilized as a creative way of leading into the congregation's prayer of petition.

SESSION BASED ON 5:9B-18

At an early point in our religious history a special day each week was set aside for the people of God to re-create. The blooming shopping malls, bustling schedules and flexible work plans seem to have confused this day's meaning as a creation of God. Those who opposed Jesus also found difficulty with what could and could not be done on the Sabbath.

1. After the class has gathered in a circle, place a pallet or cot-like bed in the center of the room. Be sure that it can be carried easily. You might ask two students to bring it into the room after the students have settled into their chairs.
2. Tell them the story of this passage. Point out that the pallet is a symbol of a deeper issue: God has created us to enjoy and glorify him.
3. Pass out newsmagazines and ask each person to tear out an article or ad that illustrates the kinds of things people tend to do on Sundays.
4. Cluster the students in pairs and ask them to share what they have chosen.
5. Give each dyad a chance to share its conclusions with the group. After the dyad finishes, the two students place the newsmagazine items on the pallet.
6. Encourage the whole group to discuss how one decides what is worthy in life and glorifies God and what is not right for the Sunday celebration. Does it have to be a choice between Jesus or soccer on Sunday morning?
7. Focus now on verse 17 by having your students prove the meaning of "work" in this passage. John is giving us several layers of meaning. The law forbids "work" on the Sabbath, but Jesus and his Father are at work doing good for people. Have the students look through the Gospel of John for an understanding of this kind of work. For example, see the story of Lazarus in chapter 11.
8. Share the fruits of this resource by adding Bible verses to the pallet.
9. You might want to arrange in advance to have the pallet carried into the worship service and the conclusions of the study shared by the students with the whole congregation.

SESSION BASED ON 5:19-24

It has been said that the experience of marvel and awe is the beginning of the religious moment. But these experiences are confusing to many at our time. The Gospel of John keeps reminding us that the experience of marveling is always directed beyond the sign. A miracle is simply the means to show people the way to God.
1. Select a box of small items that will trigger the memories of your students concerning moments of wonder, marveling and awe. You might use a baby blanket, a driver's li-

cense, a wedding ring, an item from high school, an old letter, etc. Or you might ask your students to select something in their purses or wallets that carries the deepest memories of wonder.

2. After the item has been chosen or presented, ask your students to take a few minutes and think through the circumstances of the memory. You might ask them to write it out. They might even write a description of the dialogue and events in this memory.

3. Encourage each person to share the feelings of that special moment.

4. Explore how time has changed these marvels. Why have they changed? Has nostalgia lessened or enhanced the events from the past?

5. Show some pictures from a popular magazine (tear out pages for each person) that illustrate contemporary wonder over a sporting event or some other mass gathering. You might play an audio-cassette recording of crowd sounds. This can be captured at a local sporting event or from a sound-effects record.

6. Share how these kinds of momentary marvels capture so much of our excitement. Are these distractions or valid factors for a full life?

7. Pass around a small cross.

8. Have each person share how the reality of the resurrection is still a marvelous event for him or her.

9. Close with a prayer circle of thanksgiving for the wonder of Christ and comfort of our personal marvels.

SESSION BASED ON 5:25-29

This passage raises many important questions about the faith. The theme of reward and judgment has been doubted throughout the centuries. This session will not answer all the questions. However, it should provide an opportunity to experience the lordship of God and how this reality touches our lives. How do we hear the voice of the Son of God in order to have life both now and forever more?

1. Procure a copy of the funeral service used by your pastor or denomination.

2. Create a funeral setting in a chapel or darkened classroom. Make sure the room is lighted by candles. Even flowers and black crepe paper might be used. Play somber music as students enter for class. Line up the chairs like a typi-

cal funeral home setting.

3. Read parts of the service as if you were conducting a memorial celebration for a local person. Don't mention the name of the deceased.

4. For the sermon portion of the service state that we are celebrating the resurrection on this occasion of facing death.

5. Read the passage.

6. Pass out obituaries that you have clipped from the newspapers during the past couple weeks. You might want to cut off or black out the names of the deceased persons.

7. Ask the students to share their ideas on how these persons may have died long ago. Can the living be dead if they don't hear the voice of the Son of God? You might discuss this as dyads. Let them work at rewriting the obituaries as if the person were talking about his or her life in terms of how Jesus' voice had been heard.

8. Share these new obituaries as a whole group.

9. Encourage your students to share some times they have felt that their lives were really without life, meaning or purpose.

10. Read the passage again.

11. Ask for examples of people who have apparently not heard the voice of the Son of God.

12. Discuss what might happen to those who face the resurrection of judgment.

13. Close with a prayer circle that lifts up the theme of God's love and forgiveness in the resurrection of life.

14. You might find that your church does not have a very clear process concerning the steps one needs to take upon the death of a loved one. Your class might schedule another session to prepare a booklet for the congregation for celebrating the resurrection upon the death of a loved one. They will need to do some interviews with clergy, members who have lost others in death and the local funeral directors. They might want to talk with people who direct organizations for the donation of vital organs. All of this information could be gathered by your students and prepared for printing. This would provide a very important ministry from this study group.

SESSION BASED ON 5:30-47

This passage deals with the burning light and the shadows that bear witness to the source of the light. John the Baptist is the person who gave testimony to the Christ. This session can help the students reflect on the confusion that often happens when the shadow blinds people to the source of light. It is tempting to follow the disciple rather than the Lord or worship the Bible rather than the Lord of the Bible.

1. Hold your class in a darkened room.
2. Have the students sit in a semicircle facing a blank wall.
3. Work from left to right as you invite the students to make shadows on the wall when you shine a light from behind them (e.g., a dog, swan, etc.). You can use the beam from a projector or a strong flashlight. You might modify this process by making shadow forms and have students guess what is casting the shadow. Begin with easy figures and move to more difficult shapes.
4. Have them write down the original shapes as you go through the series.
5. Project some human shapes cut in profile from paper. What can we tell about the person behind the shadow?
6. Have each person prepare a brief statement on how he or she authentically provides a shadow of Jesus in daily encounters. On the other side of the paper, have them write ways such a witness is limited and does not truly reflect the light, Jesus.
7. Share the positive statements with the whole group.
8. Now focus on the possible negative or limiting factors of being a shadow of the Lord. Read verses 33-36. Discuss how we can show others the light of Christ more than our own "shadow."
9. Pass a Bible around and have each person share in a statement just what the Word of God means. Write these down on newsprint as people share their ideas.
10. Read the passage, focusing on verses 39-47.
11. Discuss examples of how scripture can be misused.
12. Close by shining the light on each person as he or she offers a contribution to a prayer circle. Then commission them as children of the Light.
13. You might find that the class has introduced examples of cult groups. If there is interest, have them gather information about such groups and make a summary of this material available to others in the church.

Creative Speaking and Preaching Ideas

A CLUE FROM 5:1-9

This passage speaks to us on two levels. We have the story of the man being healed of his weakness. The Gospel also offers us a message about general weakness or illness faced by people of our time. It is the flow of this encounter that offers much to our situation.

The passage beckons us to enter into its message by providing us an important experiential clue. You might want to draw upon the pallet in the story for your sermon.

Place a cot or simple bed in the worship center. You can then suggest that if this simple bed could talk, it would tell us a story which touches our lives.

Then develop a first-person narrative as if you were the bed. You can talk about your master who has been weak or ill from birth. Share the sense of hopelessness that fills the 38-year-old man.

Confess that your master tended to give up and blame his failure to be cured on the fact that others didn't help him. Then talk about the day at the pool and the stranger who cut through all the sick master's mind games.

Shift your sermon to the weaknesses we bear. Pick up a copy of the Sunday paper and tear it up into strips. Pass the strips to the worshipers and ask each person to scan the section of the world as represented in the paper. What are the situations of illness that need the healing rebuke of Jesus? Ask them to share their insights. You might want to collect the pieces of paper as they are shared and put them on the bed or cot. If you feel that your congregation is not comfortable with this kind of sharing process, collect sections of the newspaper that they offer. Read them and then put them on the cot.

Close by carrying the cot down the aisle with all the weakness of the world on it. You might set it by the door as you greet people on the way out of the church.

A CLUE FROM 5:9-18

This text deals with the struggle the opponents of Jesus have with the day of rest that their faith prescribes. Jesus is teaching that he and the Father work ("helping people") continually.

You might want to pick up the struggle of the passage

and cast your congregation into a similar kind of situation. Choose several young people and adults to aid you. Ask them to suggest ways that people choose to celebrate Sunday other than worship and the church's other offerings. When the group has come up with fitting examples (soccer, TV, sleep, etc.), ask them if they will dress up in garb that illustrates these ways of spending the Lord's day.

You might ask them to come into the service just after you have started your sermon. A person speaks out why he or she wants to spend the day differently than church people usually do. Repeat verse 17 between each short vignette.

When the whole group is standing at the front of the worship area, extend your dialogue to the congregation. How do we know what is right or wrong about the celebration of this day? Does the cultural trend toward more work, business and individual recreation suggest the meaning that Jesus was giving to the Sabbath?

Close the sermon by having the co-presenters distribute glass marbles to the worshiping community. Tell them that this is a symbol of our planet and God's creative act. Ask them to carry it for the next week as they reflect on how they can do the work that the Father and Son ask of us.

A CLUE FROM 5:19-24

The passage focuses on the relationship between the Father and the Son as it touches upon the believer. Verse 24 proclaims the promise that by hearing and believing him we now have eternal life!

The passage from death to life through faith in Jesus Christ suggests that we might utilize the concept of a passport in a sermon.

The bulletin could be printed to represent a government passport. The cover could bear the form of a passport. Inner pages provide space for recording areas visited.

The sermon can be presented by asking the congregation to go through a few questions on the passport application before the passport is granted. Shape the questions in such a way that you ask about faith as it affects their lives. This can be developed in a number of different ways, such as "List five times in your life that faith has made a difference," and "How does faith relate to your family life?"

As you conclude the questions and explain their implications, "swear" people in by using a statement of faith. Close by announcing that they have now been publicly affirmed to be hearers and believers in the Son. Give them the direct assurance that they now have eternal life.

The benediction can be in the form of a blessing for the journeys they will travel under the protection of their citizenship in the kingdom of God. Remind them to use their passport to salvation faithfully.

A CLUE FROM 5:25-47

The text offers the interesting image of our salvation as the "hearing" of the "voice" of the Son of God. This manner of expression invites us to present the passage in the audible (and inaudible) mode of communication.

It is possible to focus on the "hearing" and "speaking" of the Word. The "dead" mentioned in verse 25 includes those who are living, but not alive.

Have an assistant read the passage. Present your sermon without uttering a single word! In other words, give your people a chance to understand the spiritual and emotional dimensions to the kind of "hearing" and "speaking" understood in the passage.

You might get the assistance of someone who does "signing" for the deaf. He or she could present the message in this manner. Mime could also be used. The theme of life and death can be presented in many ways without speaking.

You might also introduce another language as a means of communication. You will be surprised how a group of people can quickly establish a fresh means of communication. Your goal is to make the point that hearing and responding to Christ take place in the heart. It is more than mumbling words.

Draw upon the gifts of your people in church and the people in your community for specialized talents. They will be happy to participate in the presentation of the Gospel.

CHAPTER 6

JESUS CREATES FOOD FOR FIVE THOUSAND

After this Jesus went to the other side of the Sea of Galilee, which is the Sea of Tibe′ri-as. ²And a multitude followed him, because they saw the signs which he did on those who were diseased. ³Jesus went up on the mountain, and there sat down with his disciples. ⁴Now the Passover, the feast of the Jews, was at hand. ⁵Lifting up his eyes, then, and seeing that a multitude was coming to him, Jesus said to Philip, "How are we to buy bread, so that these people may eat?" ⁶This he said to test him, for he himself knew what he would do. ⁷Philip answered him, "Two hundred denarii[l] would not buy enough bread for each of them to get a little." ⁸One of his disciples, Andrew, Simon Peter's brother, said to him, ⁹"There is a lad here who has five barley loaves and two fish; but what are they among so many?" ¹⁰Jesus said, "Make the people sit down." Now there was much grass in the place; so the men sat down, in number about five thousand. ¹¹Jesus then took the loaves, and when he had given thanks, he distributed them to those who were seated; so also the fish, as much as they wanted. ¹²And when they had eaten their fill, he told his disciples, "Gather up the fragments left over, that nothing may be lost." ¹³So they gathered them up and filled twelve baskets with fragments from the five barley loaves, left by those who had eaten.

¹⁴When the people saw the sign which he had done, they said, "This is indeed the prophet who is to come into the world!"

15 Perceiving then that they were about to come and take him by force to make him king, Jesus withdrew again to the mountain by himself.

JESUS WALKS ON THE SEA

16 When evening came, his disciples went down to the sea, ¹⁷got into a boat, and started across the sea to Caper′na-um. It was now dark, and Jesus had not yet come to them. ¹⁸The sea rose because a strong wind was blowing. ¹⁹When they had rowed about three or four miles,[m] they saw Jesus walking on the sea and drawing near to the boat. They were frightened, ²⁰but he said to them, "It is I; do not be afraid." ²¹Then they were glad to take him into the boat, and immediately the boat was at the land to which they were going.

JESUS THE LIVING BREAD

22 On the next day the people who remained on the other side of the sea saw that there had been only one boat there, and that Jesus had not entered the boat with his disciples, but that his disciples had gone away alone. ²³However, boats from Tibe′ri-as came near the place where they ate the bread after the Lord had given thanks. ²⁴So when the people saw that Jesus was not there, nor his disciples, they themselves got into the boats and went to Caper′na-um, seeking Jesus.

25 When they found him on the

---

l The denarius was a day's wage for a laborer

m Greek twenty-five or thirty stadia

at the last day. ⁴⁰For this is the will of him, "Rabbi, when did you come here?" ²⁶Jesus answered them, "Truly, truly, I say to you, you seek me, not because you saw signs, but because you ate your fill of the loaves. ²⁷Do not labor for the food which perishes, but for the food which endures to eternal life, which the Son of man will give to you; for on him has God the Father set his seal." ²⁸Then they said to him, "What must we do, to be doing the works of God?" ²⁹Jesus answered them, "This is the work of God, that you believe in him whom he has sent." ³⁰So they said to him, "Then what sign do you do, that we may see, and believe you? What work do you perform? ³¹Our fathers ate the manna in the wilderness; as it is written, 'He gave them bread from heaven to eat.'" ³²Jesus then said to them, "Truly, truly, I say to you, it was not Moses who gave you the bread from heaven; my Father gives you the true bread from heaven. ³³For the bread of God is that which comes down from heaven, and gives life to the world." ³⁴They said to him, "Lord, give us this bread always."

35 Jesus said to them, "I am the bread of life; he who comes to me shall not hunger, and he who believes in me shall never thirst. ³⁶But I said to you that you have seen me and yet do not believe. ³⁷All that the Father gives me will come to me; and him who comes to me I will not cast out. ³⁸For I have come down from heaven, not to do my own will, but the will of him who sent me; ³⁹and this is the will of him who sent me, that I should lose nothing of all that he has given me, but raise it up other side of the sea, they said to my Father, that every one who sees the Son and believes in him should have eternal life; and I will raise him up at the last day."

41 The Jews then murmured at him, because he said, "I am the bread which came down from heaven." ⁴²They said, "Is not this Jesus, the son of Joseph, whose father and mother we know? How does he now say, 'I have come down from heaven'?" ⁴³Jesus answered them, "Do not murmur among yourselves. ⁴⁴No one can come to me unless the Father who sent me draws him; and I will raise him up at the last day. ⁴⁵It is written in the prophets, 'And they shall all be taught by God.' Every one who has heard and learned from the Father comes to me. ⁴⁶Not that any one has seen the Father except him who is from God; he has seen the Father. ⁴⁷Truly, truly, I say to you, he who believes has eternal life. ⁴⁸I am the bread of life. ⁴⁹Your fathers ate the manna in the wilderness, and they died. ⁵⁰This is the bread which comes down from heaven, that a man may eat of it and not die. ⁵¹I am the living bread which came down from heaven; if any one eats of this bread, he will live for ever; and the bread which I shall give for the life of the world is my flesh."

52 The Jews then disputed among themselves, saying, "How can this man give us his flesh to eat?" ⁵³So Jesus said to them, "Truly, truly, I say to you, unless you eat the flesh of the Son of man and drink his blood, you have no life in you; ⁵⁴he who eats my flesh and drinks my blood has eternal life, and I will raise him

up at the last day. ⁵⁵For my flesh is food indeed, and my blood is drink indeed. ⁵⁶He who eats my flesh and drinks my blood abides in me, and I in him. ⁵⁷As the living Father sent me, and I live because of the Father, so he who eats me will live because of me. ⁵⁸This is the bread which came down from heaven, not such as the fathers ate and died; he who eats this bread will live for ever." ⁵⁹This he said in the synagogue, as he taught at Caper'na-um.

MANY DISCIPLES ABANDON JESUS

60 Many of his disciples, when they heard it, said, "This is a hard saying; who can listen to it?" ⁶¹But Jesus, knowing in himself that his disciples murmured at it, said to them, "Do you take offense at this? ⁶²Then what if you were to see the Son of man ascending where he was before? ⁶³It is the spirit that gives life, the flesh is of no avail; the words that I have spoken to you are spirit and life. ⁶⁴But there are some of you that do not believe." For Jesus knew from the first who those were that did not believe, and who it was that would betray him. ⁶⁵And he said, "This is why I told you that no one can come to me unless it is granted him by the Father."

66 After this many of his disciples drew back and no longer went about with him. ⁶⁷Jesus said to the twelve, "Do you also wish to go away?" ⁶⁸Simon Peter answered him, "Lord, to whom shall we go? You have the words of eternal life; ⁶⁹and we have believed, and have come to know, that you are the Holy One of God." ⁷⁰Jesus answered them, "Did I not choose you, the twelve, and one of you is a devil?" ⁷¹He spoke of Judas the son of Simon Iscariot, for he, one of the twelve, was to betray him.

CHAPTER 6

Creative Commentary on the Scripture

VERSES 1-15: Why is this miracle reported in all four of the Gospels (twice in Matthew and Mark)? It is the only miracle reproduced in all of the Gospels. Its importance cannot be overlooked. The miraculous generosity enabled by Jesus is misunderstood and will lead his enemies to add more fuel to their hatred. This is a major sign in the revelation of the person and work of Jesus Christ. He feeds the people preceding the Passover. John again seems to suggest that Jesus replaces the Jewish festivals.

Why is there no mention of wine or water in this episode? Surely people needed something to drink. Where would that liquid have come from? There is not very strong evidence that the eucharist is intended by the writer. But scholars differ on this point. The natural place for a presentation of the Lord's Supper is chapter 13, which does not really mention it. Chapter 21 seems to have transformed the Last Supper into a fish fry. However, the motif of eating in combination with the bread-of-life statement in chapter 6 encourages us to consider this miracle as at least hinting toward the Last Supper.

Why would Jesus let himself be caught in a situation where he meets the crowd's expectations to the point that they attempt to make him their king? Is Jesus reduced to a social worker in our times? Do we simply want breadwinners/miracle workers? It is clear that the crowd can't find the correct answers to such questions. They misread the nature of this sign. There is something quite encouraging about the humanity among those who were so close to Jesus. It gives us some room for our own failure to answer the questions Jesus poses to us.

How have we misunderstood Jesus? It would seem from

this story that Jesus refused to accept the projections of the people to be their king. Instead he goes off into the hills and prays! How do we deal with the projections people place on us? We must have kings and heroes. What is the need in us to project that kind of status on others?

There is the ministry of a child here. The boy is the instrument of sharing. Does this say something to us about intergenerational education and worship? How do children trigger the miracles in our faith experience? Is our love like this boy's? There are two actions here: multiplication and sharing. Yet the miracle of the event must not be overlooked. Generosity is a wondrous gift in any age. However, it is the miracle of Jesus which triggered this release of giving. This is one of the hardest learnings for the contemporary faith community. There are many clever ways that people can be "moved" to help those in need. Witness the poster children with their hungry faces, twisted bodies and frightened eyes. Does such an emotional appeal really relate to the response called forth by Jesus Christ? It is not pity or guilt that springs the trapdoors to the goodies we hoard from others. Jesus transforms the needs and security of those who follow him. The instrument of this sign is a generous boy. But the miracle is not a human action. Jesus is the bread of life. We respond to Jesus, the bread of life, by giving bread to others.

VERSES 16-21: "It is I" reminds us of Exodus 3:14 in which God reveals who he is to Moses. The description of this scene is vivid. Again, the nature of Jesus is revealed to the reader. This sign unfolds the power and care of the Son of God. He calms both the journey and the fear.

VERSES 22-40: The strong image of Jesus as living bread dominates the passage. The Old Testament story of manna in the wilderness is compared to Jesus. Any discussion of the eucharistic theme in the fourth Gospel must include this passage.

VERSES 41-59: There is confusion in the dialogue. The opponents of Jesus don't understand how the body and blood of Jesus can be the means of life for others. The confusion over this teaching will continue to befuddle nonbelievers throughout church history.

VERSES 60-71: The toughness of Jesus' teaching surfaces strongly here. His teaching is hard and many can't bear the cost of this discipleship.

Creative Bible Study Ideas

SESSION BASED ON 6:1-15

This passage jumps out at us with many clues to our teaching. This session would work well with children.

1. Encourage the children to sit on mats.
2. Tell the story through the reading of the passage and note that the helper of Jesus is a young person.
3. Use teaching pictures as you relate the story of sharing. Your church probably has these stashed away in a closet or church library.
4. Serve every other child a roll with sardines. Ask each child to serve the boy or girl who has no food.
5. Then serve others in the Sunday school program or during a coffee hour after worship.

SESSION BASED ON 6:1-15

This is a challenging passage. The gospel provides a view of sharing that opens many opportunities to counter the philosophy of a selfish world. The child is an agent of this sharing. Jesus is also careful to have them collect the leftovers. This model could provide an excellent format for an intergenerational Bible study. Many churches enjoy occasional potluck dinners. It is possible to use the dinner to crawl inside this passage!

Have the participants bring potluck items and gather outside the fellowship hall where the meal will be held. Several people can play the roles of Jesus and his disciples. A child can provide his or her ministry by offering the bread and fish. Then enter the room.

After entering the room and offering the blessing, have the person playing Jesus give the Sermon on the Mount as recorded in Matthew.

It would be easy to help the hungry of the world through the evening dinner. At the end of the dinner, read verses 11-14 (the passage in which the extra food is collected). The participants could give canned goods and other foods that they brought to the fellowship dinner. Perhaps take a special offering for a hunger program.

To close the evening's gathering, focus on giving praise to God for the gift of the Son. You might even have the person playing Jesus depart during the worship as he does in the passage.

It would be possible to include communion as part of this biblical evening. You can easily relate this study to the various opportunities the church offers to help the hunger needs of others. The actual experience of helping in feeding the bread of life to others is suggested by this passage.

SESSION BASED ON 6:16-21

This passage invites us to enter into the frightening experience of the sea journey. Darken a room. Make a circle big enough to encompass the group of students. This can be drawn with chalk or constructed with masking tape on the floor. You might record the sounds of wind and sea on your cassette tape recorder. These sounds are available at local libraries or record stores.

A narrator can read the introduction to the story. Ask the members of the class to simulate rowing. Get them to work in unison. You might take a few minutes to get them working as a team. It is surprising how this simulated activity uses lots of energy.

Turn on a penlight across the room when you come to the time of introducing Jesus' appearance on the water. The light can represent Christ.

You might want to use a spray bottle of water to enhance the experience. Spray a fine mist of water across the group in the "boat" if they are comfortable with the experiential approach to biblical study.

Read the words of Jesus: "It is I; do not be afraid." Have them make room for Jesus in the boat. Bring up the lights as they "land." Bring in refreshments and gather in a "campfire" kind of setting.

Encourage your people to share how they felt during their "boat" ride with and without Jesus. What did Jesus mean to us in his simple statement? How does this promise say something to a situation in our past? in our present situation?

You can modify this design in many ways. Perhaps you will choose to use the sounds of thunder and slides of a stormy sea. You might ask some people in the boat to hold on to a rope while the others row. You can use the rope during your debriefing. Pass the rope around the group as you ask for the sharing of feelings after the experience.

Close the session by cutting the rope into pieces and give each person a section with a blessing that Jesus is with him or her in every moment of need.

SESSION BASED ON 6:22-40

These verses focus on the image of bread as it touches the lives of believer and Lord. One youth group has built a ministry around the making of bread. They meet every Saturday and bake 60 to 100 loaves. The regular customers for this project are from the church and in the community. The money from this task is used to finance service camps and other mission work. This text suggests a study session that finds this youth model helpful.

Perhaps you can lead a weekend study/celebration event that focuses on the "bread of life." One enabling adult or young person can help the whole group learn to bake. Use the baking procedure as a means of exploring the thrust of this section of chapter 6.

Begin by bringing the ingredients into the kitchen area. Pray together that the group might discover the bread that does not perish. You might wish to make different kinds of bread and bread products.

You might make the baking time also a time of fasting. Explore sections of the passage as you mix and knead the bread. You will find that when students are busy with their hands, the discussion will flow in a relaxed and free manner. An experienced baker can help the group make some interesting bread shapes (fish, doves, etc.).

Introduce some slides of hungry people. Discuss the different levels of Jesus' reference to bread. He has just finished feeding the crowd physically (verses 1-15) and now he moves on to the spiritual application of the experience. How do we bridge these two very different understandings from our viewpoints?

After several hours of working at this baking process and discussion, have a love feast using the freshly baked bread. Then go out from the church or retreat setting and give loaves to the needy people. Encourage the young people to share what the bread of life means to them with the receivers of the bread loaves.

SESSION BASED ON 6:41-59

The Lord's Supper plays a different role among Christian churches. In most traditions, there is something special about the image of Jesus as the bread of life. Most Christians realize that when they eat, they do so in the remembrance of their Lord. There are different conclusions among scholars concerning the implication of the Lord's Supper as suggested in this passage. It is clear that this is meant to be one of the "signs" that help us recognize the Son of God. Even with the slight link to the communion experience, the meal motif provides an excellent setting for exploring the meanings of the table in your own tradition.

Have your students gather in several different groups. You will want them to pick up the confusion and confrontation of the passage in this study. Extract several different theological positions on the Lord's Supper. Be fair with the other views. A good theological dictionary or a conversation with a friend in another denomination will provide the facts that you need. If you plan far enough in advance, you may have the students do this research.

Stage a debate similar to the dynamics of the discussion between Jesus and his opponents. Encourage the students to gather support for arguments from the Bible passage. The cross references in most Bibles will give them a good start. Then present contemporary differing views of the Lord's Supper.

At some point, provide a service of the Lord's Supper for the group. Ask each person to affirm his or her faith as the bread and cup are taken.

SESSION BASED ON 6:60-71

One of the real crises in the faith community is the lack of costly discipleship. Most traditions simply ask too little of believers. The Jesus of the New Testament demands a great deal from believers. It is indeed hard to take. The response to such a radical call to obedience is murmuring. Yet many adults and young people have wandered from traditional churches to find the discipline in cult groups. Some of these people have demanded much, but delivered little in terms of the historical message of Jesus.

This session can focus on the discipleship dynamics of this text. Every faith community struggles with the issue at hand in this passage.

1. Read the passage.
2. Pass out strips of paper upon which you have written "hard sayings" from the Gospel of John. Simply glance through John—there are plenty of them there.
3. Give each person a few minutes to look up the verses.
4. Gather in clusters of two or three. Tell them that they

will have to defend each of the hard sayings before the whole group in a few minutes.

5. Give each cluster a chance to present the saying with an explanation why it is important. Let the others challenge and discuss the verses.

6. Weave the texts together as you go around the circle and each person shares his or her verse. You might assign the verses a week in advance. Ask each person to live out the hard saying by thinking about it often and trying to express its teaching through his or her daily schedule.

7. Obtain a list of members of your church. Pass out a sheet with the names of people who no longer come to your church.

8. Discuss why these people and many others choose to "draw back" and no longer follow their path of discipleship with this congregation. What about the strangers who come once and drop away?

9. Commission the group to go forth as part of one body with the task to bear the "hard" teachings of Jesus in love to all. You might even organize a calling group to visit inactive members and visitors.

10. The group could provide a striking experience for the whole worshiping church community by telling some of their visiting experiences with the whole congregation.

Creative Speaking and Preaching Ideas

A CLUE FROM 6:1-15

This sermon can be used as a way to approach world hunger. Bake loaves of rye bread and wrap chocolate fish in foil. Ask a teenager to assist you in the sermon. He or she will take the role of an "on-the-street" reporter. You'll need a microphone with a cord for the reporter.

The story is read. Ask for volunteers from the congregation to come forward and take the roles of disciples. Give them four minutes to prepare a means of acting out the passage. Sing a few hymns while they prepare. Or, plan and rehearse the act before the service.

After four minutes the disciples come into the service and distribute the food representing the act of Jesus. The reporter then goes into the congregation and asks for responses to the gifts from Jesus. Perhaps take this a step further by asking worshipers how we should respond to Jesus' act of giving. Make sure the hymns and liturgy fit the theme of helping others in need.

A CLUE FROM 6:1-15

There is great confusion in most traditions concerning the meaning of the sacraments. This text provides an excellent opportunity to draw your people into the task of reflecting on the meaning of the bread as it relates to Jesus. Focusing on a loaf of bread, conduct a dialogue. This can be done in several different ways. You might have another person with you. Or have someone in a different room dialogue with you through use of a microphone. Rehearse the viewpoints concerning the nature of this special loaf used in the Lord's Supper. The dialogue or debate can bring out the positions in the various opinions. You can guide this discussion according to your tradition.

Conclude the discussion and invite the congregation to celebrate the Lord's Supper. You might relate aspects of the loaf to the ministry of Christ. This style will give a special meaning to the service.

A CLUE FROM 6:1-15

This text allows you to use the medium of a casserole to show the unity of all in Christ. You might ask several people to bring basic ingredients for a casserole to the service.

At the preaching time, present a small table, dishes and cooking equipment. Announce that we are hungry and a good casserole would satisfy. Mention that in this story there was a small child who gave just bits and pieces that Jesus used to feed the multitude. Where can we start?

Ask for contributions from the congregation. One of your persons who has been prepared can come forward and offer his or her contribution of food for the casserole. Make a connection between this food for flesh and a spiritual ingredient we need for the "living" bread. Repeat the process as more items are added by volunteers.

Close by noting that one of the more important aspects of Jesus' miracle was that people with very little knew that he would accept their contribution. The greatest miracle may be when we offer ourselves to God and find that that is exactly what is needed. Invite your people to stay for the eating of the casserole after the service.

A CLUE FROM 6:16-21

This passage is begging for a first-person presentation of the message. It is filled with the kind of revelation that marks the power of those who meet the living Christ.

You might remove your robe or other liturgical apparel and sit on a bench. Make the motions of rowing as someone else reads the first part of the passage. Give a first-person narrative of the events from the first five chapters from a disciple's viewpoint. Describe the fear of your character in following Jesus now that there is so much opposition to his teaching. Talk about the crowds and people wanting more miracles. Walk and talk your way through the story. You might give each person a seashell if you are in a setting where they are easy to obtain. Or you might have only one shell. Invite the children down to your imaginary boat. Pass the shell around and ask them how this shell is somehow like Jesus. Let them share these insights.

A CLUE FROM 6:22-40

The symbol of bread is highlighted in this passage. Jesus is pushing his listeners to understand the image on a couple of levels. This figure suggests that it be used in your sermon as a means of getting your listeners into the passage before us.

You might come down the aisle at sermon time dressed in the uniform of a delivery person. "Bread! Get your fresh bread!" Pause along the way in your journey from the back door to the front of the worship center. You can carry a cloth sack over your shoulder or a plastic rack filled with loaves of bread.

Make all kinds of claims for these loaves. Try to present a pitch like a traveling salesperson. Give the loaves to responsive people in the congregation.

Bring out a special loaf. It should be crude and uncomely. "This loaf is different." Continue the story that it gives life because it gives us Jesus Christ. Wrap the loaf in a towel and rock it like a baby. Explore the claim that Jesus is the bread of life. Then lead into the Lord's Supper as part of this sermon.

A CLUE FROM 6:41-59

A basic misunderstanding of Jesus' opponents seems to surface in every generation. There are many who do not grasp the meaning of Jesus as the living bread. There are diverse views on the nature of the Lord's Supper. People are often confused about their own tradition. This text raises many contemporary questions as we experience the ancient confusion of this teaching.

You might present this biblical experience from the perspective of the broken loaf and the partially filled cup. What can the elements of these symbols say to the congregation? Direct the whole sermon as a dialogue between the loaf and the cup as they look upon the confused views of your congregation. You will be amazed how easily the people will listen to direct comments concerning them when these remarks come through another medium.

Just stand behind the table or before the altar and hold the empty or remaining elements while you give them voices. Don't worry about the moving of your mouth. Just move the elements about to give them a sense of life before the congregation.

You can either tell the biblical story from their perspective or reflect on the contemporary congregation in the same manner.

If it is a small piece of bread, you might close a non-communion sermon by drinking and eating the items presented in the sermon. Of course, communion can also be served at this point.

A CLUE FROM 6:60-71

Hard sayings and controversial preaching can lose many followers of a preacher in any time and place. It is helpful to see the hard edge of Jesus' ministry. This passage invites you to explore the relationship between the work of Jesus and the ministry of the contemporary pastor. You might face the issue of a pastor's popularity within the context of this text.

Jesus gets into trouble for his verbal action and his lifestyle. Perhaps we are being told that this is the ironical fate of all who eat of this living bread: Life in Christ may lead to our own death.

You can come out from the pulpit for the sermon. Pick up a picket sign that you have prepared earlier and hidden until the time to use it. The sign should say something abstract. Just paint the words: "Peace at any cost." March around the communion table or altar chanting your slogan.

Stop and put down your sign. Ask the people how they feel about this kind of "hard" saying in worship. Encourage them to speak out. They will easily fall into the role of the opponents of Jesus in the text. Gently lead them into the passage. Tell stories of unpopular preachers, e.g., Martin Luther King, Jr., St. Paul, William Tyndale, John Huss, etc.

CHAPTER 7

JESUS SECRETLY GOES TO A FEAST

After this Jesus went about in Galilee; he would not go about in Judea, because the Jews^n sought to kill him. ²Now the Jews' feast of Tabernacles was at hand. ³So his brothers said to him, "Leave here and go to Judea, that your disciples may see the works you are doing. ⁴For no man works in secret if he seeks to be known openly. If you do these things, show yourself to the world." ⁵For even his brothers did not believe in him. ⁶Jesus said to them, "My time has not yet come, but your time is always here. ⁷The world cannot hate you, but it hates me because I testify of it that its works are evil. ⁸Go to the feast yourselves; I am not^o going up to this feast, for my time has not yet fully come." ⁹So saying, he remained in Galilee.

10 But after his brothers had gone up to the feast, then he also went up, not publicly but in private. ¹¹The Jews were looking for him at the feast, and saying, "Where is he?" ¹²And there was much muttering about him among the people. While some said, "He is a good man," others said, "No, he is leading the people astray." ¹³Yet for fear of the Jews no one spoke openly of him.

JESUS' TEACHINGS CONFOUND THE PEOPLE

14 About the middle of the feast Jesus went up into the temple and taught. ¹⁵The Jews marveled at it, saying, "How is it that this man has learning,^p when he has never studied?" ¹⁶So Jesus answered them, "My teaching is not mine, but his who sent me; ¹⁷if any man's will is to do his will, he shall know whether the teaching is from God or whether I am speaking on my own authority. ¹⁸He who speaks on his own authority seeks his own glory; but he who seeks the glory of him who sent him is true, and in him there is no falsehood. ¹⁹Did not Moses give you the law? Yet none of you keeps the law. Why do you seek to kill me?" ²⁰The people answered, "You have a demon! Who is seeking to kill you?" ²¹Jesus answered them, "I did one deed, and you all marvel at it. ²²Moses gave you circumcision (not that it is from Moses, but from the fathers), and you circumcise a man upon the sabbath. ²³If on the sabbath a man receives circumcision, so that the law of Moses may not be broken, are you angry with me because on the sabbath I made a man's whole body well? ²⁴Do not judge by appearances, but judge with right judgment."

25 Some of the people of Jerusalem therefore said, "Is not this the man whom they seek to kill? ²⁶And here he is, speaking openly, and they say nothing to him! Can it be that the authorities really know that this is the Christ? ²⁷Yet we know where this man comes from; and when the Christ appears, no one will know where he comes from." ²⁸So Jesus proclaimed, as he taught in the temple, "You know me, and you know where I come from? But I have

---

n Or Judeans
o Other ancient authorities add yet

p Or this man knows his letters

not come of my own accord; he who sent me is true, and him you do not know. ²⁹I know him, for I come from him, and he sent me." ³⁰So they sought to arrest him; but no one laid hands on him, because his hour had not yet come. ³¹Yet many of the people believed in him; they said, "When the Christ appears, will he do more signs than this man has done?"

32 The Pharisees heard the crowd thus muttering about him, and the chief priests and Pharisees sent officers to arrest him. ³³Jesus then said, "I shall be with you a little longer, and then I go to him who sent me; ³⁴you will seek me and you will not find me; where I am you cannot come." ³⁵The Jews said to one another, "Where does this man intend to go that we shall not find him? Does he intend to go to the Dispersion among the Greeks and teach the Greeks? ³⁶What does he mean by saying, 'You will seek me and you will not find me,' and, 'Where I am you cannot come'?"

37 On the last day of the feast, the great day, Jesus stood up and proclaimed, "If any one thirst, let him come to me and drink. ³⁸He who believes in me, as[q] the scripture has said, 'Out of his heart shall flow rivers of living water.'" ³⁹Now this he said about the Spirit, which those who believed in him were to receive; for as yet the Spirit had not been given, because Jesus was not yet glorified.

40 When they heard these words, some of the people said, "This is really the prophet." ⁴¹Others said, "This is the Christ." But some said, "Is the Christ to come from Galilee? ⁴²Has not the scripture said that the Christ is descended from David, and comes from Bethlehem, the village where David was?" ⁴³So there was a division among the people over him. ⁴⁴Some of them wanted to arrest him, but no one laid hands on him.

45 The officers then went back to the chief priests and Pharisees, who said to them, "Why did you not bring him?" ⁴⁶The officers answered, "No man ever spoke like this man!" ⁴⁷The Pharisees answered them, "Are you led astray, you also? ⁴⁸Have any of the authorities or of the Pharisees believed in him? ⁴⁹But this crowd, who do not know the law, are accursed." ⁵⁰Nicode′mus, who had gone to him before, and who was one of them, said to them, ⁵¹"Does our law judge a man without first giving him a hearing and learning what he does?" ⁵²They replied, "Are you from Galilee too? Search and you will see that no prophet is to rise from Galilee."

---

q Or *let him come to me, and let him who believes in me drink. As*

CHAPTER 7

Creative Commentary on the Scripture

VERSES 1-13: In the previous chapter Jesus spoke a "hard saying" that drove some of his early converts away. The hardness of the saying was in the imagery: eating his body, drinking his blood. For the Jew to eat flesh with blood in it was forbidden; to drink the blood of the animal was also against the law. It was believed that the life of the animal was in the blood. Jesus has offended their sensitivities, both legal and cultural. Jesus has also drawn a distinction between spiritual life and physical life (flesh). They do not understand because Jesus speaks the language of the spirit and the people think in the language of the physical.

The brothers' words (verses 3-4) seem a cruel mockery. They seem to bait Jesus. Jesus has already been to Jerusalem twice and traveled about Judea. He has revealed himself in signs and wonders, won some converts and spoken some difficult words for his opponents' ears. In light of this the brothers' words seem unfair. Their accusation of his refusal to reveal himself seems unfounded.

The brothers' words suggest that Jesus has something to hide, that he is afraid to reveal himself in public. Are they questioning his sense of calling? Are they probing for some doubts? Are they questioning his sense of responsibility to his mission? Is there some jealousy here? Do their words reveal a feeling of envy because they do not share the same purpose of Jesus?

In what ways do we attack the integrity of others because we feel the lack of something they seem to have? Do we envy the spiritual gifts of others or their Christian experience (because it is different and somehow "better" than ours)? Do we resent them? What does this have to say about the "secrets of the kingdom"? Are there secrets only the faithful can understand? Are we called to guard such secrets from the spiritually ignorant? Or are we called to share them? Jesus counters the brothers' words with the issue of time: God's time versus our time.

What does this say about our agendas, our strategies, our human plans and schemes? Can we get ahead of God in working for the kingdom? Do our agendas get in the way of God's kingdom? Can we plan so well that we leave no room for God's spirit? Can it be that God's time is not our time?

Jesus' sense of calling and testimony to his mission has brought upon him hatred from many quarters. He has held up a mirror to the people, the mirror of God's vision and truth. Where in our lives are we resisting the mirror of God's Word?

Jesus seems to be marching to the beat of a different drummer. In fact, the whole first part of this chapter comes together to form a picture of a Jesus who is speaking and acting not according to his own whims but in accord with the will and purpose of the one who sent him.

Following inner necessity, Jesus comes to the feast privately, but then in the course of the festival "reveals" himself in the temple.

VERSES 14-24: Verse 14 is the beginning of a controversy that rages to the end of the chapter. The controversy is over Jesus: Is he a madman or Messiah? The two conflicting groups are those who support and follow Jesus and those who seek to arrest and kill him.

The controversy is summarized in verse 24 ("Do not judge by appearances, but judge with right judgment"). The key to the whole chapter seems to lie in this: We suffer when we let our prejudices, preconceptions and faulty reasonings color our ways of understanding those different from ourselves. "You have a demon!" (verse 20) is the New Testament way of labeling a person as insane or mentally unbalanced.

VERSES 25-31: Jesus is shattering a number of myths. He teaches with wisdom but has no formal education. Jesus uses his authority to confound the authority of the official structures. Jesus claimed no authority for himself but only as a witness to the Father.

VERSES 32-36: The words of Jesus seem to be riddles to some. He is using a faith language. These words flow from a spirit-controlled life that can only be understood by those with eyes to see, ears to hear and hearts open to the stirring of the spirit.

VERSES 37-39: Those who go looking for a river will find it. Also, those who go looking for a desert will find it. Sometimes we are blind because we see only what we want to see and believe only what we want to believe. We miss truth because we look for it with a limited and constrained vision.

VERSES 40-52: The controversy that has raged since verse 14 comes out into the open here. The conflict is between those who have already made up their minds (legalists) and those who have actually encountered Jesus. Sometimes we find God's Word. Sometimes God's Word finds us. Sometimes neither happens because we aren't open to it. Nicodemus, the searcher for truth in chapter 3, encourages other Pharisees to listen to Jesus before condemning him. How could this example make a different in church disputes, gossip and interdenominational differences?

Creative Bible Study Ideas

SESSION BASED ON 7:1-13

The sixth verse focuses on the theme of time. Jesus is talking about a different flow of reality than his brothers. The fourth Gospel shows eternal life as a present reality. This clue provides a fine means to help your students crawl into this passage.

1. Appoint a timekeeper.
2. Select a certain period of time up to one minute.
3. Each person is given a chance to guess when a stated amount of time has elapsed. The timekeeper will then announce how close the person came to the actual amount of time.
4. Ask the participants how the time passed when they focused on their perception of time itself and not on a clock. What situations seem to make time pass faster or slower?
5. Talk about how our time, human time, might differ from God's time. You might encourage your students to draw upon science fiction plots that deal with the concept of different time realms. Also look at the Bible's use of time (look under "time" and "day" in a Concordance).
6. How does this concept of God's time apply to what Jesus has said about his time?

7. Form a huge clock on the floor of the room by placing chairs at the key points on the face of the imaginary timepiece. Tell the students that this is a time map of their own time line.

8. Ask each person to find a place on the clock which in some way represents a point in their own journey that they felt they were working under God's time and not their own. This is deliberately a vague exercise. We are inviting the students into a biblical experience which draws upon their own stories.

9. Share the stories.

10. Explore the common threads that led students to find the time line of God for those moments. Keep an ear for common statements.

11. Ask each student to talk to another person about his or her own clock of faith. These stories can be shared at the next session.

SESSION BASED ON 7:14-24

This passage reveals the struggle to see the real Jesus. Those around him cannot clearly see that the will of God is flowing through this person and his ministry.

1. Gather a number of pictures of Jesus from Sunday school materials and every source available. There may be pictures in old filmstrips and other unlikely places.

2. Give each person a picture to study for a few minutes. You might want to play a contemporary song or old hymn about Jesus during this period of reflection. Suggest that they might try to find an aspect of Jesus' personhood in the picture close to the biblical presentation of him.

3. Share these reflections as a group. What gets in the way of seeing Jesus fully? Why does he look different in each picture? Can our faith (law) keep us from Jesus?

4. Pass out paper and crayons or felt-tipped markers.

5. Ask each person to draw a representation of the real Jesus as he is presented by scripture.

6. Share these pictures in a closing circle. Music from a contemporary Christian song can be played during the sharing. It is easy to find albums of Christian musicians singing about seeing Jesus, the eyes of Jesus, etc. You might want to use some of your students' pictures as bulletin cover art for worship. Or make a group collage of the many images of Jesus.

SESSION BASED ON 7:25-31

1. Carry a suitcase into the classroom. You will have to prepare its contents in advance. Load it with words, images and items that reflect the kinds of "baggage" that get in our way as we seek to listen and be responsive to God's Word and the challenge of Christ. Focus on the kinds of issues that are hard for Christians (peace, minority rights, treatment of the aged, care for the unemployed, etc.). You might let them choose a pressing ethical issue for the session. The purpose of this session is to help the students focus on their "baggage" (prejudices, faulty assumptions, etc.) and unpack some of it.

2. Open the suitcase and explain how the passage suggests the prejudices we all carry in our understanding of Christ's will for our lives.

3. Ask each person to quickly choose one item.

4. Have them reflect on how this item or object symbolizes a blinder that might keep us from seeing situations from Christ's perspective.

5. Have people share these insights.

6. Read the passage to the group.

7. Talk about how preconceptions of Jesus kept many of his contemporaries from really seeing him.

SESSION BASED ON 7:14-31

A distorted sense of law fuels the accusations toward Jesus from his opponents. The tension between law and gospel whirls around the ministry of Jesus.

1. Choose an issue that closely touches the lives of those in your group. You might use a slide or individual pictures from newsmagazines to dramatize the issue.

2. Divide the group into two sections or triads.

3. Have one side or every other triad take a hardline, legalistic view on the issue. The other half of the group or the other triads are asked to take a more open, accepting view.

4. Have the students meet in their smaller units and get their position on the issue clearly organized.

5. Conduct a full debate on the problem.

6. Have the people in the group switch positions on the question.

7. Give the units three or four minutes to organize the new roles.

8. Share the discussion once again.

118   THE BIBLE CREATIVE

9. Go around the circle and share the blinders of preconceived views that keep us from hearing God speak to us freshly on issues such as this one.

10. Read the passage.

11. Talk about how our legalistic blinders put us in the same situation as the opponents of Jesus.

SESSION BASED ON 7:32-36

This text is still another example of John's style in this Gospel: Jesus speaks in a faith language that makes sense to believers and open-minded seekers. But this same language is almost a "secret code" to unbelievers. His spirit-endowed life can only be understood by those with eyes, ears and hearts tuned into the movement of the spirit.

1. Create a message written in a simple code. (Example: "PLI MO DLEM" could be the encoded version of "God is love.")

2. Give the coded message to the group.

3. Half of your students should receive the key to the code while the rest of the students don't have any guidance. The latter students will be able to read only gibberish.

4. Discuss the feelings toward the message when it is viewed from these two different perspectives.

5. Read the passage. What are the blinders worn by the critics that keep them from understanding Jesus?

6. Have the students develop a theological "code" for understanding and seeing Jesus, e.g., a list of attitudes such as "open-minded," "listen to people," "accept differences," "meet needs," etc.

7. Share the results of this session with the whole church. For example, have one of the students write an article for the church newsletter or share it on the back of the bulletin cover for Sunday worship. The reporter should give both the coded message in step 1 (above), its meaning and the results of step 6.

SESSION BASED ON 7:37-43

1. Bring to the session several items: two communion cups or small paper cups for each student, a bag of fine sand, a small wooden cross and a bowl of water.

2. Create a tight circle.

3. Pour the bag of sand on the table or floor in the middle of the circle.

4. Ask the students to imagine a long journey in the desert. You might play the sound of wind recorded on your audio-cassette recorder. Help them "feel" the heat and sun.

5. Suggest that there are dry periods of wandering in the wilderness in each person's life. Fill the small glasses or cups with sand and give one to each person. Suggest that they pour the grains into their hands. Then have them focus on one such event in their own lives. Tell them that they are thirsting for relief and help at this crisis moment.

6. Invite the students to share the feelings of those remembered moments. They don't have to share the nature of the crisis or problem unless they so desire. However, the feelings about the time should be shared. What kind of spiritual thirst does such an experience bring to each person?

7. Present the bowl of water and read the passage. Share the promise of verses 37-38.

8. Pour one cup of water and hold it. Share how Christ has met your thirst in life. Then ask the person to your right to hold out his or her cup. Pour your water into that person's cup.

9. As the members pour the "living" water of Christ, have them share how Jesus has met the thirst in their lives.

10. Close by pouring water into each small cup.

11. Each person is then encouraged to drink of this living water in order to experience the quenching of spiritual thirst through Christ.

SESSION BASED ON 7:45-52

This passage is bristling with reports concerning Jesus. His opponents are divided. Yet, the officers and Nicodemus have experienced him and are not sure that he is wrong.

The text suggests that you utilize this dynamic in order to bring your students into the message. Cast the students in the different roles of the passage (officers, chief priests, Pharisees and Nicodemus). Have the students prepare for the simulation by reading verses 14-44. Then role play the passage.

You might get the participants to describe how they felt in their roles by using a "man-on-the-street" interviewing technique. The reporter interviews them about the situation and how they came to view Jesus in a particular way. This role play and debriefing can be easily videotaped and shared with the whole congregation at the coffee hour after church.

Creative Speaking and Preaching Ideas

A CLUE FROM 7:1-13

Jesus draws the criticism of those around him once again. Why does one bringing light receive so much hatred from others? The passage suggests that Jesus holds a mirror up to the culture. His critics are really looking at their own sin. Instead of dealing with their sin, they want to kill the one holding the mirror.

You might take this clue from the text as a dynamic for your sermon. Pass out spoons to the congregation. A spoon can function as a mirror. You can have them look into the bowl of the spoon and view their upside-down image. Guide them through a time of reflection as they look at the inverted view of their world. How do we look at Jesus from the wrong perspective? Encourage them to turn to a neighbor and share the attributes of the world that are reflected in the spoon as people search for Jesus.

You might have a few people share their insights with the whole congregation. After talking to a neighbor about this experience, they will definitely have something to share with the whole gathering.

You can pick up on the examples of hatred toward Jesus by his opponents. How did these opponents actually hate their own selves? Ask everyone to turn the spoon over and look into the backside of it. This right-side-up reflection can be related to forgiveness and the gift of clear vision that Christ promises those who turn to him. The next time they use a spoon at the table, there is a good chance that they will think about this discussion of Christ's love. The possibility of carrying the worship experience into daily life is one of the strongest aspects of this kind of preaching and teaching.

A CLUE FROM 7:14-24

Verse 24 summarizes the confrontation of the passage. The people around Jesus are able to see the Son of God, yet they can't see the one who sent him.

You might utilize this clue by presenting your message through the idiom of appearance. You might not be present during the opening part of the morning worship service. When you come to the sermon time, enter through the back door and work your way down the aisle. It will be important to wear several layers of clothing. You can construct one layer for each of the several different levels of your humanity.

The outer layer could be represented by your clerical robe. Walk down the aisle and talk about the assumptions some people make about seeing such garb. Be generous in stereotypical comments. You might even invite people in the congregation to join in the process.

The next clothing layer can now be exposed. This layer is your working clothes. The costume now has the appearance of another facet of your life. Perhaps you have chosen a hobby or career (plumbing, sales, auto work, etc.). Talk about the judgments we make about a working person.

The next layer of your humanity revealed is the recreational dimension. You wear jogging or sports clothing. Talk about the generalization we can make about this appearance.

The last layer may reveal a T-shirt with a political or social slogan on it. This is the layer of social values. Share again some typical assumptions about this side of your humanity.

Repeat verse 24. What is the right judgment? How do we look into the heart of another to see the glory of God?

A CLUE FROM 7:25-31

How do we know Jesus? Those with the facts about him often miss the reality of his personhood. The difficulty facing the characters in this passage suggests that you use a reasoning method to communicate the message of the text.

Build your sermon into a detective case. Perhaps you can take the role of your favorite detective character (Sherlock Holmes, etc.). Holmes can suggest the garb you wear for this dramatic presentation of the sermon.

Tell the congregation that you have a hard case. You must solve a missing-person case. You might quiz witnesses in the congregation, present physical clues and even read letters of evidence. Some clues might be the cross, a hymn, a Bible, etc.

You are, of course, searching for the real Jesus. Don't be afraid to wander around the church. There is no reason why you have to be glued to the front of the worship area for your preaching. Close by summarizing what you have found out about the real Jesus.

122   THE BIBLE CREATIVE

A CLUE FROM 7:32-36

This text focuses on the continuing misunderstanding of those who oppose Jesus. He introduces the theme of his reunion with the Father. In a sense, Jesus is going home.

This clue offers a rich contact point between the message of the passage and the experience of the people in the congregation. Going home and/or being left behind when someone else leaves is in everyone's experience. Such an emotional moment may be the most common factor in funeral services. We feel left behind by the person who has died.

The opponents of Jesus are confused by his pronouncement. Yet, the theme of departure and separation of Jesus from his beloved is very clearly introduced here.

You might develop this clue by asking the worshipers to write on the blank part of the Sunday bulletin as they reflect on a moment in their lives when they experienced a painful passage or separation. You can suggest this participation before the sermon time. Have the choir sing while the people are reflecting on these memories.

Now ask the worshipers to focus on what they didn't understand about this sudden or expected departure of an important person in their lives.

Undertake the same exercise while the congregation is doing it. Ask your people to share some of these stories and the feelings surfaced by these memories. Worshipers who are not accustomed to sharing can be nudged into this kind of participation with patience. You might want to alert a couple of people before the service that you will invite participation in the sermon time. They can then be ready to start the sharing.

This might be an excellent context to deal with the range of situations which bring about separation (divorce, child going to college, pastor going to another church, families moving out of town, etc.).

A CLUE FROM 7:37-44

The image of a river is utilized again in this text. You might pick the sensual experience of thirsting from the passage as you preach. Bring a pail and an old-fashioned dipper to the center of the worship center at your sermon time.

You might gather the children around you and provide an intergenerational preaching event. Mention to the congregation that water is a key component in our lives. Our body is mostly composed of this ingredient as is most of the Earth. We can survive without food much longer than we can without water.

You might ask everyone to close his or her eyes and imagine a hot desert. It will be helpful if you play a recording of wind blowing during this guided journey. Take them out into the wilderness with its heat and the constant need for water.

Ask the people to share moments when a taste of water meant the most to them. The children and the adults can share these stories publicly.

Focus on the dipper and suggest how many stories this simple utensil could tell. Speak from the perspective of the dipper as if it had been present when Jesus confronted his opponents and offered them living water.

Take a bit of the water and anoint the foreheads of the children and tell them that this is a reminder of their baptism or dedication as smaller children. If your tradition focuses on adult baptism, this will be an excellent way to give them a foretaste of full baptism that will come later.

A CLUE FROM 7:45-52

The dialogue style is suggested by this passage. Again the fourth Gospel reveals the nature of Jesus through the misunderstanding of those around him.

You might follow the clue of the passage and become one of the characters in these verses. Perhaps you might be the returning officers. You are stunned by the impact of Jesus. Your superiors are furious by this turn of events. You are trying to share the power of the man. You may do the presentation from a monologue perspective. Speak as if the congregation is your superior. Build in his questions as if they were being asked. You can gather the information for your role from the verses in the whole chapter.

The character of Nicodemus also offers some fine possibilities. He has been presented in a more complete context earlier in the book. Has he grown in his understanding here?

CHAPTER 8

"LET HIM WITHOUT SIN THROW A STONE"

They went each to his own house, ¹but Jesus went to the Mount of Olives. ²Early in the morning he came again to the temple; all the people came to him, and he sat down and taught them. ³The scribes and the Pharisees brought a woman who had been caught in adultery, and placing her in the midst ⁴they said to him, "Teacher, this woman has been caught in the act of adultery. ⁵Now in the law Moses commanded us to stone such. What do you say about her?" ⁶This they said to test him, that they might have some charge to bring against him. Jesus bent down and wrote with his finger on the ground. ⁷And as they continued to ask him, he stood up and said to them, "Let him who is without sin among you be the first to throw a stone at her." ⁸And once more he bent down and wrote with his finger on the ground. ⁹But when they heard it, they went away, one by one, beginning with the eldest, and Jesus was left alone with the woman standing before him. ¹⁰Jesus looked up and said to her, "Woman, where are they? Has no one condemned you?" ¹¹She said, "No one, Lord." And Jesus said, "Neither do I condemn you; go, and do not sin again."*r*

JESUS REVEALS HIS AUTHORITY

12 Again Jesus spoke to them, saying, "I am the light of the world; he who follows me will not walk in darkness, but will have the light of life." ¹³The Pharisees then said to him, "You are bearing witness to yourself; your testimony is not true." ¹⁴Jesus answered, "Even if I do bear witness to myself, my testimony is true, for I know whence I have come and whither I am going, but you do not know whence I come or whither I am going. ¹⁵You judge according to the flesh, I judge no one. ¹⁶Yet even if I do judge, my judgment is true, for it is not I alone that judge, but I and he*s* who sent me. ¹⁷In your law it is written that the testimony of two men is true; ¹⁸I bear witness to myself, and the Father who sent me bears witness to me." ¹⁹They said to him therefore, "Where is your Father?" Jesus answered, "You know neither me nor my Father; if you knew me, you would know my Father also." ²⁰These words he spoke in the treasury, as he taught in the temple; but no one arrested him, because his hour had not yet come.

21 Again he said to them, "I go away, and you will seek me and die in your sin; where I am going, you cannot come." ²²Then said the Jews, "Will he kill himself, since he says, 'Where I am going, you cannot come'?" ²³He said to them, "You are from below, I am from above; you are of this world, I am not of this world. ²⁴I told you that you would die in your sins, for you will die in your sins unless you believe that I am he." ²⁵They said to him, "Who are you?" Jesus said to them, "Even what I have told you from the begin-

---

r The most ancient authorities omit 7.53—8.11; other authorities add the passage here or after 7.36 or after 21.25 or after Luke 21.38, with variations of text.

s Other ancient authorities read *the Father*

ning.[t] ²⁶I have much to say about you and much to judge; but he who sent me is true, and I declare to the world what I have heard from him." ²⁷They did not understand that he spoke to them of the Father. ²⁸So Jesus said, "When you have lifted up the Son of man, then you will know that I am he, and that I do nothing on my own authority but speak thus as the Father taught me. ²⁹And he who sent me is with me; he has not left me alone, for I always do what is pleasing to him." ³⁰As he spoke thus, many believed in him.

"BEFORE ABRAHAM WAS, I AM"

31 Jesus then said to the Jews who had believed in him, "If you continue in my word, you are truly my disciples, ³²and you will know the truth, and the truth will make you free." ³³They answered him, "We are descendants of Abraham, and have never been in bondage to any one. How is it that you say, 'You will be made free'?"

34 Jesus answered them, "Truly, truly, I say to you, every one who commits sin is a slave to sin. ³⁵The slave does not continue in the house for ever; the son continues for ever. ³⁶So if the Son makes you free, you will be free indeed. ³⁷I know that you are descendants of Abraham; yet you seek to kill me, because my word finds no place in you. ³⁸I speak of what I have seen with my Father, and you do what you have heard from your father."

39 They answered him, "Abraham is our father." Jesus said to them, "If you were Abraham's children, you would do what Abraham did, ⁴⁰but now you seek to kill me, a man who has told you the truth which I heard from God; this is not what Abraham did. ⁴¹You do what your father did." They said to him, "We were not born of fornication; we have one Father, even God." ⁴²Jesus said to them, "If God were your Father, you would love me, for I proceeded and came forth from God; I came not of my own accord, but he sent me. ⁴³Why do you not understand what I say? It is because you cannot bear to hear my word. ⁴⁴You are of your father the devil, and your will is to do your father's desires. He was a murderer from the beginning, and has nothing to do with the truth, because there is no truth in him. When he lies, he speaks according to his own nature, for he is a liar and the father of lies. ⁴⁵But, because I tell the truth, you do not believe me. ⁴⁶Which of you convicts me of sin? If I tell the truth, why do you not believe me? ⁴⁷He who is of God hears the words of God; the reason why you do not hear them is that you are not of God."

48 The Jews answered him, "Are we not right in saying that you are a Samaritan and have a demon?" ⁴⁹Jesus answered, "I have not a demon; but I honor my Father, and you dishonor me. ⁵⁰Yet I do not seek my own glory; there is One who seeks it and he will be the judge. ⁵¹Truly, truly, I say to you, if any one keeps my word, he will never see death." ⁵²The Jews said to him, "Now we know that you have a demon. Abraham died, as did the prophets; and you say, 'If any one keeps my word, he

---

t Or Why do I talk to you at all?

will never taste death. [53]Are you greater than our father Abraham, who died? And the prophets died! Who do you claim to be?" [54]Jesus answered, "If I glorify myself, my glory is nothing; it is my Father who glorifies me, of whom you say that he is your God. [55]But you have not known him; I know him. If I said, I do not know him, I should be a liar like you; but I do know him and I keep his word. [56]Your father Abraham rejoiced that he was to see my day; he saw it and was glad." [57]The Jews then said to him, "You are not yet fifty years old, and have you seen Abraham?"[u] [58]Jesus said to them, "Truly, truly, I say to you, before Abraham was, I am." [59]So they took up stones to throw at him; but Jesus hid himself, and went out of the temple.

---

u Other ancient authorities read *has Abraham seen you?*

CHAPTER 8

Creative Commentary on the Scripture

VERSES 7:53—8:11: This is one of the more popular stories in the fourth Gospel. Yet it does not appear in most of the early manuscripts. Everything about the story is consistent with Jesus' teaching ministry. Most modern translations use smaller type or brackets for this passage to show the nature of its textual history.

The story is very touching and cuts us as deeply now as it did the accusers around the condemned woman. The nature of Christ is revealed in a very special way in this encounter.

The verbs are interesting in this text. They track the movement of Jesus in the story. The setting for the story is sensual in many ways. There is a sin that attracts the village judges. The accusers pick up stones and Jesus writes with his finger in the sand.

The Pharisees and scribes are pointing to a particular sin and ignoring their own warts. We forget that sin is sin. They tried to trick the Lord with excuses. Jesus declared war on excuses.

The woman caught in adultery offered no excuse. She was what she was. She didn't deny her sin but stood ready to take her punishment. "The law says . . ." translates today into our love of rules, rites and ceremonies. It is easy to forget that the only law is love. Instead of pointing a finger, or grabbing a handful of stones, we must love as he loves.

The Lord forgives. It is his gift, but as with all gifts we must accept it.

VERSES 12-20: Jesus shares one of the important "I am" statements in this text. The humanity of Jesus is again defined for those who don't understand. The oneness with the Father is the thrust of Jesus' teaching here.

We are given the assurance of true leadership: Jesus knows who he is and where he is going. This points up the fact that we are to follow in faith. The implication is "follow me."

These passages urge us not to be afraid to walk through life by faith. Political and religious leaders may fail us. But we can be confident of Jesus Christ's leadership.

VERSES 21-38: The message focuses on surrender. Until the believer can surrender completely to God and his will, he or she will teeter on the edge of faith. It is not easy to surrender *totally* our very lives to God. It is a physical, difficult thing to do, because we are of this world.

Jesus sets the example in verse 29: "I always do what is pleasing to him." On our own, we cannot possibly live a life pleasing to God, but if we have surrendered completely to him, then our lives are pleasing to him. Is the believer willing to surrender completely in order to know true freedom?

VERSES 39-59: Jesus encounters his opponents in a discussion of his lineage to the Father. He responds to their children-of-Abraham claim by stating that he was before Abraham.

Why doesn't his audience understand what he says? Is it because they are afraid? Are they afraid to believe fully the words and thoughts that they cannot understand? Jesus promises that the listener is capable of understanding; all he or she needs is faith. What Jesus says is true: The believer needs only to experience it to know that. Once the person of faith surrenders in complete trust and faith, he or she will know that there is no death.

Creative *Bible* Study Ideas

SESSION BASED ON 7:53—8:11

1. Read the passage.
2. Focus on the point in the story where Jesus writes on the ground.
3. Ask each person to write on a piece of paper some things Jesus might have written on the ground.
4. Go around the group and share what the students have written. Why did he write this?
5. Repeat the exercise. What would Jesus write in the dust if *we* stood in that circle?

You might want to use blackboards for this exercise if you have enough space for the whole group. After you have shared the results of this reflection, read the passage again. Then rub out the words as a symbol of God's forgiveness of our sins.

You might want to explore some of these issues as they cut across the society in which we live. How are we going to change the sin that can be found in every mass media form? A hate campaign of letter writing is not the answer. A producer of a leading television program that has over 10-million viewers each week asked a group of religious broadcasters to guess how many suggestions for improving the program she received during the previous year. She told them that she had received only four such letters!

SESSION BASED ON 7:53—8:11

The stones that threaten the life of the woman in the passage suggest a sensual mode of studying this text. You might deal with sin that touches everyone's life. There is no distinction between little sins and big sins. All sin is the breakdown of the relationships between God, our neighbors and ourselves.

Adultery is the manifestation of the broken relationship. While the stone was an ancient instrument of punishment (death of Stephen, etc.), it is also a symbol of harshness.

If you are working with young people in a teaching situation, you might help them crawl into the passage by using stones. Give each person a small pebble. Talk about how it serves as a reflection of our sin.

Let each person share how the stone in some way reminds him or her of sin. Then ask the students to place the pebbles in their shoes. Walk around the church or room while you explore the theme of forgiveness. Sit down and talk about the discomfort of bearing the stones in this way.

Remove the stones and reflect once again as a group on how Jesus gave forgiveness to the woman in the story. You might read the story at this point. Exchange the pebbles with one another. Spend a little time getting used to the new stone and what it means to the other person. Agree that during the next week each person will pray each day for the original bearer of the stone. At the next class time, people can share their stories on how they felt being prayed for and how it was to pray for others concerning their sins. Did it help to overcome a temptation when you knew that another was praying for you?

SESSION BASED ON 7:53—8:11

Sin and forgiveness are two of the most difficult aspects of the gospel for most believers to embrace. Facing one's sinfulness leaves us helpless before God's mercy. It is at this point that the love of Jesus comes flooding into our lives. We are able to see ourselves differently (as one for whom God gave his Son) and to see others with more appreciation (other forgiven sinners). The fear of confession freezes many people into resistance at this moment of honesty. Jesus provides a graphic scene which gives the people a chance to touch and see the process of redemption.

You might design a simple moment for children concerning this theme. Glue stamps on a piece of paper. Do a good job of affixing them to the paper. Gather the children around you as you talk about removing the stamps from the sheet.

You can't get them off without destroying them. They are held fast by the glue. Ask them how this is like our desire to do things that hurt other people. You might use the pictures on the stamps to give them a story or situation for this discussion. Take some time developing the stories and how sin/separation breaks us off from a life of love.

Take the group into the kitchen and put some water into a kettle. Ask them about water as it appears in Bible stories. How does God use water for us? Don't direct their comments. Some will think of baptism and other moments when water is special for cleansing us. Heat the water on the stove as you talk.

When the steam is produced, ask them about what the steam can symbolize for us. Spirit and the word for wind are the same in the New Testament. Hold the stamps over the steam and watch them come free of the paper. Discuss this.

You might talk further about how God frees us and sends us out to carry the burdens of others. Have the children write a note or dictate a letter to someone who is sick or in the hospital. Tell them that you will glue the stamps to the envelopes containing their love notes.

SESSION BASED ON 7:53—8:11

If you have an outside setting that could be utilized for education (e.g., Vacation Bible School), you might draw upon the image of the stones from this passage to deal with sin and forgiveness. Have the students gather stones in an area that needs reclaiming or development. This might be an adjacent property that can be changed for the best.

Spend some time at making the stones special. Ask the students what is beautiful about their own and other persons' stones. Encourage them to feel the stones and share impressions of how the stones also reflect hard things about life. Put them in the center of the group and ask your students to close their eyes and take turns finding their stone just through touch.

Explore how these stones have also seen hard times as they were formed over the centuries. These stones existed when Jesus walked upon the Earth! Have them imagine that the rocks are symbols of sin. How could we label them for special sins? Let them give each one a name.

Read the passage and focus on how the stones changed from weapons of sin into harmless paving stones for the street. Lead them in the process of transforming the rocks into salvation stones. Create a garden (Eden?), a place where your students can make a beautiful statement about God's love. You might want to get some help from the gardeners and landscapers in your congregation. Don't be afraid to draw upon the rich gifts of others.

You might create a special walk in this garden. The children can invite the congregation to their salvation garden. As God has turned ugliness into beauty, so he continues to do in the lives of all his children.

SESSION BASED ON 7:53—8:11

The woman caught in adultery is an example of a woman accused by men. Is she a prostitute or a wife divorced by her husband? Who was her partner in this crime? Jesus is the only male who does not accuse her.

You might want to enable your students to experience the teaching of this passage in a dramatic manner. Select a male from the group and send him out of the room. Read the passage and arm the women in the group with stones made from wads of newspaper.

Bring the man into the room and tell him to sit down on the floor. Have the women accuse him of sinning. You might encourage this experience by having them shout judgment all at once with loud voices. Have them pummel him with the paper stones.

Stop the experience and ask them to share their feelings about this simulation. How did the man in the circle feel? How did the women feel in their judgment? Ask the rest of the class to join in this sharing.

Explore the issues they have raised. You may find yourself in a very rich and important discussion of sexuality values and abuses (incest, prostitution, adultery, pornography, etc.). These are all matters of concern for the Christian. Yet, what is Jesus really saying about the Christian's response to the abuser of sexuality?

If your class is committed to serious Bible study you might want to continue the discussion in terms of the personal responsibility for change. Can your group do something about more study on sexuality? Is there help for prostitutes in your community? Can something be started by your church?

SESSION BASED ON 7:53—8:11

There is an internal story flowing through this text. Who was this woman? How did she come to find herself in this situation? Who was the man with whom she was caught? What were the accusers like? Why were they so enraged by her sin? What is Jesus teaching us with his love and acceptance of the person, but not the sin? How can this passage be understood without tricking ourselves into taking sin lightly? Did the text's shaky history in the manuscripts come about because church people may have thought that Jesus was too accepting?

These questions from the text suggest that your people might crawl into the story in order to explore sin as it relates to sexuality in our time. This might be a particularly good session for high school youth and young adults. In this explicitly sexual age, what does Jesus say to us?

If you have a mature group of young people and some intentional time to explore this realm, you might begin by setting the scene as it comes to us in the Gospel. Create a street scene. Ask your people to play roles. Give everyone a character. You might create names and viewpoints. Put the information on a slip of paper. Use pillowcases or small towels for headdresses. You can have as many villagers as you have students. There must be the character of the woman. The role of Jesus can be an empty chair. You will give your students turns at sitting in the seat of Christ.

Create the scene of the passage. Increase the dialogue between the parties. Have a couple people resist the crowd concerning the woman. After exploring the historical situation, move some contemporary parallels into the discussion (what about those who participate in sex jokes, movies, magazines, thoughts?). When is sexual thought natural and when is it sinful?

Use the silent person in the Jesus chair as a recorder. He or she must write "on the ground" what sins are heard from the crowd. You can use a blackboard or newsprint.

Stop the scene after people have had a chance to share their feelings from their roles and from sitting in the Jesus chair. Debrief the scene by focusing on the writings in the sand. Take time with the issues and feelings.

Close with the closing moment of the biblical scene. Have each person reflect silently about the discussion and his or her sin from the perspective of the woman in the story. Ask each person to respond to your question: "Has no one condemned you?" They are to say: "No one." Then give that person the biblical assurance: "Neither do I condemn you; go, and do not sin again."

You may want to modify this process so that each person has the opportunity to give the biblical assurance of forgiveness to another. You can uncover some very deep and important concerns in the lives of these people by going into this passage. You might find that this design will work well for a lock-in (overnight retreat in a church) or retreat.

Jesus knew that God walks with us in all of our life experiences. It is a shame that the community of faith fails to deal with our sexuality from the perspective of the gospel. We leave it to the world to determine our values. Then we complain because it does such a poor job. Perhaps your class will want to suggest that a course on sexuality be offered by your church (if such an educational opportunity is not currently available).

It would also be helpful to pair this text with the story in chapter 4. The woman at the well provides another setting to address these important issues.

SESSION BASED ON 8:12-20

Jesus gives another "I am" saying as he continues to reveal his personhood to us. The image of light is important to this Gospel and to our own life experiences.

A good way to pick up the teaching clue from the passage is to utilize the presence and absence of light as a means of experiencing the message. You might create blindfolds from pieces of cloth before your session. As the students come to the room, blindfold them and tell them to trust a helper to lead them to their chairs.

Take the students to another setting with which they are unfamiliar. In fact, the bulk of the opening part of the learning session might be a walk in darkness. This "trust" walk can also be done with the whole line of students moving as they hold hands. Ask them to keep totally silent. You might play certain sounds along the way from your cassette tape recorder (traffic, crowd sounds, etc.). This can become a modern "Pilgrim's Progress" with pitfalls along the way. Describe at each stopping point a temptation or sin of the world.

When you have gathered at the final meeting place, totally darken the room before they remove their blindfolds. Talk about the walk in darkness. At what moments were they a bit afraid?

Can they describe the meaning of the places along the way where they stopped? Did the person leading them give them special care and security?

After a few minutes, light a candle. Proclaim to them that Christ is the light of the world and that there is no darkness for those who follow him. Encourage them to share the dark and fearful moments facing their lives at this time.

Close by giving each person a candle. As each one is lit from the Christ candle, ask for a one-sentence prayer for people in the group or others in darkness. Perhaps letters could be written to people with an expression of the prayer being offered on their behalf. You might even want to include a small candle and invite them to offer such prayers for others during a particular period of time (e.g., weeks before Christmas or during Lent).

SESSION BASED ON 8:12-20

The opponents of Jesus keep confusing the literal for the figurative or the figurative for the literal. Of course, Jesus is moving in both directions. He is also giving important entry points into the message of salvation. Jesus is providing directions, but they choose not to see the signposts for the direction of their own lives.

It would be helpful to focus on the aspect of direction as you explore this passage with adults or young people. Ask members of the class to bring maps from a trip they once enjoyed.

You can go to a travel club and get planning kits they offer to members. These kits have several maps. If you are not a member, just tell them that you are teaching a class and need some travel resources. In most cases, businesses and organizations are very willing to provide or lend creative materials.

After students share outlines of their trips, begin a fresh task of planning an imaginary journey as a group. Have them go through all the steps that a well-planned trip requires (places to stay, the best route, sights along the way, places to eat, etc.). If you have enough students, create several subgroups.

Report on what has been planned. Now shift the task and ask them to plot another journey. If we use the model of a real trip, how can we translate the steps into a spiritual trip to find the Father? Let them make the transformation. What preparations do we have to make? Where is our map? Who is our guide? Read the passage as you begin.

You may want to share the results of this study with the whole congregation. Perhaps a display can be designed or it can be shared during the morning worship service.

SESSION BASED ON 8:21-38

Jesus lifts up the image of slavery and its bondage (being bound) as a means to present the freedom given by the Father through his Son. This suggests that we crawl into the passage by using this textual clue with a class of young people and/or adults.

Obtain a long piece of rope. It should be thicker than string, but not so bulky that it cannot be easily cut. You will be using it in many different ways.

Gather your people in a circle. Ask them to take hold of the rope as it is passed around the group until it forms a ring. Be sure you have a long enough piece so that there are many feet left beyond the circle.

Play a recording of the passage focusing on verses 31-38. Ask them to share what ties with the past might be suggested by the rope they're holding. Go around the circle as the students share their links with the past.

Jesus suggests that such lineage can also be bondage. Ask them to make loops in the rope and bind their hands. You might have to be the one to do this for them.

Break for refreshments or some other task that will be hard to accomplish while in bondage with others. Talk about the difficulty of being bound to others. You might want to probe the many bondages of our age (Christians being persecuted in many lands, the poor, the old, the fallen, etc.).

Proclaim that Christ sets us free! Go around and bless each person with a personal affirmation of Christ's love as you cut the rope. Now each person has a bracelet. Talk about the change we have in our freedom.

Close by having people exchange their bracelets. Ask them to wear them during their personal prayers as a reminder of the freedom given to us in Christ. You might ask them to pray for the original wearer of the rope.

This design works very well in retreat settings. It is best to have the time to develop the teaching with liturgical and sharing opportunities. Don't underestimate the power of this kind of experience. I remember such a moment when we did this with a group of youth during a weekend experience. A young woman told me the story of her early life. She admitted that she had been abused by her father and could not let anyone touch her now that she was a teenager. I remember the moment of hugging and tears when she exchanged bracelets with me. I kept that piece of rope for many years.

SESSION BASED ON 8:39-59

Jesus talks about the different kinds of fatherhood. Our experience shows us that there are really three realms where this discussion of fatherhood leads us: heavenly, evil and biological.

1. You might open your class session by giving everyone a large piece of paper and a pen or felt-tipped marker.

2. Ask each person to make three columns with the markers or pens.

3. Have them make three lists of the ways they have been shaped or influenced by these realms of fatherhood. These lists can be more than words. Encourage doodles, pictures and other creative media.

4. Read the passage now to give them a picture of Jesus' discussion.

5. Form groups of two or three and share the lists. Which is longest? How do we understand these influences? Did we have a choice how we were influenced? Do we now?

6. Explore the qualities of fatherhood as revealed by the relationship between Jesus and the Father.

7. Repeat this process by substituting "mother" for "father." How does this substitution change the conclusions?

Creative Speaking and Preaching Ideas

A CLUE FROM 7:53—8:11

The sin of the woman has blinded everyone, except Jesus, to the true nature of sin: It touches all. This dramatic confrontation between sinners beckons us to present this story in a new wineskin.

Find a woman who will aid in the sermon presentation. Have her enter the service just as it begins. She should be dressed in red from head to toe: red hat, dress, stockings, shoes and red wig. Her face is plastered with strong red makeup.

At the beginning of your sermon declare that the woman in red is an outrage. State that she is disturbing the worship of God by her appearance. Ask her to move to one side of the church or altar area and sit alone.

Now add that anyone who is wearing any red (dress, tie) is a disgrace to the church on a Sunday. Ask them to join the woman at the side of the room. Expand your judgment of red by including all those who own red cars or anything else that is red.

The woman now has many companions. Warn them that next week the color of judgment may be blue or yellow or green.

Make the point that we can never be protected from having a wrong color. It is important to realize that we are loved, forgiven and accepted no matter what color we wear. You might expose your bare arm previously hidden by the sleeve of your coat or robe. It should be painted with several different bold colors. Suggest that we are not called to judge one another. Indeed, we are all sinners.

A CLUE FROM 7:53—8:11

The role of the stones appears here and at the end of this

chapter. Jesus saves the woman from death only to face the same risk to himself later. What is this saying about Jesus' compassion toward sinners? The image of the stones is too strong for us not to utilize it as a clue to our preaching of this text.

Ask a stone collector and polisher (lapidary) to help you in this task. If no such person is available, ask some of the children or young people to aid you. Gather enough small stones for everyone at worship. You might find these in your own parking lot.

Give out a stone to each person as he or she comes into the service. Use the stones in each of the prayers. Praise God by asking each person to reflect on the creative miracle of stones. Focus your prayers on the needs of others (intercession) by encouraging your people to feel the hardness in the stone and think about the suffering of others. Put the prayer of confession at the end of the sermon.

After the text has been read, share the classic short story "The Lottery" by Shirley Jackson. This tale depicts a community that annually chooses one person to represent the sins of others. They then stone the person to death. After reading the chilling story, ask them to reflect on their stones once again. How does your stone in some way reflect your own sins?

Now offer the prayer of confession. Some of your people might want to add to it from the congregation. Ask that everyone exchange a stone with another person. This act of picking up the burdens and sins of another is what the Christian life is all about.

A CLUE FROM 7:53—8:11

The stones in the passage "speak out" to us as scripture promises that they would (Luke 19:40). This clue suggests that you might present the whole message from the perspective of two stones that were present at this scene.

Read the passage. Hold two medium-to-large stones in front of you at the pulpit or communion table. Ask the question: "What could two stones that were present at this story have to tell us about it?" Then go into two voices as they have dialogue with each other about the setting and story. Use the passage to give you direction on the deep struggle between the parties in the dispute. They can describe the emotions of Jesus, the woman and the accusers.

Don't let any doubt keep you from realizing the impact of this text-inspired approach on your people. Carry the stones with you when you do the benediction. Build them into the promise you share. Put the stones on a table next to you as you greet people at the door. Watch the children hesitantly touch them.

A CLUE FROM 8:12-20

The light of the world is a wondrous gift that floods the darkness facing every person. The sin cannot overcome this light. You can utilize this clue by announcing at the beginning of your sermon that there is evidence that someone has been taking money from the offering plates each Sunday. Tell them that it is important to determine who it is and to put a stop to this stealing. Tell them that you have a process of elimination that will catch the thief and hand out the proper punishment.

Have the ushers pass out candles and a questionnaire to each person. Allow people time to answer the questions. If all of their answers are negative, they are to hold the candle up high and someone will come and light it. Tell them that when you are finished, it will be clear by the unlighted candles who could be the thief.

On the questionnaires place these six queries:
- Have you ever stolen anyone's time?
- Have you ever withheld your love?
- Is there anyone you have not forgiven?
- Have you ever told a lie?
- Have you ever lusted in your heart after someone?
- Have you ever been jealous?

When the questionnaires have been answered, there will be no lighted candles. Make the point that we are all sinners. Read the passage. There is no degree of sin before God. It is his light which keeps us in the light through the grace of his forgiveness.

A CLUE FROM 8:21-38

Walking in the truth is always hard. The strength to continue in obedience sets aside the children of God as the free persons of the world.

You might give your people a brief experience to feel and know the sense of breaking out of bondage. Point out that every person in the room is wearing a pair of shoes. This is not a natural part of the body. Invite them to take a shoe off. Let them wiggle their toes. How does one foot feel compared to the one still in the restricted space of the shoe?

If your congregation is comfortable at sharing in sermons, ask them to compare how the truth is like shoes. For example, shoes define space and yet permit the freedom to walk in snow or over blistering sidewalks.

Suggest that they try on each other's shoes. How do they fit? It is hard to put on another person's faith also. Yet, God gives each person access to the truth. And the truth fits us perfectly.

A CLUE FROM 8:31-38

Jesus was a refugee. He was carried forth from his home while he was still in his mother's womb. In this text, the listeners are refugees from their own heritage. Jesus offers them a home in his Word, but they refuse to enter.

Give your congregation a feeling for this sense of spiritual dislocation by physically relocating them. Gather about 20 of the worshipers into a small square at the center of the worship area. You can make a slight platform or some other prop that represents a raft of boat people. There must be just enough room for them to stand. Read the passage and talk a bit about it while these people are standing in this crowded space. Suggest that they imagine that they are forced to leave their land and seek another home. What will be hard to leave behind? What is fearful ahead?

Ask the people to be seated along the edge of the platform. Talk with them about the experience of being crowded and leaving home. What will be hard about resettlement?

Ask the congregation to deal with the problem. Tell them that this group has been offered some land in a rural part of the country. They want a new start. However, the people who live in this country area do not want them in their place. How would the congregation respond?

Close by having people in the pews go one at a time and bring a person back to the pew. Have the congregation sing "They'll Know We Are Christians by Our Love."

A CLUE FROM 8:39-59

There is much confusion and anger in this passage. The opponents of Jesus just can't grasp the nature of the Son of God. They call him names and finally attempt to stone him.

There is something missing from their picture of Jesus.

Draw upon the skills of a wood craftsman in your congregation. Find a picture of Jesus and glue it to a piece of plywood. Have your skilled friend cut it into small puzzle pieces. You might also have him or her drill a small hole in each piece. Number the backside of the puzzle pieces. You will need enough parts so that each person at worship will have one.

Using the offering plates, have the pieces passed out to the congregation. Encourage people to share with each other their reactions to the bits and pieces of a picture.

Talk about how a missing piece will sometimes bring about terrible results. Mad people can hurt themselves because something is lacking. Share the madness that sweeps through the opponents of Jesus when they misunderstand him.

It is the faith that enables us to receive the complete Christ and not just the piece we desire. We need everyone to be complete. Urge each person to carry or wear (chain through the hole) the puzzle piece during the next week. When people ask about your puzzle piece, share Jesus with them.

Invite everyone to bring the piece next week and tell what happened when they proclaimed Christ to others. You can number the other side of the puzzle to assemble it easily. At the following week's service, let the people share their experiences as you assemble the puzzle.

JESUS HEALS A BLIND MAN

As he passed by, he saw a man blind from his birth. ²And his disciples asked him, "Rabbi, who sinned, this man or his parents, that he was born blind?" ³Jesus answered, "It was not that this man sinned, or his parents, but that the works of God might be made manifest in him. ⁴We must work the works of him who sent me, while it is day; night comes, when no one can work. ⁵As long as I am in the world, I am the light of the world." ⁶As he said this, he spat on the ground and made clay of the spittle and anointed the man's eyes with the clay, ⁷saying to him, "Go, wash in the pool of Silo'am" (which means Sent). So he went and washed and came back seeing. ⁸The neighbors and those who had seen him before as a beggar, said, "Is not this the man who used to sit and beg?" ⁹Some said, "It is he"; others said, "No, but he is like him." He said, "I am the man." ¹⁰They said to him, "Then how were your eyes opened?" ¹¹He answered, "The man called Jesus made clay and anointed my eyes and said to me, 'Go to Silo'am and wash'; so I went and washed and received my sight." ¹²They said to him, "Where is he?" He said, "I do not know."

THE PHARISEES PUNISH THE HEALED MAN

13 They brought to the Pharisees the man who had formerly been blind. ¹⁴Now it was a sabbath day when Jesus made the clay and opened his eyes. ¹⁵The Pharisees again asked him how he had received his sight. And he said to them, "He put clay on my eyes, and I washed, and I see." ¹⁶Some of the Pharisees said, "This man is not from God, for he does not keep the sabbath." But others said, "How can a man who is a sinner do such signs?" There was a division among them. ¹⁷So they again said to the blind man, "What do you say about him, since he has opened your eyes?" He said, "He is a prophet."

18 The Jews did not believe that he had been blind and had received his sight, until they called the parents of the man who had received his sight, ¹⁹and asked them, "Is this your son, who you say was born blind? How then does he now see?" ²⁰His parents answered, "We know that this is our son, and that he was born blind; ²¹but how he now sees we do not know, nor do we know who opened his eyes. Ask him; he is of age, he will speak for himself." ²²His parents said this because they feared the Jews, for the Jews had already agreed that if any one should confess him to be Christ, he was to be put out of the synagogue. ²³Therefore his parents said, "He is of age, ask him."

24 So for the second time they called the man who had been blind, and said to him, "Give God the praise; we know that this man is a sinner." ²⁵He answered, "Whether he is a sinner, I do not know; one thing I know, that though I was blind, now I see." ²⁶They said to him, "What did he do to you? How did he open your eyes?" ²⁷He answered them, "I have told you already, and

you would not listen. Why do you want to hear it again? Do you too want to become his disciples?" ²⁸And they reviled him, saying, "You are his disciple, but we are disciples of Moses. ²⁹We know that God has spoken to Moses, but as for this man, we do not know where he comes from." ³⁰The man answered, "Why, this is a marvel! You do not know where he comes from, and yet he opened my eyes. ³¹We know that God does not listen to sinners, but if any one is a worshiper of God and does his will, God listens to him. ³²Never since the world began has it been heard that any one opened the eyes of a man born blind. ³³If this man were not from God, he could do nothing." ³⁴They answered him, "You were born in utter sin, and would you teach us?" And they cast him out.

SPIRITUAL SIGHT/BLINDNESS

35 Jesus heard that they had cast him out, and having found him he said, "Do you believe in the Son of man?"ᵛ ³⁶He answered, "And who is he, sir, that I may believe in him?" ³⁷Jesus said to him, "You have seen him, and it is he who speaks to you." ³⁸He said, "Lord, I believe"; and he worshiped him. ³⁹Jesus said, "For judgment I came into this world, that those who do not see may see, and that those who see may become blind." ⁴⁰Some of the Pharisees near him heard this, and they said to him, "Are we also blind?" ⁴¹Jesus said to them, "If you were blind, you would have no guilt; but now that you say, 'We see,' your guilt remains."

v Other ancient authorities read *the Son of God*

CHAPTER 9

Creative Commentary on the Scripture

This chapter lifts up a new sign of the Son of God: Jesus gives sight to a blind man. There is a sensual quality to this story that makes us feel as if we're there. Spittle and clay are the means for this miracle. Jesus even notes that the man must wash his dirty face.

The light of the world brings light into the life of a blind person. This burst of light sharply contrasts the people who are in spiritual darkness and ignorance.

Jesus also dismisses a common view of the day that children bore the sins of the parents through birth handicaps. He brings his listeners back to the real issue: This man's healing is a way to manifest the glory of God.

There is also the unfolding growth in the blind man's understanding of Jesus. His first explanation of the healing describes Jesus as "the man called Jesus." When he is interrogated the second time by the Pharisee, he claims that Jesus is "a prophet." As he defends his report of the healing, his sense of theological understanding sharpens. His final encounter with Jesus brings him to a new level of belief: "Lord, I believe."

Those who oppose Jesus search for ways to invalidate his work of love for the blind man. At first, they can't believe that such a miracle was possible. Then they renewed the charge that it was illegal to do work on the Sabbath.

The ministry of Jesus with the blind man is finally contrasted to his opponents' lack of spiritual sight. Jesus even says they may see. If so, they are even more guilty and blind.

Creative Bible Study Ideas

SESSION BASED ON 9:1-12

1. Blindfold the students as they come to the classroom.
2. Have a team of leaders take turns leading them into the room and sitting them down on the floor.
3. When everyone is in the room, ask them to imagine that they have been blind since birth and have had to live a life of a beggar.
4. The team can now wander around where the students are sitting and take the roles of the people around the blind man (neighbors, religious people, etc.). Finally Jesus and his disciples come by and talk about the blind person.
5. The person speaking the part of Jesus describes what he will do to heal the blind person. This will let the students know what is going to happen.
6. The team now takes pads of children's clay and places them on the eyes of the students. They will actually be placed over the blindfolds.
7. Tell the students to take the clay (and blindfolds) from their eyes and wash their faces. (You may use moist towelettes that come in individual packets.) The team is now sitting with the students in the circle. Have a bowl of water in the circle's center to indicate the pool.
8. Share the feelings they had as blind persons as they sat amidst the busyness. What sights are the most appreciated when they are able to see? Were people insensitive to their feelings and needs? Read the passage. Discuss some ways to be more sensitive to the needs of people.

SESSION BASED ON 9:1-12

This class will focus on Jesus' relationship to the man in need of healing. Invite a nurse or a doctor who has a special way of establishing trust with patients.

1. Sit in a circle with a medical bag or large first-aid kit placed in the center.
2. Ask each person to remember a time recently when he or she was cut, bruised or hurt. What was the first thing they did (kiss it, blow on it, rub it)?
3. Go around the circle sharing these memories and responses.
4. Talk about any hospital experiences the class members

JOHN 9—BIBLE STUDY 147

may have had. What was the most frightening? What was the most comforting thing that anyone did?

5. Have the nurse or doctor talk about what he or she does to heal a person other than prescribe medicine. Jesus' use of spittle was his way of personally establishing a relationship between the man and himself.

6. How do we help people who hurt? Is it something we say or do? How do we comfort?

7. Go around the circle and put a Band Aid on each person's hand with warmth and love. Tell each person that Jesus Christ comes to bring love and we are called to comfort others.

8. Ask each person to comfort someone today who is hurt in some way and tell about it the next time the class meets. The Band Aid will remind us that we have been healed by Christ and that we are called to such a ministry.

9. Explore with the class how they might participate in a ministry of healing during the next week. Perhaps they can focus on a particular person in their regular pattern of association who needs a special ministry of care. Ask them to plan how they can share the ministry of Jesus to that person. The whole group can join in and help one another plan this actual ministry of healing. This experience will provide excellent material for sharing during the next session.

SESSION BASED ON 9:18-41

The story of the blind man's journey from darkness to light is everyone's story. The experience of spiritual growth is vital to the life of every believer.

You might pick up this reflective form for your learning design with adults or young people. Ask them to listen to the story with their emotions. Read the story and then give them paper or notebooks. Be sure each person has his or her own space in the classroom for the time of reflection.

Suggest that they write a journal or dialogue concerning the blind man's emotional and spiritual growth. He moved from being treated like a child to the point where his parents affirm that he is of age. The man has to confront hostile authorities as he tells and retells his story. While the officials reject him, Jesus returns and talks with him.

Give the members of your class 30 minutes or so to write an actual dialogue with the man, Jesus, the authorities, the neighbors or the parents.

Gather and share the kinds of feelings that surfaced during this writing time. The students do not have to read their work unless they so desire. You can also do this process a bit differently. Assign the students certain characters for a role play. This model will give you the possibility of having the characters interact.

You might want to invite a blind person to visit the class. How do their dialogues relate to the experience of the visitor? The role of faith at times of physical trial can also be explored.

SESSION BASED ON 9:1-41

This passage is filled with human interaction and many layers of understanding. One of the best media suggested by this dynamic is puppetry. If you have a class of children, you have the perfect opportunity to enable them to crawl into this message in a very special way.

Don't be awed by this form of communication. Just plunge into the task and trust your hunches about the puppetry technique. You can also probably find someone in the community who will help you. Also check out resources at the public library and Christian bookstores.

This passage can be your focus for several weeks. Help the children make their own puppets, stage and scripts. The passage is perfect for this medium.

Puppets can be made out of almost any material. Old socks will work well. The stage also can be simply constructed. There are adults who will be happy to assist you in building or other skilled tasks.

One important thing to remember about puppetry is that it should be shared with others. Any learning opportunity that draws the student into *sharing* the gospel is vital to our ministry. By sharing, people learn the material most deeply.

The script will flow from the story. The characters, actions and dialogue will emerge easily from the text. Some groups record the dialogue.

You will want to see if you can arrange a way for the students to share their biblical production with others in the church. Perhaps it can be part of the Sunday morning worship experience or presented in other classes in Sunday school. This kind of learning experience is also an excellent way for your students to provide ministry to the community. The puppet presentation can be staged for community groups in hospitals, rest homes, etc.

Another excellent means of presenting this story is to pick up the clue of clay. Encourage the children to make the characters out of clay and create a setting for the scene. You might borrow a videotape unit from a church member, local school or a library center. Videotape this miniature scene and use it with different church groups.

Creative Speaking and Preaching Ideas

A CLUE FROM 9:1-41

This passage carries so much power that it is a shame to reduce it to a bland sermon. The text challenges us to let our people enter into the dramatic realm of salvation and walk with Jesus and those around him. The form for the message must be consistent with its content. Jesus teaches as he lives and works his Good News.

Ask your people to close their eyes. Guide them back into the scene at the pool with its bustling people and deformed beggars. Lead them into the sandals of the blind man. Give them clues to his hopelessness and despair.

As you describe what Jesus must have seemed like to this man who cannot see, take two pads of children's clay and put them on your eyes as you describe the scene. At the point of Jesus' healing of the blind man, ask the people to open their eyes. Then direct their attention to the packet containing the moist towelette (stapled to the bulletin). Ask them to wash their faces and hands.

Focus on Jesus' claim about being the light of the world (verses 4-5). Help them see through the eyes of the former blind man.

Take them through to the first dialogue with the neighbors. He says, "I am the man." He has been transformed from a dependent childlike person into an adult. Ask a person you've chosen beforehand to come out of the congregation and take the role of the healed man. You take the role of the Pharisees. After you work through verse 34, pause. The healed man turns about-face, then about-face again. Now you take the role of Jesus.

The final encounter with Jesus is a moment of joy. The former beggar is led to proclaim his faith in Christ. What was the miracle here? Was the manifestation of Christ the giving of eyesight or spiritual insight? or both?

A CLUE FROM 9:1-41

You might focus on the gift of sight as the entry into this message. Open the sermon in the role of the blind man. You might sit on the steps leading to the worship center. Someone else can tell the story of your plight. When the healing happens, put on a pair of sunglasses.

You can now describe what you see about life that you have not seen before. Look at the congregation and tell them what Christ permits you to see.

The rest of the sermon can be a direct monologue about the people in that congregation. Talk about the handicapped who aren't in the building this morning because no one helps them. Mention the older members of the congregation who are not included because they have been set aside.

You might also focus on the opponents of Jesus. They are the religious people of the times. They look for things to complain about—even in the presence of miracles!

This approach will give you a chance to bring forth Jesus' prophetic dimension to a blind and dark world. Near the sermon's end remove the sunglasses and tell the people that the blind man is looking at all of us. The Son of God stands with us and we fail to acknowledge him. We are as blind as the opponents to Jesus.

A CLUE FROM 9:1-12

Jesus' command that the man go and wash renews one of the more important images in the fourth Gospel. These water images help us tap into many levels of feeling and thinking. You might build a morning service around the theological theme of water.

Spread a painter's dropcloth on the floor at the front of the sanctuary. Place a children's wading pool on it. This will be an excellent setting for intergenerational preaching.

You can set the sermon at the pool. Perhaps a couple people can mime the story around the pool as it is read. This medium adds a great deal to our communication and can be done very easily by young or old.

Walk down by the water and bring the children down there with you. Have them share the different uses and meanings of this life-sustaining liquid.

Ask the adults to share how water plays a role in life and in the holy history of our people. This would be an excellent Sunday for baptism! For those traditions celebrating immersion, the setting is perfect.

You might explore briefly the symbolism and the reality of water as an agent of cleansing in the hands of believers. It would be fitting to have the children take small containers of water to the congregation. They can make the outline of a cross with water on the hand of each person as a final blessing.

A CLUE FROM 9:13-41

The adversary nature of the former blind man's story suggests that we should consider using a courtroom presentation for the sermon. You might put the congregation on trial for the defense of their faith. How do we defend what we have seen, heard and believed? Can we support our faith when others can point to the bad things that happen to Christians? Do the terrible conditions of the world undermine the Son of God?

A lawyer or judge in your church would be the ideal person to aid in the sermon. The inclusive approach to preaching will add greatly to the power of your message. God has surrounded you with a host of talented believers who are waiting to share their gifts.

Set the sermon of the service in a trial structure. Have the advocates for the officials and Pharisees quiz the congregation on the former blind man's position. Encourage people to provide responses to the questions the advocates raise. It will be quite easy to expand the trial to include contemporary parallels. To close the sermon, ask for a final witness. The former blind man comes out of the congregation and simply states the conviction of his faith. This can summarize the discussion of the trial.

A CLUE FROM 9:35-41

The last encounter between Jesus and the man he healed is very moving. This moment of the man's confession of faith comes after a long journey. It is particularly inspiring to see that Jesus follows up on his ministry to the man. After healing him, Jesus seeks him out because he has heard about the man's abuse at the hands of the officials.

You might explore this aspect of the message by picking up on Jesus' consistency of ministry. Focus on this part of the passage. Then ask your people to remember the ways their church has ministered to people in the past year. You might include sheets of newsprint or use an overhead projector to jot down their contributions. Write down all the areas (missionaries, the sick, the grieving, etc.). Ask for particular names of people.

Invite them to go back to these folks and continue the ministry of care. Pass out paper and envelopes. (Or place these in the pew racks before the service.) Ask everyone to write a note to one of these people expressing your continued love and care.

Ask them to seal the envelopes when they have finished. Have the ushers collect them. After they have been collected, offer a prayer that calls upon God to bless the messages of love, the people who will receive them and the dear people who wrote them. Then mail the messages Monday morning.

A CLUE FROM 9:1-41

The most amazing aspect of this passage is the contrast between the trust of the blind man in Jesus and the distrust of the other people. The greatest crisis facing civilization is the lack of trust and hope in the ability of God to work through us for the good of his creation. Despair seems to have overwhelmed all reason, faith and possibility.

You might explore the realm of incredible possibility as you look at faith. Draw upon a variety of your local resource people for this sermon. Talk to the science teachers and scientists, the magicians, the musicians, the doctors and the gardeners. Ask each of these people to put together the most fascinating aspect of his or her world. Invite them to share these items of awe and wonder at the sermon time. Find out what they will share and attempt to gather slides related to them. For example, a science teacher's talk about an incredible aspect of nature could be complemented with slides of nature.

Ask people to stand where they are when they share. Show the slides on the walls at the front or side of the room. Don't bother with screens. It is a background environment that you are creating, not some media show. The slides can be faded into the walls. Let them run slowly as a visual reminder of the trust that we have in the impossible.

You might want to plan a singing response to each person's sharing of the wonders in his or her life. Leave time for others to share something fascinating about their world. You will find that once we start a recital of God's impossible love for us, many people will join in with the flow. Then review Christ's incredible miracle and perhaps some of the others in John (the resurrection, the gift of life to Lazarus).

CHAPTER 10

"I AM THE GOOD SHEPHERD"

"Truly, truly, I say to you, he who does not enter the sheepfold by the door but climbs in by another way, that man is a thief and a robber; ²but he who enters by the door is the shepherd of the sheep. ³To him the gatekeeper opens; the sheep hear his voice, and he calls his own sheep by name and leads them out. ⁴When he has brought out all his own, he goes before them, and the sheep follow him, for they know his voice. ⁵A stranger they will not follow, but they will flee from him, for they do not know the voice of strangers." ⁶This figure Jesus used with them, but they did not understand what he was saying to them.

7 So Jesus again said to them, "Truly, truly, I say to you, I am the door of the sheep. ⁸All who came before me are thieves and robbers; but the sheep did not heed them. ⁹I am the door; if any one enters by me, he will be saved, and will go in and out and find pasture. ¹⁰The thief comes only to steal and kill and destroy; I came that they may have life, and have it abundantly. ¹¹I am the good shepherd. The good shepherd lays down his life for the sheep. ¹²He who is a hireling and not a shepherd, whose own the sheep are not, sees the wolf coming and leaves the sheep and flees; and the wolf snatches them and scatters them. ¹³He flees because he is a hireling and cares nothing for the sheep. ¹⁴I am the good shepherd; I know my own and my own know me, ¹⁵as the Father knows me and I know the Father; and I lay down my life for the sheep. ¹⁶And I have other sheep, that are not of this fold; I must bring them also, and they will heed my voice. So there shall be one flock, one shepherd. ¹⁷For this reason the Father loves me, because I lay down my life, that I may take it again. ¹⁸No one takes it from me, but I lay it down of my own accord. I have power to lay it down, and I have power to take it again; this charge I have received from my Father."

19 There was again a division among the Jews because of these words. ²⁰Many of them said, "He has a demon, and he is mad; why listen to him?" ²¹Others said, "These are not the sayings of one who has a demon. Can a demon open the eyes of the blind?"

"ARE YOU THE CHRIST?"

22 It was the feast of the Dedication at Jerusalem; ²³it was winter, and Jesus was walking in the temple, in the portico of Solomon. ²⁴So the Jews gathered round him and said to him, "How long will you keep us in suspense? If you are the Christ, tell us plainly." ²⁵Jesus answered them, "I told you, and you do not believe. The works that I do in my Father's name, they bear witness to me; ²⁶but you do not believe, because you do not belong to my sheep. ²⁷My sheep hear my voice, and I know them, and they follow me; ²⁸and I give them eternal life, and they shall never perish, and no one shall snatch them out of my hand. ²⁹My Father, who has given them to me,*w* is greater

---

w Other ancient authorities read *What my Father has given to me*

than all, and no one is able to snatch them out of the Father's hand. ³⁰I and the Father are one."

31 The Jews took up stones again to stone him. ³²Jesus answered them, "I have shown you many good works from the Father; for which of these do you stone me?" ³³The Jews answered him, "It is not for a good work that we stone you but for blasphemy; because you, being a man, make yourself God." ³⁴Jesus answered them, "Is it not written in your law, 'I said, you are gods'? ³⁵If he called them gods to whom the word of God came (and scripture cannot be broken), ³⁶do you say of him whom the Father consecrated and sent into the world, 'You are blaspheming,' because I said, 'I am the Son of God'? ³⁷If I am not doing the works of my Father, then do not believe me; ³⁸but if I do them, even though you do not believe me, believe the works, that you may know and understand that the Father is in me and I am in the Father." ³⁹Again they tried to arrest him, but he escaped from their hands.

40 He went away again across the Jordan to the place where John at first baptized, and there he remained. ⁴¹And many came to him; and they said, "John did no sign, but everything that John said about this man was true." ⁴²And many believed in him there.

CHAPTER 10

Creative Commentary on the Scripture

VERSES 1-6: Some scholars feel that this material doesn't flow from what has come before it. Yet, it does seem that the discussion expands the last section of the previous chapter.

The two parables in this chapter provide wonderfully rich images. The idea of a shepherd who knows the names of the sheep and the sheep recognizing the voice of the shepherd is incredibly intimate.

VERSES 7-18: Jesus uses the figure of the door as a description of his protective concern for his charges. The promise of abundant life comes at the cost of the Shepherd freely laying down his life for the flock.

He also notes the difference between the Good Shepherd and other hirelings. Verse 16 also indicates a concern for the whole flock beyond the immediate fold. The image of the voice is again utilized.

VERSES 19-21: The public rejection of Jesus is again noted. What the people can't understand they label as madness. What are the marks of the person of truth as opposed to the liar?

VERSES 22-30: The fourth Gospel seems built around the four major festivals of Judaism (Sabbath, Passover, Shelters and Dedication). Jesus appears as a fulfillment of these ancient holy days. Here he is seen as the one who is dedicated and created by God the Father.

Verse 29 picks up the theme that no one can snatch the flock from the Father's hand. These rich images are most stimulating for experiential communication.

VERSES 31-42: Jesus bases his claims on the fruits of his life and ministry. He is suggesting that we judge truth by comparing the works with the nature of the Father. His defense and life again offend his opponents. They first try to stone him and later try to arrest him.

Creative Bible Study Ideas

SESSION BASED ON 10:1-6

What does it mean to be known by name? Jesus suggests an intimate relationship in this parable. It may be helpful to build a session around how a name carries positive and negative impacts in our culture.

1. Gather your students into a circle.
2. Pass out a copy of a popular magazine to each person.
3. Have them look through the ads and tear out the names or labels that mean the most to people in general and to themselves in particular.
4. Share these findings and talk about the labels on their own clothing. Why is it important to wear someone else's name on their posteriors?
5. Pass out large sheets of newsprint and crayons or felt-tipped markers.
6. Ask each person to choose a piece of clothing and design a label using his or her own name.
7. Share these creations. How do these labels reveal things about their personalities?
8. Try the task again. This time have each person design a label that reveals exactly who he or she is to others.
9. Share these designs.
10. Close by reading the passage and offer prayers of thanksgiving that God knows our names and who we really are. Post the creations on the classroom bulletin board. These labels also could be shared with the whole church via the cover of the church bulletin.

SESSION BASED ON 10:7-10

The image of the door as used here suggests a common form for leading our students into the passage's content. Jesus has once again pulled us into his message by employing a common figure. Make this learning experience a traveling or moving event.

1. Meet in the usual classroom setting.
2. Read the passage and ask what Jesus means by his

statement in verse 9.

3. Bring the group to a door leading into the room and sit down in front of it.

4. Ask the students to imagine the different kinds of people who have used this door. What name can the students give the door based on its memories?

5. Share these speculations.

6. Go to a closet door and repeat the same reflection and sharing opportunity.

7. Take the group to a special door (outside, pastor's study, choir, etc.).

8. Repeat the process.

9. Complete your mobile study by stopping at a cross in the church. Mention that this too is a door.

10. Ask them to share their reflections on this most special door of salvation. A door can be used for coming in and for going out. Do people leave by this door? What happens to those who don't draw upon the promise of pasture and abundant life that this door offers? How do we keep people from coming in through the door of faith? How do we keep from being the thieves and robbers of the sheep?

SESSION BASED ON 10:11-18

Sacrifice is a forgotten word among Christians. In fact, many people are shocked when change in economic times calls for sacrifice. The cultural religion of our times simply has not included this quality among its attributes. Yet Jesus provides a very sacrificial model for those who would follow him. The Good Shepherd willingly risks all for the sheep. You might create a session that focuses on different kinds of risk.

1. Gather your students with the understanding that they should be dressed in comfortable clothing.

2. Lead the group on a trust walk. Ask everyone to close his or her eyes and take the hand of the persons to the left and right. You can then walk through woods, buildings, etc. Encourage your people to signal what is coming by using different hand pressures and angles.

3. Share how they felt when they depended on someone else. Were there scary points?

4. Have the members of the group share the most frightening moment of their lives.

5. Ask each person to project on paper a brief life that

traces the major changes coming before them (registration for the draft, marriage, different school, death of a loved one, etc.).

6. Have them mark the biggest challenge before them in the near future.

7. Share these anticipated moments of risk.

8. Have the whole group share how they could take on the risks of another person and help him or her. What would be the most frightening thing about doing this? What keeps us from "laying down our lives" for others?

9. Read the passage and pass around a long stick representing the staff carried by a shepherd.

10. Ask each person to feel the staff and share how Jesus, the Good Shepherd, in some way makes his or her risk more possible.

11. You might cut the stick into smaller sections and give each person a piece.

12. Ask the students to carry the wooden piece as a reminder of the responsibility to care. During the week they are to extend this gift of Jesus' love to others. Each day an actual contact with a person in need should be made. They are also to pray regularly for this person. Share these experiences with the class at the next meeting.

SESSION BASED ON 10:19-21

Who are the crazy people? What does it mean to be Christlike in an environment that is ego/self-centered? What are the demons that possess people today?

1. Divide your class into two sections.

2. Each section is to select someone to speak convincingly about something that is true.

3. Encourage both sides to shout and scream at each other while the speakers are talking.

4. Have the speakers share how they felt during this time of rejection.

5. Let the group share how it felt during the exchange. Was anything accomplished concerning the question? Was it easier to shout down the speaker than to argue with him or her?

6. List the things that Jesus did and said in this chapter that might have led some contemporaries to think that he was mad. Then list the things that would deny this charge. How do we distinguish the madman from the prophet?

SESSION BASED ON 10:22-39

Jesus uses the feast of the Dedication to proclaim that he is the one who has been dedicated and sent by the Father. How do we know the truth of this claim in our contemporary world? An interesting session can evolve from this passage.

1. Research cults and focus on several characteristics common among them.

2. Give the students a chance to join one of two groups as they arrive for the class. One group offers popcorn and Pepsi. The other promises potato chips and Seven-Up for refreshments. This is the lure.

3. After they have chosen a group, tell them that they must sign a sheet that does not need to be read. (This sheet specifies in small print that they will give all their possessions to the group, obey the leader, etc.).

4. Give each group a name and tell the students that they are to be called by that name while they are in the session.

5. After they have eaten the goodies, change the pace by becoming more direct and demanding with them. Give them rules:

A. Everyone is important.
B. You must wear these handbands.
C. We believe in the sanctity of life.
D. The leader is the boss over all things.
E. We only sin when we go against the wishes of the leader.

Put the rules on the points of a star and ask them to put the star on their foreheads as the mark of their membership in the group.

6. Develop a chant and a code of ethics.

7. After 30 minutes bring the groups back together and discuss what happened. How do we know the truth when it sounds *almost* true? Compare the truth of Jesus as you read this passage and discuss it.

8. You might have the class develop a report of the conclusions they reached about cults from this experience. This report can be shared with the whole church. It might be interesting to create a booklet for parents from this session. The young people will be providing a ministry to parents as an extension of their Bible study.

SESSION BASED ON 10:40-42

How do we know the truth? Can we tell by the way things

are said whether the message can be trusted? Which is more important, the message or the messenger? These three verses deal with testimony. They suggest an important resource for your learning environment.

Interviewing with audio-cassette recorders is an important form of communication. This process is very affirming to those who are asked to tell their stories. They know that the interviewer is offering the most important compliment one can extend to another: hearing another's story.

The audio-cassette recorder's presence makes this kind of human exchange very special. The hesitation a person might experience in giving such an interview depends on his or her uncertainty about the value of his or her story. Or, the interviewee might be afraid of the interviewer. There is no fear of microphones.

You might devote a couple hours for the introductory session. Take the students through the process of basic listening skills. Equip them with two questions: "If you were God reviewing the life of our church, what would make you happiest about how we have witnessed to the truth of your Son?" and "If you were God reviewing what we have done as a people, what would you want us to change to be closer to the truth?"

There is no way people can answer these kinds of questions incorrectly. The person seeking a testimony about the faith will need to encourage interviewees to tell their stories in their own ways. Also snap a color slide of your person if he or she allows you to.

Return to a session after a number of these interviews have been collected. Share bits and pieces about these stories. Are there some situations when the story sounds off center, but the person telling it is irresistable? Are there other times when the person is unappealing, but what he or she says is inspiring? How do we know the truth?

Your students will quickly learn how to probe for feelings and values. The more we get stories or examples from their lives, the more clearly we can understand their faith in Christ.

You might want to interview non-Christians or even some cult members. Try to draw the people into the conversation. Break into set speeches with probes for personal feelings and ideas. This may be hard if people present a memorized pat answer.

This course of study would make an excellent Advent or Lenten series as you prepare for Christmas or Easter. It is quite easy to get broadcast-quality material. Follow these six simple rules:

A. Always clean the recording heads with alcohol and cotton swabs before going out to interview.

B. Use an extension microphone when possible. Built-in mikes do not give you the best-quality recordings.

C. Use quality tapes.

D. Keep your battery charged.

E. Pick good sound environments. Stay out of the wind especially.

F. Hold the mike close to the face of the interviewee. Do not fondle the mike. You'll get bad rattles if you do.

You might want to utilize these interviews (or sections of them) for a multimedia presentation for the whole congregation at a family dinner. Gather some slides from those taken of your interviewees or from other sources (filmstrips, etc.). Use two projectors if possible. The students might want to play one interview that speaks positively about a different religious expression. After showing a slide and sharing the comment, ask the audience to respond with their opinions. This use of media and discussion will quicken the pace of the evening and give the audience a better sense of involvement. It will also give the students a chance to get close to the material.

Creative Speaking and Preaching Ideas

A CLUE FROM 10:1-6

The importance of a name emerges in this passage. The sheep respond because they know the voice of the shepherd when he calls them by name.

The church tends to adhere to the social glue of formality. I love those traditions (e.g., Brethren and Mennonite) that encourage young people to call adults by their Christian names. The elders of the tribe (the old) may have the prefix of "brother" or "sister." Yet, they remind us that it is the name we are called in our baptism that is honorable and known to God.

In these few lines, Jesus seems to beckon us back to an intimacy that honors persons with names. If you have a smaller congregation, you might want to present a message that incorporates the names of everyone present! Pass the attendance pad early in the service. Or have people sign in as they come into worship. Use this to get the names for placement in your sermon.

Introduce each person to the Shepherd. Call upon God to know these good sisters and brothers. Affirm them before God. Or, create a poetic hymn of petition that includes slots of six or eight names between a biblical refrain. Your music and poetry people will be a great help here. There are more closet poets in your congregation than you can imagine! These wonderful skills are just waiting to be released to the glory of God.

Perhaps the people can sing or say "amen" after each transition point in your poetic sermon. No one will be bored when they realize that they will be named. You might even leave a spot at the end where you can ask any people who have been missed to raise their hands. Then make them known to the Good Shepherd.

A CLUE FROM 10:1-18

Jesus reveals himself through these important images: shepherd, door and Son of God. This threefold process is an important clue to those presenting Christ in preaching. How do we permit the many layers of understanding to unwrap through comparisons for the person worshiping? It might be interesting to draw upon the triptych (or three-panel painting) mode of presentation for this passage. A triple-faced mirror such as those used in clothing stores might be used in your sermon.

Walk to the middle of the worship center and stand in front of the three mirrors with your back to the congregation. Reflect on your reflection concerning how you look from different angles. It is all you. But each image is different: flattering, embarrassing, surprising, etc.

Read the passage and place the Bible in the three-mirror space. Ask the congregation to imagine the person of Jesus taking shape from the description of the text. You might cover each pane with a sheet as you work through the three descriptions. Save the Son of God for the central image.

Remove the sheets from the mirrors. Now the congregation will see itself reflected in the three mirrors. You will have to experiment to get the right angle so that all the people can see themselves in the mirrors. You can now close by sharing how these gifts of Jesus' character live in us.

A CLUE FROM 10:1-6

The concept of the flock hearing the voice of the Good Shepherd suggests a way of presenting the sermon. Tape short segments (15-20 seconds each) of popular voices. Choose from a whole spectrum of well-known people (the president, evangelists, comedians, TV personalities, cartoon characters, etc.). Be sure also to have some people who are not known by voice quality, but by what they are saying.

Have the congregation check a list on the back of the bulletin or have them call out the names of the people on the recording. After playing all of the voice tracks, share some ways that we knew the voices (e.g., familiarity, subject matter, etc.). Then go to the passage and discuss how the flock would know the shepherd by voice.

A CLUE FROM 10:7-10

Jesus' proclamation that he is the door of the sheep is the perfect guide for the form of your sermon. Use the doors to the worship area. Take the congregation on a tour of these openings and their barriers. Have them imagine all those who have responded to the voice of the Good Shepherd and entered to worship over the years. Respond to the clue of verses 1-6 and mention names. The door to the worship center area has been the entry way for the pastors and choir people who have gone before.

These doors also have seen sinners seeking the mercy of the Shepherd. Name some of these—including yourself. The Shepherd has come to protect these fallen people. Indeed, our entry into this realm promises that we might live abundantly.

This form can easily evolve into a dialogue with people in the pew. Ask them for examples of the joy and sadness these doors have seen. This would be the perfect sermon for a homecoming, anniversary or New Year's Sunday service.

You might invite a few people forward to touch the door. As they feel the door to the sanctuary of God, what brings them the greatest joy?

A CLUE FROM 10:11-21

Draw upon the powerful promise of Jesus that he will willingly lay his body and life down for the sake of others.

Borrow a medical examination table from a doctor or local hospital. (By the way, community companies and organizations are always very helpful in loaning material like this for creative teaching and preaching.) Also get a basic white or green hospital staff gown. This can be worn under your clerical robe if you wear one. The last resource you will need is a mannequin from a clothing store. Again, you will have to look to your community connections for this item.

After the passage is read, have the table wheeled or carried to the center of the worship center. The dummy is on the table covered with a sheet. Remove your clerical robe, revealing your hospital garb. You will become a theological pathologist who is taking us through a review of the victim.

The person is dead, but parts of him or her can bring life to others. Describe how transplants help people. There is information on the procedure for donation that you can get from local hospitals. The giving of blood can also be cited as a way to lay down your life for another. You might provide forms for donation of one's body for others (in the pews or attached to the bulletins).

If this application is too threatening or you do not want to focus on it for some reason, you might conduct a spiritual autopsy. Analyze how this person risked his or her life for others (loving, healing, praying, etc.).

Feel free to end your sermon with the acknowledgment that this is simply a dramatic way to crawl into the gospel. The flow of this passage is not a simulation. Jesus, the Good Shepherd, has given his life freely for us.

A CLUE FROM 10:22-42

Verse 29 offers a promise of security to face any situation threatening our spiritual and physical existence. No one can snatch us from the love of the Father and Son.

There is much fear about losing young and old to those outside of the church family. Many youth are following cults and numerous adults seem to be enticed by faith groups that overemphasize only one or two parts of the gospel. Many more people simply "fall through the cracks" and rarely ever set foot in church again.

This passage suggests that spiritual kidnapping is not a new worry. You might build upon this image for your sermon. Utilize several of your folks in preparing two short cassette tapes. One features a young girl or boy talking about joining a cult. This story should sound fairly positive. The young person is glad to have left family and church to follow a leader. He or she gives a few reasons why he or she left.

You might ask the members of the congregation to listen to this story with the perspective of a family member who loves this young person. After you have played the tape segment (not more than three or four minutes in length!), ask people to write a note to this person about their feelings.

Collect these unsigned notes and read sections of them. Ask anyone to speak out if they want to add something to the statements. You will want to push the folks to add positive comments about the person and the source of hope in Christ for him or her. Read the passage. Then focus on verse 29.

Pose the question: "How would we have to change the life of our church to make the person feel comfortable here?" Accept the suggestions. Perhaps write them on newsprint. Conclude with the assurance that no one can snatch people from God's love. Pray that those separated from God's people will come back soon.

CHAPTER 11

THE ILLNESS AND DEATH OF LAZ′ARUS

Now a certain man was ill, Laz′arus of Bethany, the village of Mary and her sister Martha. ²It was Mary who anointed the Lord with ointment and wiped his feet with her hair, whose brother Laz′arus was ill. ³So the sisters sent to him, saying, "Lord, he whom you love is ill." ⁴But when Jesus heard it he said, "This illness is not unto death; it is for the glory of God, so that the Son of God may be glorified by means of it."

5 Now Jesus loved Martha and her sister and Laz′arus. ⁶So when he heard that he was ill, he stayed two days longer in the place where he was. ⁷Then after this he said to the disciples, "Let us go into Judea again." ⁸The disciples said to him, "Rabbi, the Jews were but now seeking to stone you, and are you going there again?" ⁹Jesus answered, "Are there not twelve hours in the day? If any one walks in the day, he does not stumble, because he sees the light of this world. ¹⁰But if any one walks in the night, he stumbles, because the light is not in him." ¹¹Thus he spoke, and then he said to them, "Our friend Laz′arus has fallen asleep, but I go to awake him out of sleep." ¹²The disciples said to him, "Lord, if he has fallen asleep, he will recover." ¹³Now Jesus had spoken of his death, but they thought that he meant taking rest in sleep. ¹⁴Then Jesus told them plainly, "Laz′arus is dead; ¹⁵and for your sake I am glad that I was not there, so that you may believe. But let us go to him." ¹⁶Thomas, called the Twin, said to his fellow disciples, "Let us also go, that we may die with him."

JESUS COMFORTS MARY AND MARTHA

17 Now when Jesus came, he found that Laz′arus[x] had already been in the tomb four days. ¹⁸Bethany was near Jerusalem, about two miles[y] off, ¹⁹and many of the Jews had come to Martha and Mary to console them concerning their brother. ²⁰When Martha heard that Jesus was coming, she went and met him, while Mary sat in the house. ²¹Martha said to Jesus, "Lord, if you had been here, my brother would not have died. ²²And even now I know that whatever you ask from God, God will give you." ²³Jesus said to her, "Your brother will rise again." ²⁴Martha said to him, "I know that he will rise again in the resurrection at the last day." ²⁵Jesus said to her, "I am the resurrection and the life;[z] he who believes in me, though he die, yet shall he live, ²⁶and whoever lives and believes in me shall never die. Do you believe this?" ²⁷She said to him, "Yes, Lord; I believe that you are the Christ, the Son of God, he who is coming into the world."

28 When she had said this, she went and called her sister Mary, saying quietly, "The Teacher is here and is calling for you." ²⁹And when she heard it, she rose quickly and went to him. ³⁰Now Jesus had not yet come to the village, but was still in the place where Martha had met

---

x Greek *he*
y Greek *fifteen stadia*
z Other ancient authorities omit *and the life*

him. ³¹When the Jews who were with her in the house, consoling her, saw Mary rise quickly and go out, they followed her, supposing that she was going to the tomb to weep there. ³²Then Mary, when she came where Jesus was and saw him, fell at his feet, saying to him, "Lord, if you had been here, my brother would not have died." ³³When Jesus saw her weeping, and the Jews who came with her also weeping, he was deeply moved in spirit and troubled; ³⁴and he said, "Where have you laid him?" They said to him, "Lord, come and see." ³⁵Jesus wept. ³⁶So the Jews said, "See how he loved him!" ³⁷But some of them said, "Could not he who opened the eyes of the blind man have kept this man from dying?"

JESUS GIVES LIFE TO LAZ'ARUS

38 Then Jesus, deeply moved again, came to the tomb; it was a cave, and a stone lay upon it. ³⁹Jesus said, "Take away the stone." Martha, the sister of the dead man, said to him, "Lord, by this time there will be an odor, for he has been dead four days." ⁴⁰Jesus said to her, "Did I not tell you that if you would believe you would see the glory of God?" ⁴¹So they took away the stone. And Jesus lifted up his eyes and said, "Father, I thank thee that thou hast heard me. ⁴²I knew that thou hearest me always, but I have said this on account of the people standing by, that they may believe that thou didst send me." ⁴³When he had said this, he cried with a loud voice, "Laz'a-rus, come out." ⁴⁴The dead man came out, his hands and feet bound with bandages, and his face wrapped with a cloth. Jesus said to them, "Unbind him, and let him go."

THE JEWS PLAN TO KILL JESUS

45 Many of the Jews therefore, who had come with Mary and had seen what he did, believed in him; ⁴⁶but some of them went to the Pharisees and told them what Jesus had done. ⁴⁷So the chief priests and the Pharisees gathered the council, and said, "What are we to do? For this man performs many signs. ⁴⁸If we let him go on thus, every one will believe in him, and the Romans will come and destroy both our holy place*a* and our nation." ⁴⁹But one of them, Ca'iaphas, who was high priest that year, said to them, "You know nothing at all; ⁵⁰you do not understand that it is expedient for you that one man should die for the people, and that the whole nation should not perish." ⁵¹He did not say this of his own accord, but being high priest that year he prophesied that Jesus should die for the nation, ⁵²and not for the nation only, but to gather into one the children of God who are scattered abroad. ⁵³So from that day on they took counsel how to put him to death.

54 Jesus therefore no longer went about openly among the Jews, but went from there to the country near the wilderness, to a town called E'phraim; and there he stayed with the disciples.

55 Now the Passover of the Jews was at hand, and many went up from the country to Jerusalem before the Passover, to purify themselves.

a Greek *our place*

⁵⁶They were looking for Jesus and saying to one another as they stood in the temple, "What do you think? That he will not come to the feast?" ⁵⁷Now the chief priests and the Pharisees had given orders that if any one knew where he was, he should let them know, so that they might arrest him.

CHAPTER 11

Creative Commentary on the Scripture

VERSES 1-16: The gift of life to Lazarus is the crowning sign of the Son of God. Ironically, Jesus' opponents respond to his gift of life by plotting his death (verse 53). Mary, who anointed Jesus (12:1-3), pleads for her brother's life. The story builds dramatically toward its incredible conclusion.

The writer of the fourth Gospel reveals the deep emotional ties between Jesus and members of this family. The disciples know that they are headed in the wrong direction if they wish to avoid a confrontation between Jesus and his opponents. Perhaps they have a hunch that the ministry to Lazarus and his family will be a turning point in their relationship with the religious authorities. Thomas' comment (verse 16) underscores the resignation among the disciples concerning their fate: "Let us also go, that we may die with him."

VERSES 17-27: Jesus draws near to Jerusalem as he stops at Bethany for his ministry to Lazarus. Mary and Martha profess their faith in Jesus to raise their now-four-days-dead brother.

VERSES 28-44: Jesus is surrounded by a loving family in grief. He is deeply moved and sheds tears. Lazarus is buried in a cave. Jesus orders the stone removed. Martha lets us know that Lazarus is absolutely dead by noting that he might smell from decay. Our Lord notes that this act will glorify God.

After praying to the Father, Jesus calls out in a loud voice and Lazarus comes out of the tomb. Jesus' voice acts much like God's in the act of creation and similar to the role of the Word at the opening of the fourth Gospel. Lazarus is unbound and seen fully alive.

VERSES 45-57: The opponents of Jesus finally decide definitely to kill him. How ironic: The more Jesus gives, the more his opponents hate him. It is the visible reality of his work that forces their hatred to find a way to stop him. The final act of the drama of salvation is now set in motion.

Creative Bible Study Ideas

SESSION BASED ON 11:1-44

This section is a foreshadow for the greater miracle of Jesus' death and resurrection. The drama and emotion in this scene are stunning for anyone who has lost a loved one in death. The flow of the story builds to the final moment at the door of the tomb. This form suggests that we help our students enter into the message through such a form.

It might be helpful to provide children the opportunity to deal with the hope and joy of this passage by using a dramatic form. One excellent mode is the use of sock puppets.

This technique is very simple. Some old socks and perhaps a few buttons are all the materials you need. The most important thing is *how* you utilize this medium to enable your children to enter into this passage.

Don't be concerned about technique and the complications of scripting, staging, etc. Every medium of communication used by the faith community for education and proclamation should always be seen only as a way to experience the gospel. Resist the temptation to permit a communication art form to become an end in itself.

Tell the story of the passage to the children. Develop the characters in the story. Note particularly how Jesus felt about the death of his friend. He shed tears. Jesus is saying that it is acceptable to feel sad at times. It is this kind of emotional flow that can be explored by your students.

Let the puppets become a way that the children tell the story. Perhaps the puppet characters can be people who saw the miracle. What did they say about the events? Let the children take turns talking in the voices of these imaginary people.

You may want to arrange a presentation to the whole congregation. This would be an excellent part of a Lenten worship service.

SESSION BASED ON 11:1-57

It is possible to look at this passage as it unfolds in five acts: verses 1-16 (death of Lazarus); verses 17-27 (Jesus the resurrection and the life); verses 28-37 (Jesus' sorrow); verses 38-44 (the raising of Lazarus); and verses 45-57 (the reactions of Jesus' opponents). Divide the class into five clusters. Give each unit a section of the story.

Have each group study its section of the passage and develop a mime. Everyone in the cluster must participate in presenting the story to the whole group. Share these nonverbal vignettes.

Discuss the feelings of the students when they participated in the mime. Encourage the other students to reflect on how they felt when other clusters presented a mime. Did it remind them of a recent death in their school, office, neighborhood or family? How does the gospel address our own feelings toward death?

Pass out copies of recent obituaries from the local newspapers. Ask the students to imagine that they are sitting with the survivors mentioned in the articles. What does the passage suggest that they do to comfort the grieving? Role play this situation.

The class could take a few minutes writing letters to people who have recently lost a loved one in death. What does one say in light of this chapter's message? What can we say so that a grieving person can feel the love of Christ and not just a string of words? These letters can be discussed and then sent to the people who are grieving.

SESSION BASED ON 11:1-16

1. Read the text to the class.
2. Explain that there are really two journeys about life and death told here: one about Jesus and one about Lazarus. Yet they are really related to one another.
3. Divide the group into two sections.
4. Tell the students that they have been given the role of two detective agencies. It is the task of each to find all of the facts and hunches about the journey of Lazarus or Jesus. Assign Jesus to one group and Lazarus to the other. The groups are to work on these verses carefully and find every bit of information revealed. The facts and hunches can be written on pieces of newsprint. They might note the roles

played by the people around the main characters in the story.

5. Give each group the physical clues from the case. The Jesus group receives a bag containing a linen strip and a stone. The Lazarus group also receives a strip of linen and a stone.

6. Call the groups together as a whole.

7. The leader plays the role of the one who engaged the agencies. He or she now calls for a full report. Raise questions about the characters and their motivations. Why did they act the way they did?

8. Ask students to choose a character in the chapter with whom they were best able to relate. Pass around the physical evidence for the case (stone, linen strip).

9. Share the feelings about the persons in the case.

SESSION BASED ON 11:17-27

1. Before this session meets, ask several of your students to secure interviews on cassette tape with people in the church who have gone through the experience of losing someone in death. Provide audio-cassette tape recorders. Take some time with these students and help them realize that they are gathering something very special. Encourage them to let people talk freely about pain and sadness. They might ask about the lowest point in the grief process and also what helped the most. Check with the students a few days before the class. Ask them to isolate certain sections for class use. You don't want to have them play more than three or four minutes at a time.

2. Read the passage.

3. Share the first story from the interviews.

4. Ask the interviewer and the students to share reactions to the story. What kinds of feelings did the man or woman express about death and grief? What kinds of feelings were touched in the listeners? Is there something that you could particularly feel in yourself?

5. Repeat the process and read the passage each time. Take the time you need for sharing the interviews. You may have to take another session on these stories. If there is a strong response from your students, assign some more interviews to other members of the class. Don't be surprised if some people find it difficult to respond. It is sometimes hard for us to express our deepest feelings in class situations.

Public schools tend to demand only certain segments of a student's thinking. Christ calls us to share all of ourselves. This difference must be won by patient care and trust. You might debrief the students' feelings by role playing the situation on the tape. Suggest that the man or woman on the tape has come to you. How would you respond? Play the section and have two people sit in chairs. You might ask them to mime the encounter. Then use spoken language. This is very important material for those serious about equipping people for discipleship.

6. You might spend some time talking about how your students can minister to people who have lost a loved one. The people who were interviewed need love and care. Ask the students to return to the people and extend a ministry in light of the resurrection.

SESSION BASED ON 11:28-44

1. Read the passage.
2. Tell the students that they are finely honed instruments that reflect human emotions. They are going to graph the emotions in this text.
3. Place long strips of paper (like that used to cover tables for church suppers) along all the walls of the room.
4. At the left side and right side of each of four strips write "verse 28" and "verse 44," respectively.
5. Draw a horizontal line in the center of each sheet from end to end. Then draw intersecting vertical lines (one line for each verse) on the horizontal line. It should look like this:

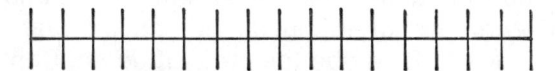

├┼┼┼┼┼┼┼┼┼┼┼┼┤

6. Divide the class into four sections.
7. Read each verse aloud several times using a different translation each time.
8. Ask each group to discuss the emotions that the biblical characters seem to be feeling at this point.
9. Using a different-color marker for each character (four or five colors), each group should mark a series of peaks and lows for each character's emotions. Above the line are highs and beneath the line are lows. It is not important that each group has the same understanding of the markings.
10. Read the passage and go around to the groups asking them to share their emotional charting of the people in this

moving story.

11. Ask the whole group to compare the results. Where are the differences? Could several feelings within a character be true?

12. Ask the students to share their own feelings as they encountered the story. What was the most moving point? What enabled them to be this sensitive? Perhaps something in their own experience?

13. Read the passage once again.

14. Ask them to reflect on how the passage encourages us to deal with the difficult times of life.

SESSION BASED ON 11:38-44

The sheer power of this moment is overwhelming! The love and hope of Jesus before the cave is a powerful sign that the Father and Son are one. This passage begs that we give our students a chance to grasp the power of the teaching through the physical reality of this scene.

Take your students to a cemetery or natural setting that in some way represents the tomb in this story. Weather and other factors may discourage you from such a learning experience. However, you can also utilize the church building (basement, etc.) to give an environmental texture to this session.

You might prepare the students by placing one member or the whole group in the "tomb" place. They are told to move quietly with no talking. You could even blindfold them, if they are older. Wrap each of their hands with crepe paper. Do not wrap the hands together. Ask them to close their eyes (if they are not blindfolded) and imagine that they are deep in the earth. Describe the state of death. Don't be too vivid. People can be frightened easily.

Play an audio-cassette tape recording of crying. Allow a pause. Then play a voice speaking the words of Jesus in verses 41-43. At that point play a recorded reading of the whole passage. Meanwhile unwrap the students' hands.

Spend the rest of the time sharing the feelings they had. Was there a moment that touched them the most? You might pass a linen strip and ask them to reflect on the feeling of being bound as they hold the strip.

Cut strips from a piece of linen. Tie a piece to each person's wrist. Tell the class that this is a resurrection tag. Ask them to wear it for a day during the week. If they feel comfortable, they are to tell people that the strip celebrates the resurrection of Lazarus, Jesus and all of us. The experiences they have can be shared at the next session of the course. Ask them to bring the linen strips with them when they come.

You can open the session by reading the passage again. Go around the circle and have them share their tags and the stories that developed from them.

SESSION BASED ON 11:45-57

There has been a misunderstanding about faithfulness in the popular mind. Cultural religion has suggested that discipleship will lead to popularity and success. Yet, this passage shows us the biblical message that one is called to faithfulness and most often the world does not appreciate what God leads us to do. This text will be an excellent way of exploring this aspect of the Christian faith.

This session might follow a pre-session suggestion. Ask the students to collect stories from people in the congregation and their families about times when they did the things God led them to do but were misunderstood by others. It will be best if the students can tape record these stories.

Gather the class and read the passage. Ask them to share the stories they found in their talks with others. List the kinds of reactions people had to their good deeds or well-meaning Christian acts.

How does Jesus look at the fact that this very gift of raising a person from the dead will only intensify the plans of others to kill him? Discuss the basis for our discipleship. What gives us the strength to do works the world will not like?

Ask the students to share their own experiences when they acted out of their faith and were misunderstood. How do we keep at our ministry when others don't support us at school or work?

Have the students draw up a list of unpopular people who need our ministry. How can your church help these unpopular people? Spend some time preparing a document that lists some proposals for your church's ministry to the oppressed. Present the proposals to the church board or committee.

Creative Speaking and Preaching Ideas

A CLUE FROM 11:1-16

This passage reveals a tension between impending good news and bad news: Lazarus will be risen and Jesus will die. Such a texture makes a strong connection to our situation as people living in the everyday world.

Ask each person in the congregation to write on both sides of a "news" card (a standard 3×5 card). On one side encourage them to share something good about themselves. On the other side, something bad. Have these cards collected while you go through the passage with a "good news/bad news" motif: God accepts both the good and bad in us. Have the cards redistributed so that different people receive the cards.

Ask people to share good news/bad news items. After each story, repeat verse 9. Conclude that the Good News is able to use our good news and transform the bad news about ourselves.

A CLUE FROM 11:17-44

This text is one of the more dramatic in the fourth Gospel. It deserves the full freedom in our preaching to touch the lives of the worshipers.

Enter into the experience of Lazarus as a way of bringing your people to the message. Have yourself wrapped with strips of cloth in the manner of a grave wrapping. You may be at a door or behind the partition separating the choir area from the worship center. As the passage is read, remain out of sight. Come into the room or stand up when verse 43 is read. You will need to get someone who reads well to present the passage.

As verse 44 is read, have a couple people unwind the cloth covering you. You can be wearing a simple robelike garment under the linen binding.

Present your message from the perspective of Lazarus. Do a stream-of-consciousness monologue about the silence of death. Continue the stream with the booming words of life that Jesus spoke to awake Lazarus. Reflect on how life will be for you now. Look at your hands. Take in the view. Mention the people who see now that you have life. The drama of the text will touch the lives of your people.

A CLUE FROM 11:45-57

Jesus' command in verse 44 triggers an intriguing preaching clue. The people around the tomb are ordered to "unbind him." The motif of cloth binding and protecting is a consistent motif in the story of Jesus' ministry.

Begin the sermon experience by introducing a large piece of linen cloth. It can be simply folded and not in any special shape. As you preach, allow the cloth to play a role in the sermon's focus and appearance.

Gather a series of texts in which cloth plays an important role: baby's clothes—Luke 2:12; woman touching Jesus' robe—Mark 5:27; taking off clothing to wash feet—John 13:3-4; soldiers gambling over clothing—John 19:23-24; and grave clothes—John 20:5-7. Develop the relationship between the Good News presented in these passages and the connecting "thread" of the cloth. For example, as you talk about the manger scene, move the cloth over your head as if you were Mary. When the baby Jesus is described, move the cloth into the form of swaddling a baby. In the same manner, the cloth can take on the changing roles as the story is told. You will want to conclude the journey of the cloth with the empty tomb and discarded grave clothes.

If you are celebrating communion, you might want to put the cloth on the table or altar for this part of the service.

A CLUE FROM 11:45-57

In verse 47, the opponents of Jesus summarize their reason for acting against him: "What are we to do? For this man performs many signs." This important theme in the fourth Gospel suggests a clue for our preaching.

1. Study the key signs or miracles in the fourth Gosepl: water into wine (2:1-11); healing the official's son (4:43-54); healing the lame man (5:1-18); feeding the crowd (6:4-14); walking on water (6:16-21); healing the blind man (9:1-41); the raising of Lazarus (11:17-44) and the catch of fish (21:4-12).

2. Select an object that symbolizes each of the miracles (water jar, hourglass, a cot, loaf of bread, bowl of water, clay, stone from a tomb and fishing net).

3. Add mobility to your preaching of these texts by moving to different places in the sanctuary during the sermon. Place an item at many different points. You can help the congregation walk with Jesus in his ministry. Don't worry about some of the people having to turn in a different direc-

tion at certain points. We tend to lock people into one viewing area during worship. The whole room is important. You might have some of the young people go and get the item representing the story. They can carry it to a central area.

4. Conclude with questions focusing on the irony of killing Jesus for giving life. Are there contemporary situations in which the ministry of Jesus by people of the congregation brings down criticism and misunderstanding? Do we suppress the signs of God in order to keep the peace among the faithful? You might plunge into the particulars of these questions by noting the ministries of your denomination in some of the following areas: peace, the poor, minority action groups, Third World issues, etc. There are Christian ministries in these and many other controversial areas. Would we once again plot to kill Jesus if he returned and again undertook his radical ministry among us today?

CHAPTER 12

JUDAS CHALLENGES JESUS

Six days before the Passover, Jesus came to Bethany, where Laz′arus was, whom Jesus had raised from the dead. ²There they made him a supper; Martha served, and Laz′arus was one of those at table with him. ³Mary took a pound of costly ointment of pure nard and anointed the feet of Jesus and wiped his feet with her hair; and the house was filled with the fragrance of the ointment. ⁴But Judas Iscariot, one of his disciples (he who was to betray him), said, ⁵"Why was this ointment not sold for three hundred denarii*ᵇ* and given to the poor?" ⁶This he said, not that he cared for the poor but because he was a thief, and as he had the money box he used to take what was put into it. ⁷Jesus said, "Let her alone, let her keep it for the day of my burial. ⁸The poor you always have with you, but you do not always have me."

9 When the great crowd of the Jews learned that he was there, they came, not only on account of Jesus but also to see Laz′arus, whom he had raised from the dead. ¹⁰So the chief priests planned to put Laz′arus also to death, ¹¹because on account of him many of the Jews were going away and believing in Jesus.

A GREAT CROWD WELCOMES JESUS TO JERUSALEM

12 The next day a great crowd who had come to the feast heard that Jesus was coming to Jerusalem. ¹³So they took branches of palm trees and went out to meet him, crying, "Hosanna! Blessed is he who comes in the name of the Lord, even the King of Israel!" ¹⁴And Jesus found a young ass and sat upon it; as it is written,
¹⁵"Fear not, daughter of Zion;
behold, your king is coming,
sitting on an ass's colt!"
¹⁶His disciples did not understand this at first; but when Jesus was glorified, then they remembered that this had been written of him and had been done to him. ¹⁷The crowd that had been with him when he called Laz′arus out of the tomb and raised him from the dead bore witness. ¹⁸The reason why the crowd went to meet him was that they heard he had done this sign. ¹⁹The Pharisees then said to one another, "You see that you can do nothing; look, the world has gone after him."

JESUS FORESHADOWS HIS DEATH

20 Now among those who went up to worship at the feast were some Greeks. ²¹So these came to Philip, who was from Beth-sa′ida in Galilee, and said to him, "Sir, we wish to see Jesus." ²²Philip went and told Andrew; Andrew went with Philip and they told Jesus. ²³And Jesus answered them, "The hour has come for the Son of man to be glorified. ²⁴Truly, truly, I say to you, unless a grain of wheat falls into the earth and dies, it remains alone; but if it dies, it bears much fruit. ²⁵He who loves his life loses it, and he who hates his life in this world will keep it for eternal life. ²⁶If any one serves me, he must follow me; and where I am, there shall my servant be also; if

---

ᵇ The denarius was a day's wage for a laborer

any one serves me, the Father will honor him.

27 "Now is my soul troubled. And what shall I say? 'Father, save me from this hour'? No, for this purpose I have come to this hour. ²⁸Father, glorify thy name." Then a voice came from heaven, "I have glorified it, and I will glorify it again." ²⁹The crowd standing by heard it and said that it had thundered. Others said, "An angel has spoken to him." ³⁰Jesus answered, "This voice has come for your sake, not for mine. ³¹Now is the judgment of this world, now shall the ruler of this world be cast out; ³²and I, when I am lifted up from the earth, will draw all men to myself." ³³He said this to show by what death he was to die. ³⁴The crowd answered him, "We have heard from the law that the Christ remains for ever. How can you say that the Son of man must be lifted up? Who is this Son of man?" ³⁵Jesus said to them, "The light is with you for a little longer. Walk while you have the light, lest the darkness overtake you; he who walks in the darkness does not know where he goes. ³⁶While you have the light, believe in the light, that you may become sons of light."

A Summary Of Jesus' Teaching

When Jesus had said this, he departed and hid himself from them. ³⁷Though he had done so many signs before them, yet they did not believe in him; ³⁸it was that the word spoken by the prophet Isaiah might be fulfilled:

"Lord, who has believed our report, and to whom has the arm of the Lord been revealed?"

³⁹Therefore they could not believe. For Isaiah again said,
⁴⁰"He has blinded their eyes and hardened their heart,
lest they should see with their eyes and perceive with their heart,
and turn for me to heal them."
⁴¹Isaiah said this because he saw his glory and spoke of him. ⁴²Nevertheless many even of the authorities believed in him, but for fear of the Pharisees they did not confess it, lest they should be put out of the synagogue: ⁴³for they loved the praise of men more than the praise of God.

44 And Jesus cried out and said, "He who believes in me, believes not in me but in him who sent me. ⁴⁵And he who sees me sees him who sent me. ⁴⁶I have come as light into the world, that whoever believes in me may not remain in darkness. ⁴⁷If any one hears my sayings and does not keep them, I do not judge him; for I did not come to judge the world but to save the world. ⁴⁸He who rejects me and does not receive my sayings has a judge; the word that I have spoken will be his judge on the last day. ⁴⁹For I have not spoken on my own authority; the Father who sent me has himself given me commandment what to say and what to speak. ⁵⁰And I know that his commandment is eternal life. What I say, therefore, I say as the Father has bidden me."

CHAPTER 12

Creative Commentary on the Scripture

VERSES 1-8: The anointing at Bethany presents an interesting collection of people. They respond differently to the ministry of Jesus. We are given a moving moment of adoration in the anointing of Jesus closely followed by the first step in his betrayal by Judas. The fragrant ointment and the jingling of coins are suggestive to the experiential Christian communicator.

Note the important discussion of priorities for the use of time. The ministry to the poor is inseparable from the gospel. But Jesus knows that this moment must be celebrated because it will not come again. Does he mean that nothing can be done, ultimately, to improve the lot of the world's poor? Or is he being blunt and realistic: We are sinners at heart, and only by the grace of God will we ever begin to show concern for others before ourselves?

VERSES 9-19: We are moved from an intimate scene to the roar of the crowds. The celebration of this joyful moment is placed in the context of Jesus' sadness that the people still don't understand the source of their joy. Perhaps we only appreciate the reason for celebration after the fact. If we had been there, would we have been any more understanding than the disciples? The resurrection straightened it all out. Without the resurrection, all is in confusion, chaos. Once again God brings order out of chaos!

VERSES 20-26: The Greeks' quest to "see Jesus" comes in the form of friendship or personal evangelism. The role of the believer in taking a brother or sister to Jesus is vital.

This passage also introduces the image of the grain that must die to bring life. The communion or love feast is indicated by this image.

186   THE BIBLE CREATIVE

The concepts of love and hate again flourish in this text. The use of "love" indicates "to embrace" and "hate" indicates "to be separate" in this text.

VERSES 27-36: Jesus seeks solitude for his prayer. The quality, rate and flow of time concepts surface in a special way. Why can't they grasp how Jesus is working with time? The voice that can be understood or rejected is an interesting clue for experiential communicators.

The text returns to the use of light and darkness. It is important to remember in reading translations of this passage that "sons" and other male language include both males and females. We need to be quite consistent about making this clear. Jesus Christ redeems all people—male and female, Greek and Jew, young and old, rich and poor, those at home and those far off. Verse 36 really means "sons and daughters" of light.

VERSES 37-43: What more need Christ do before we totally trust and believe him? Fear is a major stumbling block for faithful people of every age. Acceptance from others will often blind us to our own commitment to Christ.

VERSES 44-50: Jesus speaks out loudly. His appeal directs listeners to hear his sayings and do his word. The logos of the opening chapters has become both spiritual and practical. Jesus, Father and Word are all intimately woven together.

Creative Bible Study Ideas

SESSION BASED ON 12:1-8

1. Divide the group into five clusters: (a) Martha; (b) Mary; (c) Judas; (d) Jesus; and (e) Lazarus.
2. Read the story.
3. Have each cluster discuss the story only from the perspective of the person it represents.
4. Establish the biblical scene with chairs placed for each of the characters.
5. Role play the scene with representatives from each group.
6. Discuss the interaction dynamics between the characters in the story.
7. Pass around a jar of ointment or perfume.
8. Ask each person to smell it and share how she or he

has publicly witnessed on behalf of Christ this last week.

9. Go around the group and anoint the hands of each person as an act of dedication to witness for Christ during the coming week.

10. Ask each person to focus on someone who might receive his or her ministry during the coming week. These experiences can be shared with the class at the next session.

SESSION BASED ON 12:1-8

The text radiates the feeling of an evening family dinner. There are food odors, conversations and even arguments. You might hold a family-night supper. Role play this scene from John. Have a woman wash and anoint the feet of someone else in the group. Perhaps she might choose one of the older, respected persons in attendance. You might even have someone object to the waste of good oil and perfume when the money could have been spent to help people.

Spend some time sharing the feelings experienced by the participants in this short role play. How did it feel to have your feet washed by another? What was it like serving another in this humble way?

You might bring in the reality of Judas' complaint by having some guests who are hungry. Maybe they are the ones whose feet are washed! It might even be possible to have the church group work in a local soup kitchen as part of the evening's experience.

SESSION BASED ON 12:1-8

1. Place a bottle of perfume and a check for $1 million in the center of the group. The check can be created by writing out one from your checkbook. You won't have to cash it! You might also purchase one of those novelty items containing $1 million of shredded bills.

2. Read the passage and focus on Judas' criticism of Jesus (verses 4-5).

3. Pass the money or check around the circle and dream about how this money could be used to help people in need. You might pursue this process in small groups.

4. Make a list of the good things that could be accomplished.

5. Read Jesus' response (verses 7-8).

6. Meet in small groups and go over the list from the perspective of verses 7-8.

188   THE BIBLE CREATIVE

7. Anoint each person with the commission to go forth and serve the Lord through love for the poor. Ask for a specific act of helping the poor from each student.

SESSION BASED ON 12:1-8

1. Share dreams, intuitions and foreknowledge experiences you may have had or have heard about concerning other persons.
2. Tell about the most practical person you have ever known.
3. Place pictures of Jesus before the group.
4. Invite the group members to look at Jesus from a purely analytical basis. If you were Sherlock Holmes, what would you deduce from these pictures about Jesus? Make a list.
5. Look at Jesus as a dreamer. List things about him that indicate that he was a dreamer.
6. Ask the students to bring together both sides of Jesus as dreamer and practical person.
7. Introduce ointment. Look at it as a chemist might. Now talk about the other perceptions of this product (burial, healing, etc.).
8. Apply this discussion to the lives of the students. Ask them to describe themselves from a purely analytical position. Then ask them to describe their value as a child of God.
9. Ask each person to exercise in the coming week the two natures of Jesus.

SESSION BASED ON 12:9-19

1. Play the sounds of a crowd from your audio-cassette tape recorder. You can record these sounds at sports events or check out a sound-effects record from a local library.
2. Read the text.
3. Organize a musical parade with class members. Pass out simple items that can be used to create musical sounds (blocks of wood, etc.).
4. Using the words of the text, start building the energy for the parade. You might start with simple swaying, humming, chanting, etc. Move around the room, go down the hall, march around the building and maybe even into the neighborhood if the weather and setting permits.
5. Spend some time talking about how the students felt giving this kind of public praise. What kind of reaction did they get from others?

6. Discuss when the students last did something to make others amazed at Jesus. When have they last been amazed by what Jesus did for them?

7. Ask the students to design a "hosanna" week. How can each person alter his or her life so that others can experience the joyous aspect of Jesus? It might be the wearing of a flower or some other small change in appearance. The response of others can be shared at the next session.

SESSION BASED ON 12:20-26

We are given an example of the role of friendship in evangelism. When a person seeks Jesus, he or she can best find him through the aid of a friend.

1. Read the passage with special focus on verses 20-22.
2. Pass out pieces of paper to the students. Fold them into halves. On the front of the folded sheets print the words: PASSPORT TO THE KINGDOM OF GOD. Ask each student to write his or her name on it. Then open the papers.
3. Ask students to write the history of how they came to see Jesus. They may want to draw a little map using symbols for the key spots in their journey. They may want to draw a timeline. Let them create their own history. Be sure that they record the people, events and places that were important in their faith journey.
4. Share the passports.
5. Have each person make another passport.
6. Have each student fill in the name of someone who doesn't know Jesus but could with the student's help. If they can't think of a particular person, you might suggest a public person or a category of persons who need Christ in a special way.
7. Help the students develop a plan for helping this person see Jesus. What is the first step to be taken?
8. Share how the process is working at the next session.

SESSION BASED ON 12:27-36

1. Organize the group into two units.
2. Ask the units to listen to a reading of the text from two different perspectives: the words of Jesus and the words of the Father. You might want to put the students in two different classrooms for this part of the session. You can record verses 27-28a on one tape and verses 28b-29 on another tape. Have 10 to 15 people read the passage onto the tape

for you. Encourage them to use different speeds and inflections.

3. Let each group discuss the following considerations: (a) the emotional quality of the text; (b) the sensuality of the passage; (c) the teaching thrust of the verses; and (d) the implications for my life in this portion of the Bible.

4. Gather together once again.

5. Share the insights gained from this session.

6. Read the texts in unison as one passage.

SESSION BASED ON 12:35-36

1. Meet in a dark room with no light.

2. Talk about students' feelings in this sudden darkness. What are the fears and uncertainties in such an experience?

3. Light a very small candle that has only a limited amount of burning time left in it.

4. Read verses 35-36.

5. Share how the light brings something new to the room. What does the light do to change the room? How does Jesus bring light to our personal lives in a similar way?

6. Pass the candle around the circle.

7. Ask each student to share how faith in Jesus makes a person a son or daughter of the light.

8. Put a drop of wax on each person's hand. You might want to drip the wax into a shallow container of water. You can then take the wax out and give it to your students. The hot wax is not really hot, but its warmth says something about the cost of the light in the life of Jesus.

9. Have the students share how this drop of light in some way symbolizes or reminds them of some darkness in their lives.

10. Ask the students to share the darkness of another person's life during the next week. This will mean that each person will have to listen to another person's story. It will take courage to let the light of Christ shine into the darkness of another's life. These experiences can be explored at the next session.

SESSION BASED ON 12:37-50

1. Give each person a Manila folder containing stapled sheets of paper.

2. Tell the students that this file represents their "permanent record."

3. Ask them to fill in the first page with things about themselves they like the most.

4. Read four paragraph-length stories concerning people in need of friendship and help: a drug user, a person with a bad reputation in sexual matters, a loner who dresses poorly and is considered "out of it" and lastly a story about a religious fanatic. You might want to type these stories and include them in the folders.

5. Ask each student to choose a story and write some thoughts on how he or she could help this person.

6. Exchange folders.

7. As a total group ask the students to pretend that they are an admissions officer or some other person who must "judge" the person whose file he or she is reading.

8. Share positive and negative conclusions about a person who tries to help someone in trouble.

9. Discuss the fear in risking.

10. Read verses 42-43.

11. Talk about the fear which keeps us from ministering in the name of Jesus. Why are many people hesitant to join volunteer organizations to help others? Have you been embarrassed to tell your friends about Christ?

12. Return the folders to each person.

13. Close with a prayer circle. Focus on God's help in enabling the students to be witnesses to Jesus. Ask for strength to overcome the fear that holds many Christians. You might ask them to use the folders as a journal of their witness. This can be kept and the results shared from time to time.

Creative Speaking and Preaching Ideas

A CLUE FROM 12:1-8

The ointment of this text seems to be the catalyst for people to reveal their true feelings toward the ministry of Jesus. You might utilize this clue by developing a sermon that explores the different attitudes toward Jesus.

Have someone bring to the front of the worship center a "pound of costly ointment" during the reading of the text. This person can use mime or simply bring a container to the worship center. You will also want to have several people gathered around the place where you set the ointment. They represent the people in the story: Mary, Martha, Jesus, Judas and Lazarus. They are to sit in a frozen tableau setting.

Walk into the middle of the group and pick up the ointment. Ask a rhetorical question: "I wonder what kind of story about Jesus this jar of ointment could tell?"

Move into the sermon by telling each person's story as the jar might relate it. You can use a different voice or your natural one. Be sure to hold the jar and give it some animation as one would a puppet.

This perspective for the sermon will permit you the freedom to say some very direct things to the congregation. Perhaps the sermon could end with the jar speaking about the faces of the worshipers. Use the first-person voice.

Close by anointing each person in the circle. Then have them go into the congregation and begin a process of anointing each worshiper. One person can anoint the hands of the person next to him or her.

A CLUE FROM 12:9-19

Many congregations have picked up the clue of this passage by giving out palm branches on the Sunday before Easter. The people in the story used palm branches so it is natural that we follow the same process. However, we should really use them in the same way and not simply drop them in worshipers' hands on the way home.

Make your sermon a celebration of the recognition that Jesus Christ is Lord over all! Lead the congregation back into the crowd of the ancient world. Have several young people pass out the palms as you read the text. They can call yells of joy as they encourage others to be excited about the fact that the Lord of life is coming to town. Incorporate sections from John that are mentioned in this passage (the story of Lazarus).

Your sermon can be presented from the perspective of the Gospel's writer. He comments on Jesus' entry and the crowd's reaction. This can be the perfect form of your narration. Use a hand-held microphone and wander back and forth across the front of the worship center. Give a running account of what is happening. Explain the dynamics of the situation.

A CLUE FROM 12:20-26

This is an excellent passage for a communion service. The

text utilizes the image of the grain of wheat. Perhaps the usual bread and juice/wine could be accompanied on the communion table by a bushel of wheat and a bunch of grapes. Have the elements carried to the table by several people.

Pass out the wheat and grapes in the offering plates. Ask each person to take a grain or two of wheat and a grape. Encourage each person to consider the ministry of these two simple items. Talk about how the grain and the grape must suffer death and transformation before they can be gifts of life for us.

You might ask the worshipers to reflect on the grain and grapes and share moments in their lives when they have experienced physical and emotional dying and suffering. If the congregation is not used to this kind of open sharing, ask them to write the examples on cards and pass them to the front.

Share these moments. Build on these contributions as you move into the communion service itself.

A CLUE FROM 12:27-36

Time is a key concept in this text. Jesus suggests a concept of time misunderstood by his followers and opponents. You can draw upon this clue by using an hourglass. Pass it around the congregation as you reflect on this passage. Keep it moving from hand to hand until the sand has run through. Don't use one that takes more than 15 minutes.

Present your message from the perspective of a person who has only 15 minutes to live. He or she tries to fill this time with a special appreciation for the life God has given. Draw particularly from verses 35-36 as you cast the message into the life of the dying person. Conclude that time is a most precious resource. How we use it should be well-planned and honorable to God.

A CLUE FROM 12:37-43

This text reveals the unwillingness of people to give themselves to Christ in spite of the many ways he has shown his love for us. You might build your sermon upon this clue by reviewing the many signs in this Gospel. Instead of simply talking about them, create experiential moments in the lives of the worshipers. For example, you might open your sermon as if you were a salesperson on a television ad. Set a table in front of you as you face the congregation. Use the "tell-you-what-I-am-going-to-do-for-you" pitch of the stereotypical late-night commercial.

Focus on several of the signs Jesus gave for us. Connect an object or symbol with each one. These might even be passed around after they have each been introduced. After each sign, add the salesperson's pitch: "Still not convinced? Tell you what I am going to do!"

Close by dropping the character and summarize by directly offering Jesus to the people. He can be embraced without fear of others.

A CLUE FROM 12:44-50

This highly emotional passage concerns the unity of the Father and the Son. John promises that we know the Father by following the Son and keeping the sayings of the Son. This clue offers us a marvelous speaking opportunity!

Gather some people to help you prepare for this service. Work carefully through the Gospel of John (and perhaps the other Gospels) as you and your people gather the sayings of Jesus. Select enough for each person at worship. Your helpers can write them out on individual pieces of paper. Again, this process is an excellent opportunity to involve youth and adults in a co-proclamation of the Word.

You might also enlist the help of instrumental musicians for your sermon. Select a musical effect that expresses a subdued but painful tone. Describe the frustration Jesus must have felt as he tried once again to help his listeners understand the Good News. The music can play all through your sermon.

Jesus called his listeners to hear and keep his sayings. Have your partners in the sermon distribute the sayings of Jesus. Call for a few minutes of meditation (music playing all the time) in which they are to reflect on how they can follow this saying the following week. What will be the hardest part of the task? What will keep them from being faithful to Jesus?

Now ask the people to share these "yes, but" worries about following the sayings of Christ. You might have them memorize the saying and write their needs on the paper and return it. You can read them aloud and ask others to respond.

I fully realize the fear you may have at the suggestion to

interact with your people within a sermon. However, the entire fourth Gospel is propelled through the interaction between Jesus and his listeners. It begs for this kind of contemporary presentation. You are not Jesus. However, you are called to follow him faithfully in the presentation of the Word. It deserves the best our people can offer.

Ask your people to report back next Sunday, ready to share their experiences during a week of intentionally living a particular saying of Jesus. This could be the whole sermon for the following Sunday.

JESUS WASHES THE DISCIPLES' FEET

Now before the feast of the Passover, when Jesus knew that his hour had come to depart out of this world to the Father, having loved his own who were in the world, he loved them to the end. ²And during supper, when the devil had already put it into the heart of Judas Iscariot, Simon's son, to betray him, ³Jesus, knowing that the Father had given all things into his hands, and that he had come from God and was going to God, ⁴rose from supper, laid aside his garments, and girded himself with a towel. ⁵Then he poured water into a basin, and began to wash the disciples' feet, and to wipe them with the towel with which he was girded. ⁶He came to Simon Peter; and Peter said to him, "Lord, do you wash my feet?" ⁷Jesus answered him, "What I am doing you do not know now, but afterward you will understand." ⁸Peter said to him, "You shall never wash my feet." Jesus answered him, "If I do not wash you, you have no part in me." ⁹Simon Peter said to him, "Lord, not my feet only but also my hands and my head!" ¹⁰Jesus said to him, "He who has bathed does not need to wash, except for his feet,^{c} but he is clean all over; and you^x are clean, but not every one of you." ¹¹For he knew who was to betray him; that was why he said, "You are not all clean."

12 When he had washed their feet, and taken his garments, and resumed his place, he said to them, "Do you know what I have done to you? ¹³You call me Teacher and Lord; and you are right, for so I am. ¹⁴If I then, your Lord and Teacher, have washed your feet, you also ought to wash one another's feet. ¹⁵For I have given you an example, that you also should do as I have done to you. ¹⁶Truly, truly, I say to you, a servant^d is not greater than his master; nor is he who is sent greater than he who sent him. ¹⁷If you know these things, blessed are you if you do them. ¹⁸I am not speaking of you all; I know whom I have chosen; it is that the scripture may be fulfilled, 'He who ate my bread has lifted his heel against me.' ¹⁹I tell you this now, before it takes place, that when it does take place you may believe that I am he. ²⁰Truly, truly, I say to you, he who receives any one whom I send receives me; and he who receives me receives him who sent me."

"ONE OF YOU WILL BETRAY ME"

21 When Jesus had thus spoken, he was troubled in spirit, and testified, "Truly, truly, I say to you, one of you will betray me." ²²The disciples looked at one another, uncertain of whom he spoke. ²³One of his disciples, whom Jesus loved, was lying close to the breast of Jesus; ²⁴so Simon Peter beckoned to him and said, "Tell us who it is of whom he speaks." ²⁵So lying thus, close to the breast of Jesus, he said to him, "Lord, who is it?" ²⁶Jesus answered,

---

c Other ancient authorities omit *except for his feet*
x The Greek word for *you* here is plural

d Or *slave*

"It is he to whom I shall give this morsel when I have dipped it." So when he had dipped the morsel, he gave it to Judas, the son of Simon Iscariot. ²⁷Then after the morsel, Satan entered into him. Jesus said to him, "What you are going to do, do quickly." ²⁸Now no one at the table knew why he said this to him. ²⁹Some thought that, because Judas had the money box, Jesus was telling him, "Buy what we need for the feast"; or, that he should give something to the poor. ³⁰So, after receiving the morsel, he immediately went out; and it was night.

31 When he had gone out, Jesus said, "Now is the Son of man glorified, and in him God is glorified; ³²if God is glorified in him, God will also glorify him in himself, and glorify him at once. ³³Little children, yet a little while I am with you. You will seek me; and as I said to the Jews so now I say to you, 'Where I am going you cannot come.' ³⁴A new commandment I give to you, that you love one another; even as I have loved you, that you also love one another. ³⁵By this all men will know that you are my disciples, if you have love for one another."

36 Simon Peter said to him, "Lord, where are you going?" Jesus answered, "Where I am going you cannot follow me now; but you shall follow afterward." ³⁷Peter said to him, "Lord, why cannot I follow you now? I will lay down my life for you." ³⁸Jesus answered, "Will you lay down your life for me? Truly, truly, I say to you, the cock will not crow, till you have denied me three times."

CHAPTER 13

Creative Commentary on the Scripture

The setting for this scene is *before* the Passover. The other Gospels give the account of the Last Supper at the Passover celebration. Jesus, true to the Gospel of John, again replaces one of the festivals of the Jews.

The author of the fourth Gospel does not include the institution of communion. Some have concluded that John is being anti-sacramental by such an omission. These scholars believe John downplays communion in order to make a statement against gnostics. Gnosticism developed an extensive system of sacramental or secret rites.

John's imagery (wine, grapes, living water), however, does indicate a love for a fuller understanding of baptism and the eucharistic feast. The banquet on the beach in chapter 21 seems to be the displaced feast which is not described here. The rich detail of this act of servanthood provides an important aspect to any understanding of the sacraments.

The table setting provides the backdrop for the disciples to define their journey of faith against the background of Jesus' ministry. Judas falls into temptation and betrayal. Peter lurches from one direction to another as he seeks faithfulness.

The servanthood model of Christ leads the believer to a humble and selfless lifestyle. The footwashing is a compelling act of discipleship. We are given a pattern of relationship between Lord and follower and between believers.

Guilt about the impending betrayal sweeps through the disciples. It is a morsel of Christ's bread that sends Judas off to his mission of sin. The act is done and we are told that it is night. The darkness is about to challenge the light.

The theme of the glorification of the Father emerges. It

will be with us for the rest of the book. The pain of impending separation is acknowledged.

Verses 34-35 are classical statements of the Christian life. Jesus provides the benchmark for his people. The fourth Gospel also gives us the true basis of outreach and evangelism. The presence of God's spirit as reflected in his love determines whether or not others will be drawn to the faith community.

The text records Peter's attempt to give himself totally to Christ. His mind is willing, but he can't yet embrace the full discipleship until the Son has been glorified. Only the death and resurrection of Christ will enable his followers to undertake their calling.

The rich storytelling character of this passage suggests exciting ways to draw students and worshipers into the message.

Creative Bible Study Ideas

SESSION BASED ON 13:1-11

Much is revealed about the people at this gathering. The text suggests that we use the group's reflective mood in our class.

1. Find a large collection of old photos from family albums, magazines, old catalogs, etc. Every picture should feature the image of one person.

2. Divide the photos among the students. They should be in triads.

3. Read the passage.

4. Ask each group to choose pictures for the different personalities in the story. Make a collage from these photos. What does a face tell us? What kind of characterization does the passage provide? You might want to use different translations.

5. Share the pictures for the character. Discuss some things that they have learned about the people in this passage.

SESSION BASED ON 13:1-11

1. Gather the group around the table.
2. Pass a small mirror from person to person.
3. Ask students to share what they think Jesus would

know about them if he looked into the mirror of their hearts.

4. Pass the mirror around once again and ask them to share what they see of God when they look into their own faces.

5. Ask the students to mirror the love of God to others in the coming week.

SESSION BASED ON 13:1-20

The central act of this section is the washing of the disciples' feet. This action nudges us into using this creative servanthood medium.

1. Wash the feet of the students. If you wish to perform this biblical act, wear very humble garb. Perhaps you can put on a robe or exercise outfit (sweat pants). Kneel before each student to perform this act.

2. Dry each person's feet and anoint them with a scented lotion or oil. You may wish to add a little salt to the water. This will loosen dry skin and make the feet more sensitive. When the lotion is added, the students will feel the comfortable sensation of the lotion. A variation of this act is the washing of hands. This is less embarrassing to people wearing pantyhose and non-removable apparel.

3. Alert one person to give Peter's reaction at some point in the process.

4. Close by repeating Jesus' statements to Peter.

5. Suggest that the students find a way to provide a ministry of servanthood to others during the next week. What are some "footwashing" ministries that we can do for others?

SESSION BASED ON 13:12-20

1. When the class is settled, ask that all the chairs be turned so that everyone is facing the center of a circle.

2. Go around and wipe the shoes of everyone in the gathering. Kneel before each person and do the task carefully and lovingly.

3. Read the passage or play a recording you have made of the verses.

4. Talk about the scene and what Jesus has done for all of us.

5. Pass the towel around the circle and have each person share something that we, as disciples, do that soils the purity of Christ.

6. Ask them to reflect on this more deeply by writing (in words or doodles) things that have happened in the past 24 hours of their lives that have been inconsistent with discipleship. Tell them that they will not have to show this material to anyone. You may want them to turn chairs in different directions so that they are isolated from one another.

7. Play reflective music (instrumental, classical or reflective pop/rock) while this task is being done.

8. Gather the group.

9. Ask your people to share their general emotional responses to the task. What general areas arose in which we were denying Christ?

10. Close by reading the passage once again as the towel is passed around.

11. You might cut the towel into strips and give each person a section as a reminder of our servanthood in Christ.

12. Ask each person to make a commitment to pick an eight-hour period during the next week in which he or she will consciously live all of life without denying Christ. Encourage the students to keep a nightly journal. General reflections on the experiences will be shared next week. You may ask them to keep the strip of towel and return it with the journal next week.

This session would work well into a pre-Easter series on discipleship. The elements of this passage that inspired this design will work well with youth as well as adults. Don't underestimate the spiritual power of your people. They are waiting for the experience of the fourth Gospel to take hold on their lives.

SESSION BASED ON 13:12-20

This session might follow the towel session suggested above. Your people have contracted to two or more weeks of experiential study of this text. They return with their discipleship thoughts and their strip from the servanthood towel.

1. Open the session with prayer of thanksgiving for bringing these forgiven disciples together again.

2. Have each person place the towel strip in the center of the table.

3. Read a few sections from your journal. Remind them that no one will have to read from theirs unless they wish.

4. Ask the group to share feelings about the week of servanthood. Probe for emotions and some examples from the group.

5. Ask them about the most difficult aspect of this task. How many times did they demand to be served rather than a willing servant?

6. Affirm their successes and failures. Write them on newsprint or on a blackboard.

7. Close by reading the passage again. Note the forgiving spirit of Christ. Even the betrayer is loved by Jesus!

8. Ask each person to pick up a different piece of towel than the one they carried last week. This is the symbolic act of bearing another's sin. Suggest that each person clean the strip before he or she brings it back next week.

9. Agree to pray for the person whose strip of towel you now bear. This could be done just before sleep or after each person has written in the journal of discipleship.

10. Let each person participate in the final act. Offer affirmation to each other that in Jesus Christ our sins are forgiven.

11. Your class might take the idea of this session to the church board with the suggestion that the towel be used as a symbol of service when officers are installed to lead the church, the youth groups or other congregational positions.

SESSION BASED ON 13:21-30

This section relates the betrayal of Judas in the midst of the disciples' innocence. Jesus hastens the will of God and doesn't provide a "super-spy" response of foiling the evil one at the last minute. Jesus' acceptance cuts against the grain of cultural conditioning.

1. Read the passage.

2. Invite the students to direct an imaginary film of this story. Begin by having a story conference (a meeting in which the film's writers plan the story line).

3. Form triads and give each unit a section of the passage.

4. Create a movie story that is consistent with the scripture.

5. After they have written notes on this task, gather the whole class.

6. Share story ideas.

7. Have the students describe the hardest part of the story for a general audience to accept.

8. Discuss how we know the will of God. When should we

take action to change things and when should we permit events to take their own course?

9. Close by passing out a "morsel" of bread to each person.

10. Offer a concluding prayer that we may know the will of God and not betray him in the course of our everyday lives.

SESSION BASED ON 13:31-38

Verses 34-35 ring in our ears and stir our hearts. What judgment falls upon every youth group and church community when we face this criterion of faithfulness? The realm of religion has been one of the most angry and hate-filled arenas of human history. In the name of faith, terrible things have happened. Yet, Jesus established a simple standard for how we Christians are to be judged.

1. Create pairs or triads of people.

2. Give each unit a phrase from verses 34-35. There are six sections if you take the material from punctuation mark to punctuation mark. You may have to give the same section to more than one unit if you have a larger class.

3. Ask the subgroups to create a mime that expresses their section of the verses. All members must become involved. They are to become living extensions of the material.

4. Have the groups share the mimes. Some of it will be humorous. Don't worry about good laughter. The people of God often take their humanity far too seriously.

5. Invite the whole group to reflect on how this living commandment appears to the outside world. Could a stranger know Jesus from what was taking place during the sharing? Does the love of Christ appear in laughter? anger? tears?

6. Have the students go out at this time or during the week and interview a person in the congregation with an audio-cassette tape recorder. Ask these questions: "How have you experienced the love of Christ from other Christians? Does the world know Jesus by experiencing us?" This process is beneficial to both student and interviewee.

7. Debrief the experience. Deal with both the positive and negative results.

8. List findings on newsprint.

9. Develop a way to heal some of the negative things damaging the quality of love in your congregation. Even small suggestions reap large doses of love. For example, one group suggested that worshipers hold hands during the

pastoral prayer. This simple touch helped the congregation to simply reach out to another person.

Creative Speaking and Preaching Ideas

This chapter bristles with possibilities for creative preaching and worship. Indeed, in some traditions footwashing plays an important role. The eucharistic implications are important to most Christian traditions.

It is ironic that even with the clear biblical imperative to experience the faith physically, the faith community has a hard time living up to the servanthood acts of this passage. It is very hard to fill the gap between Christ as a living event and our traditional ways of doing things.

Experiential preaching is difficult only because someone must bear the risk alone. But the biblical material mandates creative expression!

A CLUE FROM 13:1-11

The setting for this service could be very simple. Instead of placing the usual symbolic objects on the communion table or altar (cross, chalice, candles, etc.), place on it an old pitcher, basin and a small towel.

The actual footwashing can be done in a number of ways. You might perform the act with the church board sitting at a large table. You could have two people from the congregation. There are many combinations available. An older person can wash the feet of a young person and then reverse the process.

It is possible that footwashing can be combined with a communion service. One way of crawling into the Bible story is to wipe the shoes of the worshipers with towels as they come to receive communion.

A CLUE FROM 13:1-11

Judas stands out as a complex and contradictory person in the faith community. He is an instrument of the will of God and yet he is a victim of the evil one. History has judged his guilt. Only occasionally has he found a sympathetic word. The character of Judas offers another excellent opportunity to present the sermon from the inside out. Become Judas. You might consider costume and makeup. Enter the worship area in character and offer the conflicting feelings that fill you as you betray Christ. Help the congregation to experience the betrayer in all of us. End the sermon by slipping away after you have taken the morsel of bread.

A CLUE FROM 13:12-20

Verse 15 places the point of this chapter clearly before the believer. Jesus has washed their feet as an example. Servanthood is the inescapable theme of discipleship. He even washed the feet of the betrayer.

Print a special page in the church bulletin that is headed: "Pattern." The rest of the sheet should be blank. Be sure there are pencils in the pew racks.

Open the sermon with a reading of the passage, focusing on verse 15. Take a towel and talk about the many uses of this single piece of cloth. Model the uses by putting it on your arm when you mention how a waiter uses it, or around your neck when you suggest the way joggers use it.

The last illustration should be Jesus' use of this simple piece of cloth. Kneel down on the floor and show how he did it. Note that "models" and "examples" are important to our development as persons. Ask the people in the pews to take a few minutes to write down the names of people who have most influenced their lives. Jot down a sentence beside the persons' names describing the small actions or behaviors that made the persons special.

Give the people in the pews a chance to share their role models. Explore the role models' humility, wisdom and patience. Then go back to Christ as our model. Have each person turn to a neighbor and offer a word of affirmation to him or her.

A CLUE FROM 13:12-38

Verse 38 reveals another example of human fallibility. Peter means well in his compulsive commitment to Jesus. But Jesus is aware of his limitations.

We know the first disciples were a mixture of many different qualities and attributes. They were both good and evil. They were faithful and weak.

You might beckon your people into this passage's message by setting up the problem of our search for the accused: the real Christian. Give instructions to the congregation about being alert and observant as they face this task.

Call for a lineup of suspects. Have five different people come forward and stand in a police-type "lineup." Have each person wear a set of numbers on a piece of cardboard around his or her neck.

Question these people concerning who is the real Christian. Make sure that there are a number of different ages and personalities among the people in your "lineup." Is there enough evidence to convict a person for being a Christian?

Perhaps the congregation can also raise some questions about the things they do. The answer is, of course, that all of them, regardless of strengths and weaknesses, are Christians. God calls us as we are.

CHAPTER 14

JESUS AND THE FATHER ARE ONE

Let not your hearts be troubled; believe[e] in God, believe also in me. ²In my Father's house are many rooms; if it were not so, would I have told you that I go to prepare a place for you? ³And when I go and prepare a place for you, I will come again and will take you to myself, that where I am you may also be. ⁴And you know the way where I am going."[f] ⁵Thomas said to him, "Lord, we do not know where you are going; how can we know the way?" ⁶Jesus said to him, "I am the way, and the truth, and the life; no one comes to the Father, but by me. ⁷If you had known me, you would have known my Father also; henceforth you know him and have seen him."

8 Philip said to him, "Lord, show us the Father, and we shall be satisfied." ⁹Jesus said to him, "Have I been with you so long, and yet you do not know me, Philip? He who has seen me has seen the Father; how can you say, 'Show us the Father'? ¹⁰Do you not believe that I am in the Father and the Father in me? The words that I say to you I do not speak on my own authority; but the Father who dwells in me does his works. ¹¹Believe me that I am in the Father and the Father in me; or else believe me for the sake of the works themselves.

12 "Truly, truly, I say to you, he who believes in me will also do the works that I do; and greater works than these will he do, because I go to the Father. ¹³Whatever you ask in my name, I will do it, that the Father may be glorified in the Son; ¹⁴if you ask[g] anything in my name, I will do it.

15 "If you love me, you will keep my commandments. ¹⁶And I will pray the Father, and he will give you another Counselor, to be with you for ever, ¹⁷even the Spirit of truth, whom the world cannot receive, because it neither sees him nor knows him; you know him, for he dwells with you, and will be in you.

18 "I will not leave you desolate; I will come to you. ¹⁹Yet a little while, and the world will see me no more, but you will see me; because I live, you will live also. ²⁰In that day you will know that I am in my Father, and you in me, and I in you. ²¹He who has my commandments and keeps them, he it is who loves me; and he who loves me will be loved by my Father, and I will love him and manifest myself to him." ²²Judas (not Iscariot) said to him, "Lord, how is it that you will manifest yourself to us, and not to the world?" ²³Jesus answered him, "If a man loves me, he will keep my word, and my Father will love him, and we will come to him and make our home with him. ²⁴He who does not love me does not keep my words; and the word which you hear is not mine but the Father's who sent me."

THE PROMISE OF THE HOLY SPIRIT

25 "These things I have spoken to you, while I am still with you. ²⁶But

---

e Or *you believe*
f Other ancient authorities read *where I am going you know, and the way you know*
g Other ancient authorities add *me*

the Counselor, the Holy Spirit, whom the Father will send in my name, he will teach you all things, and bring to your remembrance all that I have said to you. ²⁷Peace I leave with you; my peace I give to you; not as the world gives do I give to you. Let not your hearts be troubled, neither let them be afraid. ²⁸You heard me say to you, 'I go away, and I will come to you.' If you loved me, you would have rejoiced, because I go to the Father; for the Father is greater than I. ²⁹And now I have told you before it takes place, so that when it does take place, you may believe. ³⁰I will no longer talk much with you, for the ruler of this world is coming. He has no power over me; ³¹but I do as the Father has commanded me, so that the world may know that I love the Father. Rise, let us go hence."

CHAPTER 14

Creative Commentary on the Scripture

This passage is an easy target for those who rearrange the fourth Gospel according to their theory of its content. In verse 31 Jesus seems to be concluding his comments to his disciples while the discourse continues through chapter 17. But who is to say that the author was following the kind of logic we wish to impose on the Bible?

VERSES 1-14: Jesus recognizes the natural tendency of his followers to be troubled over his passion and death. He suspects they will feel that their relationship with him and the Father will be threatened. The text is loaded with prepositional phrases assuring a close relationship between Father/Son/Holy Spirit and the believer. The image of a home with many guest rooms is utilized.

The misdirected dialogue is again used as Thomas tries to comprehend this word of hope. Another "I am" passage is offered. The unity of Jesus with truth and life joins the previous litanies of promise. Philip also evokes a clarification from Jesus.

Jesus places great hope and trust in his anticipated passion. It will make his other signs pale by comparison.

VERSES 15-31: It is confusing to hear Jesus talking about obeying commandments and being free in the Holy Spirit at the same time. For many people, this is an either/or proposition: Either we are bound by someone else's commandments, or we are free to choose for ourselves. In the Gospel of John we are given a very different picture: Obedience and Christian freedom in the Spirit are intimately related to each other.

It is important that those who love Jesus keep his words. He provides the gift of the counselor in order that the Word will become a constant part of the believer's life.

Jesus apparently closes his discourse to his disciples in verse 31. Yet we know that this discussion continues for several more chapters in the fourth Gospel.

Creative Bible Study Ideas

SESSION BASED ON 14:1-7

1. Have your class make a floor plan of your church or meeting building.
2. When you have all the rooms identified, tour the facility.
3. Spend a bit of time in each room while the students give the area a symbolic quality as if this were "the Father's house." For example, the worship area might be the place of praise or the kitchen might become "the place of the heavenly feast." Urge the students to express a feeling for each place. You might assign each student an area and have him or her spend some time in a particular environment. Have each person (or cluster) develop this room so that it communicates its spiritual and emotional qualities to others. Or each person (or cluster) might develop a mime or monologue that communicates the room's special qualities.
4. Gather the group.
5. Read the passage.
6. Visit each room as a group. Allow each person or cluster to present the creative decoration, mime or monologue.
7. Spend a couple minutes talking about a few things in students' lives that are troubling their hearts.
8. Relate the concerns to the qualities in each room of the Father's house. For example, if your group is in the sanctuary and someone says he or she feels there is no purpose in life, look toward the cross and ask the other students to share how the cross gives meaning and purpose to life.

This kind of traveling class will give your students a whole new sense of comfort in the building. Once they have explored the church they may always have a special love for the symbolism of this passage.

SESSION BASED ON 14:1-14

This section is filled with concepts and terms that make experiential learning a challenge. However, the passage's literary style still bristles with opportunities to help students crawl into the message. It is tempting to cast this expression of the Good News into a comfortable intellectual form. The material beckons in this direction, but our commitment here is to enable the students to translate the message into their lives.

1. Arrange the room with tables and chairs in a horseshoe shape. Everyone should be facing others when he or she is seated. Post newsprint at the open end of the horseshoe. You will also need paper and crayons or markers.

2. When the students have been seated, tell them they have been chosen as a special intelligence (as in "spy") team. They have been chosen to decode a secret document and discover the nature of Jesus.

3. Divide the group into four teams. Give each team a copy of the passage. Each team has a mission:

- Team A: Examine the relationship between Jesus and others by looking at the prepositional phrases (e.g., see "in the Father" in verse 10).
- Team B: Examine what Jesus claims about himself.
- Team C: Examine how others view him.
- Team D: Examine his relationship to the Father.

Urge the students to mark the words and phrases that apply to their team's mission.

4. Ask each team to crystalize its conclusion into a picture or diagram.

5. You might collect a number of pictures from Sunday school teaching posters, magazines, etc. or a number of slides. Ask teams to choose pictures that share what they've found.

6. Ask each team to translate the message into a mime.

7. Share the mimes with the whole group.

8. Read the text once again.

This process might be an uncomfortable leadership experience for you. It puts a great challenge before your class to be creative. You cannot be sure what the students will create. It is more than likely that they will focus on particular parts of this complex message. Accept their perspective and discovery. For example, their struggle with verse 6 may result in a fresh understanding of Jesus' self-revelation. Trust God to work through your students. You may go into this session without the answers to the questions. This is an acceptable situation. It is our responsibility to confront the

Word as seekers of truth. It is NOT our calling to merely teach the comfortable or predictable.

SESSION BASED ON 14:15-31

This text expresses the linkage between Father, Son and believer. Indeed, the counselor is the glue that seals this special relationship. The passage contains many prepositional phrases, e.g., "in my Father," "in that day," "If you love me."

1. Read verses 15-16. Remind the students that Jesus promises an ongoing relationship with us that spans all time, every situation and every need.

2. Read the passage. As you come to a prepositional phrase, assign it to a person in the class. If you have too many or too few students for the number of prepositions, make double assignments or create subgroups.

3. Ask the students to create little theological "diagrams" that show how the prepositional phrase shows a relationship between God and us. This can be done very simply. For example, "If you love me" can be diagrammed like this:

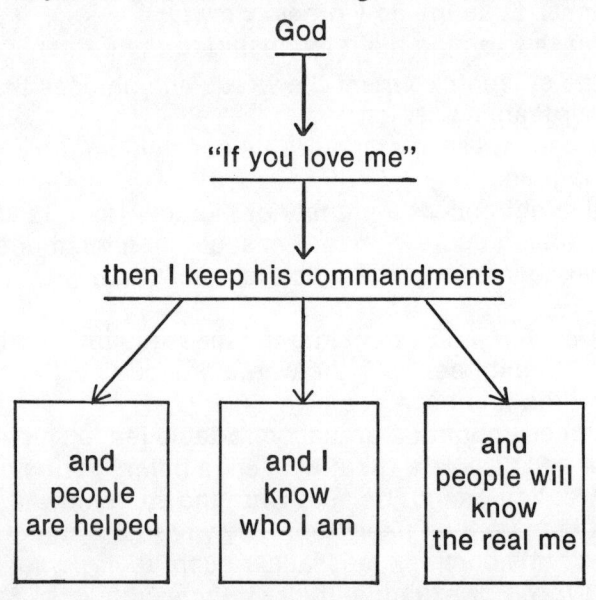

```
            God
             │
             ▼
      "If you love me"
             │
             ▼
   then I keep his commandments
       ╱     │     ╲
      ▼      ▼      ▼
  ┌──────┐ ┌──────┐ ┌──────────┐
  │ and  │ │ and I│ │   and    │
  │people│ │ know │ │people will│
  │ are  │ │who I │ │  know    │
  │helped│ │  am  │ │the real me│
  └──────┘ └──────┘ └──────────┘
```

Encourage them to use the prepositional phrase's context to spark ideas for the diagram.

4. Have them transform the diagram into a symbol that expresses what God is telling us in these statements. For example, "If you love me" could be a symbol of a contract. They might even sign the contract.

5. Share these symbols of our relationship to the Father and the Son.

Creative Speaking and Preaching Ideas

A CLUE FROM 14:1-14

This passage offers the image of the Father's house as a place promised by Jesus. We are assured that there is room for many. The idea of a home stands as a source of hope somewhere in every person's imagination. Human beings have always searched for a place to belong, a people to belong to. This search is a good clue for a talk on this passage.

Open your sermon by asking everyone to close his or her eyes. Lead your listeners on an imaginary journey into their own areas of concern and worry. How are their hearts troubled at this moment? Guide them to look at unemployment, illness, loneliness, family worries, etc.

Read the verses. Ask them to open their eyes. Introduce a large skeleton key. Suggest that this symbol represents entry into a house where there is a place for everyone. This home is free from life's fears and worries.

Pass the key around the congregation. Ask people to suggest what kinds of peace and comfort can be found in this special place. Or have people write out these qualities and you can read them.

The key to this place is Jesus Christ. The Father's house is not in the future, but it is present for those who believe! You might want to adjust this clue by actually giving a key to everyone at worship. Old keys can be picked up at auctions and other resale stores for pennies. Don't cast this message of hope into some other age. The gift of the Holy Spirit has come and the home to belong to is present with the house of faith.

A CLUE FROM 14:12-14

Jesus claims that his miracles will be surpassed by his reunion with the Father. This is hard for his disciples (and all of us) to comprehend. Restored eyesight is nothing big compared to the glorification of the Father in the death and resurrection of the Son. You might build upon this clue by asking your people to participate in the claim of this passage.

List the important signs or miracles that Jesus has performed thus far in the fourth Gospel. Have two or three people mime them while they are read. Draw upon the skills of youth and others to provide this simple and moving art.

Now ask the congregation to utilize the 3 x 5 cards you have included in the pew racks. On one side they should write down the names of 10 people for whom they have prayed. On the other side they should list 10 crises in their lives that God has used to bless them.

Collect the cards. Read items from them and lead the congregation in a litany (a phrase of spoken or sung response: "thanks be to God") after each card is read. Or you might want to place them on the altar or communion table and offer a prayer of thanksgiving for what God has done in the past and what he will do in the future.

You might extend the participatory level of this sermon by asking the congregation to focus on the promise that anything prayed in the name of Jesus will be honored. This can lead into a sharing public prayer in which people call out petitions or requests. After each request, the body responds: "Lord, hear our prayer."

A CLUE FROM 14:15-31

As we have noted in our comments on this chapter, this text is more theologically intellectual and suggests an academic treatment. How do we keep the integrity of the passage's nature while remaining faithful to our experiential approach?

One model for this kind of presentation could combine the clues of the text with the insights of noted theologian Paul Tillich. Tillich provides a perspective that encourages us to crawl into the text by using three intriguing terms: heteronomy (other authority), autonomy (self-authority) and theonomy (God's authority).

These approaches offer three ways to make decisions about life. In order to draw people into this struggle, develop an experiential way to personalize the words of Jesus. You could suggest three ways that hands could identify each approach to making decisions (e.g., other authority: a fist; self-authority: a finger pointing to the head; and God's authority: hands raised with palms pointing upward).

You can also show a few slides to provide examples of the different ways we face moments of decision (e.g., other authority: policeman; self-authority: newlyweds; God's authority: St. Francis of Assisi). Choose a variety of slides for this visual representation of the content.

You may not be attracted to Tillich's theological construct as it is here. That's fine. Our point is this: Any biblical content can be creatively communicated in experiential biblical speaking and preaching. We're only limited by our decision to be creative or simply comfortable.

CHAPTER 15

JESUS THE TRUE VINE

"I am the true vine, and my Father is the vinedresser. ²Every branch of mine that bears no fruit, he takes away, and every branch that does bear fruit he prunes, that it may bear more fruit. ³You are already made clean by the word which I have spoken to you. ⁴Abide in me, and I in you. As the branch cannot bear fruit by itself, unless it abides in the vine, neither can you, unless you abide in me. ⁵I am the vine, you are the branches. He who abides in me, and I in him, he it is that bears much fruit, for apart from me you can do nothing. ⁶If a man does not abide in me, he is cast forth as a branch and withers; and the branches are gathered, thrown into the fire and burned. ⁷If you abide in me, and my words abide in you, ask whatever you will, and it shall be done for you. ⁸By this my Father is glorified, that you bear much fruit, and so prove to be my disciples. ⁹As the Father has loved me, so have I loved you; abide in my love. ¹⁰If you keep my commandments, you will abide in my love, just as I have kept my Father's commandments and abide in his love. ¹¹These things I have spoken to you, that my joy may be in you, and that your joy may be full.

12 "This is my commandment, that you love one another as I have loved you. ¹³Greater love has no man than this, that a man lay down his life for his friends. ¹⁴You are my friends if you do what I command you. ¹⁵No longer do I call you servants,[h] for the servant[i] does not know what his master is doing; but I have called you friends, for all that I have heard from my Father I have made known to you. ¹⁶You did not choose me, but I chose you and appointed you that you should go and bear fruit and that your fruit should abide; so that whatever you ask the Father in my name, he may give it to you. ¹⁷This I command you, to love one another."

THE WORLD PERSECUTES THE DISCIPLES

18 "If the world hates you, know that it has hated me before it hated you. ¹⁹If you were of the world, the world would love its own; but because you are not of the world, but I chose you out of the world, therefore the world hates you. ²⁰Remember the word that I said to you, 'A servant[i] is not greater than his master.' If they persecuted me, they will persecute you; if they kept my word, they will keep yours also. ²¹But all this they will do to you on my account, because they do not know him who sent me. ²²If I had not come and spoken to them, they would not have sin; but now they have no excuse for their sin. ²³He who hates me hates my Father also. ²⁴If I had not done among them the works which no one else did, they would not have sin; but now they have seen and hated both me and my Father. ²⁵It is to fulfil the word that is written in their law, 'They hated me without a cause.' ²⁶But when the Counselor comes, whom I

---

h Or slaves
i Or slave

shall send to you from the Father, even the Spirit of truth, who proceeds from the Father, he will bear witness to me; ²⁷and you also are witnesses, because you have been with me from the beginning."

CHAPTER 15

Creative Commentary on the Scripture

Tangible images in this chapter include those found in nature's growth cycle (vine, branches and fruit) and those in the human growth cycle (vinedresser, disciples, Father, friends, servants, master and counselor). God is viewed as the vinedresser in the opening metaphor, "I am the true vine, and my Father is the vinedresser."

Verses 1-2, 4-8 and 16-17 all carry the same group of images, figurative and literal, based on the growth cycle in the horticultural/agricultural world. The flow follows a route from the vine (Jesus) through the branches (disciples) overseen by the vinedresser (God) resulting in fruit (love).

This combination of images and dynamics of the life/growth process suggests an alternative to the traditional view of the relationship between God and the people of God. We have been taught, generally, to look skyward for God (heaven), to look at both heaven and Earth for Jesus (mediator), to look around us for humanity (made in the image of God) and beneath the Earth for those fallen from grace (Satan). The horticultural vine and vinedresser metaphor, however, suggests the dynamic process of growth begins, literally, from the ground up.

We know that all plants, crops, trees, grasses and bushes that grow on land have roots that are the source of their strength and sustenance.

Lesson 1: Instead of looking "up" to know God, we must look "down." The stem, through the process of capillary action, gains its strength and reason for being from the roots.

Lesson 2: Jesus knew enough to look in both directions for his Father. Branches, like other appendages, receive their nurture from the tree.

Lesson 3: "Apart from me you can do nothing." The vinedresser holds the power to maintain the health of the plant and sustain its life and growth.

Lesson 4: Jesus understood that God is everywhere: below, above, around us. God is wise and wishes the best for us. When this life/growth process is functioning the way it is intended, the fruits of it are love.

Lesson 5: Trust God and the life/growth process established by God. We shall then know and become part of the love of God.

The implications of the process don't stop there. Our knowledge comes from the light and the moisture. Both come from above. This adds to the images of God the Father (protector, authority, strength) and God the Provider (supplier, steward, sustainer). The heart of the life/growth process, the fruit, is the seed that contains the formula for the immeasurable, unsearchable, eternal love that unfailingly renews itself.

The "hate" passages (verses 18-27) are not tied directly to the pastoral life/growth imagery. They do, nonetheless, reflect the nature and fate of those who deny Jesus as Son of God. Their fate is like withered branches that are pruned and burned. It is worth noting, too, that though Jesus says hate fosters hate and perpetuates persecution, room is allowed for a remnant of people of good will in this often hateful world: "If they kept my word, they will keep yours also."

The entire chapter, literally and figuratively, is something of an organic gardener's prescription for the divine/human relationship established by God and nurtured in life by Jesus Christ.

Creative Bible Study Ideas

SESSION BASED ON 15:1-11

The imagery of the vineyard suggests an obvious clue to experience the teachings of Jesus in this passage. It would be ideal if you could teach this session during the time that grapes mature. Find someone who will permit you to pick from his or her grapevines.

1. Take the students to the home of the person who owns grapevines.
2. Pick the grapes from the vines.

3. Wash, sort, press, cook and strain them.
4. Prepare both grape juice and jam. Find people around the church to help if you are not experienced in this kind of cooking.
5. Read the text at several points during the project.
6. The juice can be given to the church for future communion services.
7. The jam, if produced in quantity, could be given away or sold and the money given to hunger programs.

SESSION BASED ON 15:1-4

1. Bring in a bundle of grapevines. Be sure to include old, dry ones along with the new. Find someone in your church or community who will give these to you.
2. Make a circle with your class members.
3. Spread the vines around the group so that everyone can touch them.
4. Encourage each person to pick up a leaf or a piece of vine and explore it with senses of sight, smell, touch, taste and even hearing.
5. Have them share how the vine in some way symbolizes their own lives.
6. Read the verses.
7. Ask them why the dead vines are cut away and the healthy ones are pruned. They can guess without having specific knowledge. How is the vine similar to your local church?
8. Read the verses once again.
9. Ask students to share what the promise of Christ means in terms of being able to overcome weaknesses and difficulties as a disciple.

SESSION BASED ON 15:5-10

1. Use two vine branches: one fresh vine and an old, withered and dead one.
2. Read the passage and ask how we might know whether people are with the true vine or the rejected one.
3. Have students name some people who might belong to either vine.
4. Place a bunch of grapes in the center of the group.
5. Invite each person to take a grape and look at it carefully.
6. Ask everyone to share how Jesus expects the true vine

to bear fruit. About what kind of fruit is he talking? Make a list of this fertile fruit of faith (good works, lifestyle, etc.).

7. Invite everyone to eat the grape as a sign of God's gift to him or her.

8. If you can get some kind of safe container, burn a small piece of the withered branch as an act of confession for the fruitlessness of our spiritual life. Then close with positive affirmations of faith in a circle prayer.

SESSION BASED ON 15:11-17

1. Find a simple friendship ring with vine images engraved on the band. If this isn't possible, use a Celtic cross. These old silver crosses usually have vines woven into the design.

2. Read the passage and focus on the thought that we are now friends of the Father and the Son!

3. Have each member of the group describe the best friend he or she has ever had. What made this person a friend?

4. Discuss what one expects from a friend. What does a friend have the right to expect from us?

5. Pass the ring (or the cross) around the circle.

6. Ask each person to put it on and share how the friendship of Jesus touches his or her life. Ask each person to show how he or she might be a better friend to Jesus.

7. If you have an ongoing class, you might give the ring or cross to a different person each week. Ask this person to share the following week something about friendship that happened during the week.

SESSION BASED ON 15:18-27

The contrast between the love of God and the hatred of the world is sharply etched in these verses. The conflict is described in the images of a courtroom battle. There is persecution, witnessing and a counselor or advocate.

1. Create a courtroom scene. If you have a lawyer in your congregation, be sure to utilize his or her skills.

2. Draw upon some of the earlier charges against Jesus by his opponents.

3. Give roles to members of your class (judge, jury, lawyers, witnesses for each side, etc.). Role play a trial of the charges against Jesus.

4. Discuss how the students felt playing the different

characters in the courtroom scene.

5. If this model develops and works well you might want to approach the pastor about presenting this drama of salvation to the whole church at morning worship.

SESSION BASED ON 15:12-17

Love is probably the most misused word in our cultural vocabulary. Products exploit this deep human longing by promising, frightening and teasing us in the quest for sales.
Jesus defines the meaning of love in a very special way. The gospel provides no confusion when we are told to love as he has loved us.

1. Collect popular magazines and provide one for every student.

2. Ask class members to tear out ads that reflect some views of love.

3. Share these findings and discuss the views of love represented.

4. Invite each person to list five people who have professed love to him or her.

5. Talk about these moments of love. How were they different from each other? Were there some people in your past who loved you, but never said it in so many words?

6. Name four people you have loved (outside your family).

7. Talk about the difficulties in loving someone.

8. Read the text.

9. Close by praying for those we are called to love, but have difficulty loving.

10. Ask the students to focus on a person who seems hard to love. Ask them to write notes to themselves. Each note has the hard-to-love person's name and one thing the student can do to show God's love. Pass out envelopes. Have each student seal the note in the envelope and address the envelope to himself or herself. Collect the envelopes and mail them to the students in two weeks.

Creative Speaking and Preaching Ideas

A CLUE FROM 15:1-6

In order to bring the people into this passage, have everyone stand up and form a circle around the outside walls of the worship area.

Ask them to close their eyes and imagine that they are part of the vine. Have them hold hands as you read the six verses. Then have them keep their eyes closed and move apart as far as they can without letting go of the other persons' hands. Read the section about the withered branch.

Talk about being the living vine. Now they are the withered piece that must be broken off. Can they feel the separation? Think of severed relationships: families, parents, siblings, friends, spouse.

Ask them to separate even more. Encourage them to think about the brokenness of the world (refugees, etc.). There are so many broken people in the world: the old, the handicapped, etc.

Now have them move close to each other once again. Ask them to imagine the touch of Jesus. Have them think about their own brokenness. Make them become aware of the hand they are holding. Is that person broken over something? Ask what each person feels broken about in life.

Ask everyone to move in as close as possible. Closer. Instruct participants to put their arms around each other's shoulders. Tell them that they are grafted together in the vine.

Now read verses 7-11. Close with a prayer for the gift of Christ who makes us one body.

A CLUE FROM 15:1-11

Use an actual grapevine as you build your sermon experience from this passage. Obtain a couple sections of grapevine and pass these around the congregation as you share the passage.

This would work well at a communion service. You might serve bread and grapes; give each person a grape instead of juice in cups.

A CLUE FROM 15:1-11

You may want to focus on verse 8 although this section is a single unit that defines and develops the source of love. Most Christians are curious about Jesus' demand in this passage. How do we bear fruit in order to glorify the Father? As an old teaching reminds us, our chief reason for living is "to glorify God and enjoy him forever."

The fourth Gospel is not suggesting that we can earn God's love. It calls us to be true to our legacy as disciples.

What kind of fruit have we produced as a result of our faith?

Prepare the table or altar with a large display of fruit. There should be enough grapes so that each person will have one. You will also want to have an apple for each person. Get the spiritual fruit ready by seeing that each grape is solid and polished. The apples should be polished and wrapped in foil.

Distribute the grapes as you talk the congregation through this chapter and its imagery of the true vine. When everyone has a grape, ask people to reflect on the significance of this small piece of fruit. The grape is a foretaste of the blood Jesus will surrender for the sake of our sins.

Ask the worshipers to eat the piece of fruit together as an act of dedication and thanksgiving. Have them bite at it so that they really taste the refreshment of this gift from God.

Restate the commandment of Jesus that we are called to be instruments of love and reach out to others. Give out the apples and tell the worshipers that they are to bear this piece of fruit as a means of creating more fruit. Send the community of faith (both young and old) out to the world with the task to give the apple to a stranger during the next week. The apple should be given as a symbol of the fruit given to us by the Father: "I give you this apple with the spirit of God's love."

Close by commissioning them to return next Sunday and share what happened when they went out to bear fruit in the name of Christ. This will be your sermon for the next week.

A CLUE FROM 15:12-17

The commandment to love one another is hard to celebrate in most churches. We are just too busy and often too large to feel the impact of special moments of love.

The boldness of this passage suggests that you use your sermon time to enable your folks to express the love they feel. Love notes are a good practice.

You can equip each pew rack with a pad of paper and a pencil or pen. Focus on a beloved person who has not been affirmed for a long time. Perhaps it is an absent choir director or someone in the community. Share Jesus' call to be loving to one another. Then ask the people to write a "love" note to him or her.

You can collect the notes and send or take them to the person. Or you might ask your people to exchange the notes among themselves.

One pastor was visiting in a church served by a friend. He asked all the people to write love notes to the church's full-time pastor. The visiting preacher then left them on the pastor's desk.

A CLUE FROM 15:18-27

The fourth Gospel presents the conflict between Jesus and the powers of the world in the dramatic context of a courtroom. A good way to utilize this clue is to provide an equally stunning presentation of the message.

Have a liturgical assistant take care of the opening parts of the service. When it comes to the preaching time, enter dramatically on the arms of two policemen. They may have you handcuffed!

One of them states that you are charged with being a Christian. You then undertake a dialogue in defense of your position.

Encourage people in the pews to join in, giving testimony, etc. If your people are not used to participating in this kind of dialogue with you, ask them to write comments on cards and pass them up to the front. The policemen read some of the notes. Be sure to make the point of the passage: If people will hate Jesus, they will also hate those who follow him.

There are policemen and other people in the community who will be happy to assist you in this kind of approach to your preaching. These resource people need not be members of your congregation.

You might also bring your people into the passage by a less dramatic design. Borrow handcuffs from the police department. Hold them before the congregation and explain that people are still being imprisoned for their faith.

Pass the handcuffs among the worshipers and ask them to imagine a prison cell and the persons who are persecuted for their faith. Pray for those whom the world hates because they love Jesus.

have said all this to you to keep you from falling away. ²They will put you out of the synagogues; indeed, the hour is coming when whoever kills you will think he is offering service to God. ³And they will do this because they have not known the Father, nor me. ⁴But I have said these things to you, that when their hour comes you may remember that I told you of them.

"I did not say these things to you from the beginning, because I was with you. ⁵But now I am going to him who sent me; yet none of you asks me, 'Where are you going?' ⁶But because I have said these things to you, sorrow has filled your hearts. ⁷Nevertheless I tell you the truth: it is to your advantage that I go away, for if I do not go away, the Counselor will not come to you; but if I go, I will send him to you. ⁸And when he comes, he will convince[x] the world concerning sin and righteousness and judgment: ⁹concerning sin, because they do not believe in me; ¹⁰concerning righteousness, because I go to the Father, and you will see me no more; ¹¹concerning judgment, because the ruler of this world is judged.

12 "I have yet many things to say to you, but you cannot bear them now. ¹³When the Spirit of truth comes, he will guide you into all the truth; for he will not speak on his own authority, but whatever he hears he will speak, and he will declare to you the things that are to come. ¹⁴He will glorify me, for he will take what is mine and declare it to you. ¹⁵All that the Father has is mine; therefore I said that he will take what is mine and declare it to you."

THE DISCIPLES' SORROW WILL TURN INTO JOY

16 "A little while, and you will see me no more; again a little while, and you will see me." ¹⁷Some of his disciples said to one another, "What is this that he says to us, 'A little while, and you will not see me, and again a little while, and you will see me'; and, 'because I go to the Father'?" ¹⁸They said, "What does he mean by 'a little while'? We do not know what he means." ¹⁹Jesus knew that they wanted to ask him; so he said to them, "Is this what you are asking yourselves, what I meant by saying, 'A little while, and you will not see me, and again a little while, and you will see me'? ²⁰Truly, truly, I say to you, you will weep and lament, but the world will rejoice; you will be sorrowful, but your sorrow will turn into joy. ²¹When a woman is in travail she has sorrow, because her hour has come; but when she is delivered of the child, she no longer remembers the anguish, for joy that a child[j] is born into the world. ²²So you have sorrow now, but I will see you again and your hearts will rejoice, and no one will take your joy from you. ²³In that day you will ask nothing of me. Truly, truly, I say to you, if you ask anything of the Father, he will give it to you in my name. ²⁴Hitherto you have asked nothing in my name; ask, and you

---

x Or convict

j Greek a human being

will receive, that your joy may be full.

25 "I have said this to you in figures; the hour is coming when I shall no longer speak to you in figures but tell you plainly of the Father. [26]In that day you will ask in my name; and I do not say to you that I shall pray the Father for you; [27]for the Father himself loves you, because you have loved me and have believed that I came from the Father. [28]I came from the Father and have come into the world; again, I am leaving the world and going to the Father."

29 His disciples said, "Ah, now you are speaking plainly, not in any figure! [30]Now we know that you know all things, and need none to question you; by this we believe that you came from God." [31]Jesus answered them, "Do you now believe? [32]The hour is coming, indeed it has come, when you will be scattered, every man to his home, and will leave me alone; yet I am not alone, for the Father is with me. [33]I have said this to you, that in me you may have peace. In the world you have tribulation; but be of good cheer, I have overcome the world."

CHAPTER 16

Creative Commentary on the Scripture

VERSES 1-4a: Jesus provides us with a "reality check" on the faith message. There is no cheap grace in this Gospel. The believer should be prepared to think "Why not me?" when the forces of evil attack the community of faith.

VERSES 4b-15: The Holy Spirit is promised. Jesus tries to prepare us for his departure. We are called to be expectant because the one who comes will give us even more. We do not need to worry about the Son; he will be with the Father. Our advocate will take on the sin of the world.

VERSES 16-24: The Gospel offers frustrating words for the child in each of us: "a little while." The disciples are impatient and don't understand what Jesus is saying about his death and resurrection. Several different ideas of time are offered her. There is travail, much like the birth process awaiting the Christian. Pain and suffering are natural and real. No art or faith exists without discipline and cost. Yet joy awaits those who endure.

VERSES 25-28: Jesus makes an incredible claim of prayer. He promises new possibilities of communication through him which provide a whole new realm of freedom. Everything we ask in Jesus' name will be ours. But prayer in this context is not an extension of tooth-fairy theology.

VERSES 29-33: More is revealed here about the disciples (us) than about Jesus. We try to control God by our understanding. We think that we understand—only to realize how far we are from grasping the truth. Jesus tells the disciples that hard times await them, but that he will give them peace and courage.

Creative Bible Study Ideas

SESSION BASED ON 16:1-4

Jesus' prediction that disciples will be misunderstood and persecuted is in sharp contrast to the way Christians live in the Western world. Being members of Christian churches brings at least some social status in most communities. It is no wonder that the cost of discipleship (as Jesus explained it) surprises most contemporary believers.

1. Read the passage.

2. Share a letter from a mother who is concerned that her daughter has become a religious "zealot." You may write this letter, which should list examples of the daughter's fanaticism (attending prayer meetings, talking to strangers on the streets, studying all the time, etc.). You might record the letter on an audio-cassette tape so that it can be played for the group. Of course, the "mother" is describing her daughter's membership in an ordinary church group. The daughter has simply taken her discipleship seriously. Don't make the letter too long. Have the mother end her letter with sadness and fear for her daughter.

3. Ask your students to write a letter to the mother about her worries and fears.

4. Share the letters and discuss the kind of persecution a believer may face from his or her own community.

5. Ask if anyone present has faced pressure and criticism for being a Christian. Do peers make it difficult to confess your faith?

6. Pass out a full page from your newspaper to each student.

7. Ask the class members to study the stories, ads and other items from Jesus' perspective. The culture is not Christian. If we are bearing the cross of Jesus, why aren't we in more conflict with society? Have your students circle items and apply a radical Christian interpretation to them. What would happen if we pursued the call to radical obedience in these cases? Discuss individual examples.

8. Invite each student to choose an area of life in which he or she could become more radically obedient to the will of God. It will be best if this new life pattern could be experienced each day during the next week. This will make excellent discussion material for the next session.

9. Use verse 4 as a benediction.

JOHN 16—BIBLE STUDY   235

SESSION BASED ON 16:5-15

The Holy Spirit is promised in these verses. The one who is coming will be with us when Jesus must leave.

1. Gather the group in a circle.
2. Read the passage.
3. Hold a simulation of a press conference for Jesus and the counselor. Ask someone in your group to play the role of Jesus. Invite a stranger to be the comforter. He is like a twin brother to Jesus. Your students will play the news people. They ask questions about the coming of the new "brother" and the "brother" who is leaving. Be sure that someone asks how this new coming will add something that wasn't provided before (verses 13-15 answer the question).
4. Debrief. What feelings did participants have during this experience? Was there a sadness about losing Jesus? Is it hard to think about the stranger taking his place? Who is the Father of these two brothers? How do we glorify the Father through our relationship with the offspring?

SESSION BASED ON 16:16-22

1. Read the passage.
2. Gather the group into units of four or five each.
3. Be sure that there is at least one woman in each unit who has given birth to a child.
4. Ask her to share the experience in order that the students (especially men) can understand the passage (verse 21). Did the anticipated joy of the results help make the pain of birth more bearable? Did it help to be prepared before the birth event? How is Jesus able to help the disciples by trying to prepare them for his death and resurrection?
5. Assemble the whole class and share insights and questions that arose as you dealt with Jesus' words of comfort.
6. Encourage each student to spend some time during the next week talking with others about the person they miss the most among those who have passed away. Have them explore in these interviews how comfort came to them after such a sad separation.

SESSION BASED ON 16:23-28

How do we come before God in prayer? If Jesus is our link to the Father, what happened when he was in the tomb before the resurrection?

You might prepare a series of questions about different prayer avenues to God. In other words, what are different forms of prayer (pastoral, pre-game, silent, etc.) and which is the best one. Make statements which can be marked as "agree" or "disagree."

Make this questionnaire and the responses from your students the basis for your discussion of making requests to God. You may want to explore the understanding of prayer forms held by Christians from different traditions. Close this session by taking turns leading the group in prayer by using different approaches.

SESSION BASED ON 16:29-33

Jesus gives his disciples permission to experience difficulties in their faith journey. He is honest about the pain and persecution that results from following the Son.

You might want to utilize this form by airing the confusion that is experienced, but rarely shared about living faithfully in a difficult time

1. Pass out paper and pencils and ask members of the class to list questions of faith that disturb people. What confuses the Christian in our times? For example, if God is a loving God, why does he allow innocent children to die?

2. Collect the questions and have the class deal with them as Jesus might in the fourth Gospel. Interview others with audio-cassette recorders. Simply ask a person to answer one of the questions raised by the group. Play these tapes and discuss them in class in this session or the following week.

3. Discuss verse 33 and Jesus' promise of peace and good cheer to his followers. How do we know this? How does this promise help us in time of trouble?

Creative Speaking and Preaching Ideas

A CLUE FROM 16:1-4

Jesus informs us that he knew the temptations and despair that awaited his followers. He was preparing us for the difficult times ahead. He did not want us to "fall away" because of these predictable trials.

The text suggests that you deal with people in your congregation who have fallen away. Every church seems to have lists of members who never come to worship. Why have they fallen away? Have we even missed them?

Print a Sunday morning bulletin as if it were a "membership" book. Design a cover that proclaims that it is the directory of church members. Inside you can feature a list of those who have fallen away. Also add created names and, next to them, "notes of visitation"—comments supposedly recorded by callers who visited the fallen-away people. The notes should explain reasons why some people don't attend church anymore. They could also include common criticisms about the church.

Make this presentation dialogical. Ask people to volunteer responses to the comments. Ask to be positive more than defensive. The goal is to air some good ideas for reaching out to others.

A CLUE FROM 16:5-15

1. Open the sermon experience by having someone carry in a suitcase and set it in the middle of the worship center.

2. Invite a couple of people to join you around it.

3. Tell all present that "He is going away. I wonder what we can remember about him from what he packed in his bag?" Pull out and talk about a few things that symbolize, in some way, Jesus' ministry (sandals, bread, stone, etc.). Let the other couple of people and maybe some others in the congregation make these suggestions.

4. Summarize how you feel about Jesus and how you are going to miss him.

5. Have another suitcase carried in as the other is carried out.

6. This is the bag of the counselor. Jesus kept his promise to send the counselor.

7. Go through the same process of unpacking a few symbolic things that reflect the gift he brings us.

8. You might want to unpack the wine (juice) and put it with the bread from the other bag as the elements for communion.

9. Then celebrate the Lord's Supper as a way of experiencing our relationship with Father, Son and Holy Spirit.

A CLUE FROM 16:16-22

1. Create a collage of news headlines. Get some young

people and others to help you. Imagine how much more the worship will mean to young people if they are encouraged to become real partners with you in the speaking or preaching opportunity. Meet for a couple hours and utilize their insights and skills. Go through all kinds of magazines and newspapers. Look for words and phrases that suggest confusion about what is happening to our world in transition. Try to compress these bits and pieces into a collage that will cover both of the inside pages of the Sunday bulletin. You should be able to include 50-80 items. It might be possible to use one of those photocopiers that can reduce print down to another size.

2. When you come to the sermon time, play an audio montage of confusing sounds and voices on a cassette tape created by your support group. Keep the level low.

3. Mention the fact that these are confusing times.

4. Invite people to share some bits and pieces from this world that make things difficult to understand. Point out the collages in their bulletins. Encourage them to let their eyes wander over all the items. They will pick out those things that already disturb them.

5. Stop the sound and ask for silence.

6. After a calm has settled, share the message of Jesus from this passage. He tells us that we won't understand, but the comforter or counselor will come to help us.

7. If your congregation is comfortable with participatory worship, encourage them to make paper airplanes from their bulletins. The people can move around and help others with the task.

8. As a final act of commitment, ask them to sail the planes into the air. Read the passage in the chapter about the Holy Spirit coming. Or sing a hymn about this Good News while the planes sail. Encourage people to pick up landed planes of others and sail them again.

A CLUE FROM 16:23-28

This section of the fourth Gospel offers an important discussion on prayer. Utilize the suggestion from the passage to carry the worshipers through different avenues of prayer.

Focus on one particular prayer concern: for peace, for the unemployed, for the hungry, for the ill, etc. While preparing your service, contact different people in the congregation;

ask them to name their most helpful modes of prayer. Just the fact that you've had input from 20 to 30 people will liven the message. Use the phone for your discussion. Pastors often overlook the importance of the telephone. Properly utilized, the phone can expand the outreach of a pastor by 30 or 40 percent.

Gather a list of 10 or 15 different ways to approach prayer for the chosen concern. Search through your collection of prayer books and the Bible for examples.

The key to bringing your people into this passage is being experiential. Do the prayers with them! Prayer is too vital to simply mumble through clever words. For example, you might work through gestures for each prayer avenue (facing different directions, standing or sitting, hands up, hands folded, hands clapping, eyes open or eyes closed, arms in front, arms over head, arms folded, arms down at sides, feet on floor, feet stomping, body swaying, body erect, body bent forward). What does the content suggest about the form? This is the most important factor guiding your choice of prayer.

You might label the whole service: A Special Service. Explore what you can do with your own voice. What and how do people hear? We have assumed that written words can be heard and followed in public worship. But is this the best way to capture the whole person? You might explore the use of stream-of-conciousness thought that Jesus uses in this passage. God understands when minds stray from the voice of the worship leader. How do we help people to utilize the distraction of personal needs and thoughts as moments of encounter with the Good News?

A CLUE FROM 16:29-33

What a blessing we have in these verses! Jesus acknowledges the hard times we will have and at the same time affirms that "good cheer" can be ours! This is the tough faith we are called to bear. There are no simple answers, but there is still peace in Christ.

The focus on faith-challenging tribulations or suffering cuts very close to every person's experience. You might develop this sermon out of your time for prayers and concerns. If you do not have a time when people get up and share these vital moments during the worship service, simply ask people to write out the most pressing tribulation facing them. Don't ask for names. Have the ushers collect these slips of paper.

Share the passage once again. Amplify the hope it proclaims to people in hard times. Invite the congregation to work with you as the Word of God is heard. Read the note on a slip of paper and ask the worshipers what Jesus is saying to this person. This process may sound frightening or impossible; I hope you don't think that such a participatory sermon won't work because your people are not capable of making contributions. God is working in the lives of your people. Trust God and his love through other believers.

If you are worried about a lack of response from your people, alert a few of them before the worship service. Ask them to contribute ideas when the opportunity is present.

You may hear words that don't express your exact thoughts. Please be patient and let the Holy Spirit work within this community. You will find that another comment will be added by another person that will balance the situation.

After several concerns have been addressed, ask the community of faith to do something about the situation. Where do we go from here? Perhaps someone will suggest prayer in small groups right there. Don't rescue your people (or yourself) by stepping in with all the answers.

This passage suggests that Jesus knew our weaknesses and failures but that he really trusted those who would follow. We cannot do less in our preaching.

End with the incredible peace and hope that Jesus has paid to give us. Move into a litany. After a concern is read, have the congregation say: "Be of good cheer!" A sensitive musician could work on song responses for you. Perhaps clapping and other natural responses by the people can be incorporated into this sermon.

CHAPTER 17

JESUS' PRAYER FOR HIMSELF

When Jesus had spoken these words, he lifted up his eyes to heaven and said, "Father, the hour has come; glorify thy Son that the Son may glorify thee, ²since thou hast given him power over all flesh, to give eternal life to all whom thou hast given him. ³And this is eternal life, that they know thee the only true God, and Jesus Christ whom thou hast sent. ⁴I glorified thee on earth, having accomplished the work which thou gavest me to do; ⁵and now, Father, glorify thou me in thy own presence with the glory which I had with thee before the world was made."

JESUS' PRAYER FOR HIS DISCIPLES

6 "I have manifested thy name to the men whom thou gavest me out of the world; thine they were, and thou gavest them to me, and they have kept thy word. ⁷Now they know that everything that thou hast given me is from thee; ⁸for I have given them the words which thou gavest me, and they have received them and know in truth that I came from thee; and they have believed that thou didst send me. ⁹I am praying for them; I am not praying for the world but for those whom thou hast given me, for they are thine; ¹⁰all mine are thine, and thine are mine, and I am glorified in them. ¹¹And now I am no more in the world, but they are in the world, and I am coming to thee. Holy Father, keep them in thy name, which thou hast given me, that they may be one, even as we are one. ¹²While I was with them, I kept them in thy name, which thou hast given me; I have guarded them, and none of them is lost but the son of perdition, that the scripture might be fulfilled. ¹³But now I am coming to thee; and these things I speak in the world, that they may have my joy fulfilled in themselves. ¹⁴I have given them thy word; and the world has hated them because they are not of the world, even as I am not of the world. ¹⁵I do not pray that thou shouldst take them out of the world, but that thou shouldst keep them from the evil one.ᵏ ¹⁶They are not of the world, even as I am not of the world. ¹⁷Sanctify them in the truth; thy word is truth. ¹⁸As thou didst send me into the world, so I have sent them into the world. ¹⁹And for their sake I consecrate myself, that they also may be consecrated in truth."

JESUS' PRAYER FOR THE CHURCH

20 "I do not pray for these only, but also for those who believe in me through their word, ²¹that they may all be one; even as thou, Father, art in me, and I in thee, that they also may be in us, so that the world may believe that thou hast sent me. ²²The glory which thou hast given me I have given to them, that they may be one even as we are one, ²³I in them and thou in me, that they may become perfectly one, so that the world may know that thou hast sent me and hast loved them even as thou hast loved me. ²⁴Father, I desire that they also, whom thou hast given me, may be with me where I am, to

---

k Or *from evil*

behold my glory which thou hast given me in thy love for me before the foundation of the world. ²⁵O righteous Father, the world has not known thee, but I have known thee; and these know that thou hast sent me. ²⁶I made known to them thy name, and I will make it known, that the love with which thou hast loved me may be in them, and I in them."

CHAPTER 17

Creative Commentary on the Scripture

VERSES 1-5: Jesus did not glorify the Father on Earth with pomp, tanks or marching armies. What does this indicate about the theological meaning of glory? Jesus reveals God's will to us through his style of life, his deeds, his relationships and his modesty. We tend to be clever and pompous in our use of elitist language for the experience of Christ. But the scripture is known through "common" Greek, used in daily life in the ancient world.

How do we know God? What skills should be honed for this encounter? Perhaps Jesus is saying that the Word of God comes to us through his prayer. The concept of glory can best be understood by perceiving Jesus' life on this planet. His life tells us something quite important about creation. His life also tells us a great deal about the kingdom of God that we'll know after passing through the door of death.

VERSES 6-8: Jesus gives us over to someone else. He surrenders us in order that we may have more life. How hard it must have be for Jesus to give up those who have been his. He also calls us into a position of response. We must choose to accept his kinship.

The author challenges us to keep God's words. Jesus reports our faithfulness to the Father. Jesus believes in us!

Jesus prays for the people. He does not focus on the world's institutions, customs, ways and other systems.

Jesus does not condemn us for still being in the world. We need prayers because we are here. The world will not make it easy for us to maintain our faith. The world encourages us to separate, alienate and push apart from the unity of the Son, the Father and the faith community.

VERSES 9-19: The role of scripture suddenly becomes important to those who live out the reality of this prayer.

Jesus is coming to the Father. Yet he and the Father are one. This paradox is noteworthy. We are called to face the spacial and relational possibilities of this relationship. The author forces us to stretch our thinking about the faith. We are also faced with the difference between time and eternity.

Because of the life, ministry, death and resurrection of Jesus, we have joy. What is this joy like? What experience with Jesus must we have to live joy-filled lives? The results of living with the Word and not being of the world leads to being hated by the world. The cost of this oneness with Jesus leads to joy even when we must suffer for it.

The Word that brought creation into being, which became flesh and dwelt among us, is truth. This truth frees us for what? from what? We are called to experience a new kind of freedom.

VERSES 20-23: Jesus now directs his prayer to those who will come after the disciples. He prays across centuries, past national boundaries and beyond our narrow theological games. We can be one with Jesus and with each other as the Father and Jesus are one. We are distinct from each other, but one! What is our unity, and how must we express it? This question raises an important challenge for all Christians. Unity in Christ seems impossible without some sort of organic structure of the church. Without a united church, how can the world believe in the unity of Jesus and the Father? Yet our fractured structures seem to have taken the Lord's name in vain.

We have seen how God loved Jesus. Often it is hard to realize that God loves us exactly the same way. It changes our lives to experience our Creator's love. We seem to want it both ways: We want to be loved by God, but we shy away from loving our neighbor.

VERSES 24-26: If Jesus has his way, we will be with him to see his glory. It is hard to accept this gift if his glory comes in a nonglorious manner to us.

His name and his love, if not synonymous, are parallel to each other. God, known through a specific person named Jesus, has a particular character, a specific identity. We are called to show how the love of God makes a difference in the way we live, perform our jobs and raise our families.

The prepositions for love ("in me," "in you" and "in us

all") can make a difference in our lives. The cost of discipleship is clearly spelled out. There is no room for cheap and easy grace.

Creative Bible Study Ideas

SESSION BASED ON 17:1-5

How did Jesus glorify God on Earth? How did the Father glorify Jesus?

1. Pick out four or five different popular figures or causes (for example, sports figures, issues in industry, national concerns, etc.) familiar to your students.

2. Collect materials about these figures or causes from magazines, newspapers, etc.

3. Form triads from the class.

4. Ask each group to develop an ultimate media campaign through which their famous person or cause could be honored and glorified before the world. What kinds of praise could your glory program create?

5. Gather and share the conclusions.

6. Read verses 1-5.

7. Contrast the way we glorify important people with how Jesus was glorified by the Father. How does Jesus' glorification help us live our lives to the glory of God?

SESSION BASED ON 17:1-5

1. Ask each person to create a power map on a piece of paper: Each student draws a circle in the middle of the sheet, and lines from the circle to the edges of the sheet. The lines signify the arms of power that act upon the student. These strings of power are to be labeled. For example, one arm could be labeled "boss," another "parents," etc.

2. Work alone on these power maps. Then form dyads and share each other's maps.

3. Share the maps with the whole group. You may want to encourage students to copy their maps on the blackboard or display their actual maps if they were created on a large piece of newsprint.

4. Compare these sources of power with those that had power 50 years ago. Mark power sources that will still have power 50 years from now.

5. Read verses 1-5.

248 THE BIBLE CREATIVE

6. Discuss the power sources that affected Jesus. Perhaps the whole group can create a power map of his life.

7. Explore the kind of powers he exercised. How do they compare to the power forces in our lives?

8. Ask the students to become free of one of the negative power influences in their lives. Have them describe their struggles for freedom at the next session.

SESSION BASED ON 17:6-8

This section of the text includes Jesus' prayer about the foundation of the community. The people of God are those given by the Father to the Son.

This sense of being chosen for membership in the body of faith suggests that we give our people a chance to explore their kinship. You might come into the room shortly after the starting time for the class. Announce that everyone who is a member of such and such a class should go to another room. Or you might ask each person as they come into the room, "Are you a Christian and a member of this class?"

When everyone is gathered and checked in, tell them that they are people who belong to Jesus. How in the world have they come to be in this same faith family? Spend time helping them work out the common factors of their kinship.

Divide into small groups and create a coat of arms that illustrates their common beliefs, actions, values, etc.

Share these symbols of oneness with the whole group. Make one collective coat of arms for the whole class on a large piece of newsprint.

How much of our life together is based on the action of God and how much of it is based on our initiative? What about those who don't follow Christ? Have they chosen not to respond or has God not beckoned them? What does this say about evangelism?

SESSION BASED ON 17:9-19

Jesus prays in this section for the blessing of the kinship of the faith. He is speaking to the Father and talks about joining him soon. How is Jesus one with the Father but apart from him?

1. Read the text.

2. Explore this paradox by having one person play the role of God the Father and another person play the role of God the Son.

3. Ask them to show the relationship spatially (join hands, etc.).

4. Encourage them to express the relationship as Father and Son.

5. Repeat the two roles in terms of time (eternity and human time).

These are difficult tasks. Rotate different students into the process. You might let them suggest different ways to look at the relationship between the Father and the Son. You can run the whole process over again in terms of how they are different from one another.

6. Read the passage.

7. Have the students, one at a time, stand in front of a full-length mirror. Ask them to describe their relationship to God in spatial, personal and chronological terms.

8. Ask the group to share how this experience relates to the relationship between the Father and the Son.

SESSION BASED ON 17:20-23

1. Distribute pieces of string, pebbles or some other material to the students. The items should be in different colors and should be large enough and strong enough to be used in different ways.

2. Read the passage.

3. Ask each person to reflect on how his or her materials in some way symbolize an aspect of God's truth.

4. Share these ideas with the whole group.

5. Ask them to compare their Christian tradition to other Christian traditions.

6. Discuss the concept of this passage: unity in diversity.

7. Close by using the materials to create a floor design that says something about the oneness we have in Jesus Christ. Encourage students to mesh the differently colored materials into the final design. You will be amazed at the beauty of this floor design.

8. Form a circle and pray for unity in Christ. If you have met in a room that could host a coffee hour or some other meeting, invite the whole church to see the session's creation.

SESSION BASED ON 17:24-26

1. Ask the students to bring information about their names and family trees.

2. Write each person's name on the board as he or she shares background material on it, particularly information about people who carried the name in the past.

3. Look at the use of names in the Bible. God's name is very important (Exodus 3:14).

4. Read the text.

5. Discuss what Jesus' ministry revealed about God the Father.

6. Have the students create something that illustrates how their names can show they are instruments of God. For example, acrostics could be made. Take the name "Dennis": D—Doing creative work for God; E—Energetic; N—Now is the time for creative ministry; N—Never take local people for granted; I—If I'm indeed a new creation, I owe God my best; S—So be it! Share these names.

Creative Speaking and Preaching Ideas

A CLUE FROM 17:1-8

Knowing God has always been a blessing and curse for seekers of truth. In this text Jesus reports that we as his people know the only true God. What difference does this knowledge make in our contemporary life? How do we see God more clearly and know him more nearly?

Your sermon can explore these important questions about the quality and validity of the Christian faith in our time. Introduce the questions by wandering into the worship center with a symbol of Jesus' life. Perhaps you are holding a piece of cloth that represents his robe.

Lead the congregation through some of the options for "knowing the only true God." Suggest areas of seeking (listening to the witness of others, paraphrasing, giving and receiving, praying, studying the Bible, etc.). You might have a dialogue with the congregation as you explore each area. What can we say about God from a particular line of inquiry?

What does the passage mean that such knowledge is eternal life? Again, use the robe (and other objects) to help people focus on this question.

A CLUE FROM 17:9-19

Jesus prays for his people, not the institutions and structures of the world. We are not judged for being in the sphere of the world. We are called to live in the Word while living in the world.

Tape a brief section of the morning's news from the radio. It is easy to play cassette tapes over the sound systems used in most places of worship. Don't record more than two to four minutes of the news. Be sure that the newscast covers five or six different areas of concern.

Read the text and play the tape. Ask your people to close their eyes and absorb the world's feelings as they listen to the cries of this age.

Ask each section (rows or areas divided by aisles) to focus on a particular concern. Encourage your people to write down several ways that Christians can show their faith.

Spend a couple minutes talking about the prayer of Jesus in this text. Instead of our being trapped in despair and wanting to escape the world, Jesus releases us to be the truth.

Encourage people from each section to share some stories from their lives that illustrate the joy of Christ.

A CLUE FROM 17:20-23

Our unity as the family of God is affirmed in this moving text. Jesus has come that we might know the unity of the Son, the Father and those who believe. The reality of the fractured world (and church) offers an excellent preaching opportunity. We love our traditions more than Jesus.

As people come into the worship area, give out individual sheets of paper. Each one bears one of these labels: Presbyterian, Methodist, Lutheran, Catholic, Orthodox, Baptist, etc. The label is followed by a short paragraph that lifts up that tradition's major focus.

At the time of the sermon, ask people to move into designated areas that match the label on their sheets. The ushers can help people move to these new areas.

Each section is to brainstorm what its members know of the tradition. Then each group chooses a spokesperson to present their findings. Affirm all the points made by these denominational groups. But note with sadness the universal church's fragmentation and the world's continued suffering. We are weak in our ministry because of our separation.

Lead prayers of confession for the body of Christ. Read this text and note the price paid by Christ that we may be one.

Close with a prayer of a uniting faith. This might be an excellent moment for the Lord's Supper if your tradition celebrates Worldwide Communion Sunday. Use different kinds of homemade bread. It will be easy to note the reality of the church's diversity and the hope for its eventual unity.

A CLUE FROM 17:24-26

Jesus prays for the believers who will come later. He suggests that the Father's love is in us as he himself will be in us.

Explore this clue. Draw your people into the text by finding an image that helps them experience this love.

Have the ushers pass around (via collection plates) nuts in their shells to each worshiper. Use the nuts for each part of the service. For instance, in the prayers the nut can be used differently for confession ("What sins hide within you at this moment?"), pardon ("Give your nut to someone else as you cast your sins upon the Lord"), intercession ("How does the roughness of the shell represent the needs others have for God's special care and love?"), thanksgiving ("Find the beauty in this simple nut and focus on the gifts that God has given you") and petition ("Like the nut meat inside the shell, what gifts from God will meet your personal needs?").

At your sermon time, focus again on the nuts. Read the text and ask people to share how this simple item tells us something about the latter part of verse 26. You will be amazed how sensitive your people are to God's Word.

At some point, have them break open the shells to experience the merging of the nut with their lives. It will be in us as it was once in the shell. Don't worry about instruments for breaking the nuts. Even the harder ones can be broken by crushing two of them together. It is fitting that the people work together just as Christ and the Father work together.

They can eat the nuts to symbolize God's love in them. Then have the ushers pass the collection plates for the shells. This act can symbolize God taking away our sins, freeing us to be new creations.

CHAPTER 18

JESUS ARRESTED BY NIGHT

When Jesus had spoken these words, he went forth with his disciples across the Kidron valley, where there was a garden, which he and his disciples entered. ²Now Judas, who betrayed him, also knew the place; for Jesus often met there with his disciples. ³So Judas, procuring a band of soldiers and some officers from the chief priests and the Pharisees, went there with lanterns and torches and weapons. ⁴Then Jesus, knowing all that was to befall him, came forward and said to them, "Whom do you seek?" ⁵They answered him, "Jesus of Nazareth." Jesus said to them, "I am he." Judas, who betrayed him, was standing with them. ⁶When he said to them, "I am he," they drew back and fell to the ground. ⁷Again he asked them, "Whom do you seek?" And they said, "Jesus of Nazareth." ⁸Jesus answered, "I told you that I am he; so, if you seek me, let these men go." ⁹This was to fulfil the word which he had spoken, "Of those whom thou gavest me I lost not one." ¹⁰Then Simon Peter, having a sword, drew it and struck the high priest's slave and cut off his right ear. The slave's name was Malchus. ¹¹Jesus said to Peter, "Put your sword into its sheath; shall I not drink the cup which the Father has given me?"

12 So the band of soldiers and their captain and the officers of the Jews seized Jesus and bound him. ¹³First they led him to Annas; for he was the father-in-law of Ca′iaphas, who was high priest that year. ¹⁴It was Ca′iaphas who had given counsel to the Jews that it was expedient that one man should die for the people.

PETER'S FIRST DENIAL

15 Simon Peter followed Jesus, and so did another disciple. As this disciple was known to the high priest, he entered the court of the high priest along with Jesus, ¹⁶while Peter stood outside at the door. So the other disciple, who was known to the high priest, went out and spoke to the maid who kept the door, and brought Peter in. ¹⁷The maid who kept the door said to Peter, "Are not you also one of this man's disciples?" He said, "I am not." ¹⁸Now the servants[1] and officers had made a charcoal fire, because it was cold, and they were standing and warming themselves; Peter also was with them, standing and warming himself.

THE HIGH PRIEST QUESTIONS JESUS

19 The high priest then questioned Jesus about his disciples and his teaching. ²⁰Jesus answered him, "I have spoken openly to the world; I have always taught in synagogues and in the temple, where all Jews come together; I have said nothing secretly. ²¹Why do you ask me? Ask those who have heard me, what I said to them; they know what I said." ²²When he had said this, one of the officers standing by struck Jesus with his hand, saying, "Is that how you answer the high priest?" ²³Jesus answered him, "If I have

---

1 Or slaves

spoken wrongly, bear witness to the wrong; but if I have spoken rightly, why do you strike me?" ²⁴Annas then sent him bound to Ca′iaphas the high priest.

PETER'S SECOND AND THIRD DENIALS

25 Now Simon Peter was standing and warming himself. They said to him, "Are not you also one of his disciples?" He denied it and said, "I am not." ²⁶One of the servants � of the high priest, a kinsman of the man whose ear Peter had cut off, asked, "Did I not see you in the garden with him?" ²⁷Peter again denied it; and at once the cock crowed.

JESUS FACES PILATE

28 Then they led Jesus from the house of Ca′iaphas to the praetorium. It was early. They themselves did not enter the praetorium, so that they might not be defiled, but might eat the passover. ²⁹So Pilate went out to them and said, "What accusation do you bring against this man?" ³⁰They answered him, "If this man were not an evildoer, we would not have handed him over." ³¹Pilate said to them, "Take him yourselves and judge him by your own law." The Jews said to him, "It is not lawful for us to put any man to death." ³²This was to fulfil the word which Jesus had spoken to show by what death he was to die.

33 Pilate entered the praetorium again and called Jesus, and said to him, "Are you the King of the Jews?" ³⁴Jesus answered, "Do you say this of your own accord, or did others say it to you about me?" ³⁵Pilate answered, "Am I a Jew? Your own nation and the chief priests have handed you over to me; what have you done?" ³⁶Jesus answered, "My kingship is not of this world; if my kingship were of this world, my servants would fight, that I might not be handed over to the Jews; but my kingship is not from the world." ³⁷Pilate said to him, "So you are a king?" Jesus answered, "You say that I am a king. For this I was born, and for this I have come into the world, to bear witness to the truth. Every one who is of the truth hears my voice." ³⁸Pilate said to him, "What is truth?"

After he had said this, he went out to the Jews again, and told them, "I find no crime in him. ³⁹But you have a custom that I should release one man for you at the Passover; will you have me release for you the King of the Jews?" ⁴⁰They cried out again, "Not this man, but Barab′bas!" Now Barab′bas was a robber.

CHAPTER 18

Creative Commentary on the Scripture

VERSES 1-11: Jesus' arrest takes place in a garden. It is the site of betrayal and sin. Is there the shadow of the Garden of Eden in this passage? Is it significant that Jesus as goodness and righteousness returns to the garden, where humanity originally fell into sin?

Judas and the guards come for Jesus. We are told that Jesus "knows" all that will come to pass. How does he have this knowledge? Some people in the early church exaggerated cases like this one and considered Jesus a "gnostic" god who simply resided in a human body. Later in this chapter (verses 19-23), Jesus underscores the fact that he spoke in an open manner and did not secretly carry on his ministry. There are no secrets about the gospel.

Impulsive Peter turns to violence to protect Jesus. He attacks a slave. We are given particulars, such as his name and which ear is damaged. Why are these details important to the sweep of this ageless message?

This is an excellent place to note the difference between the gnostic view and that of the fourth Gospel concerning the person of Jesus Christ. As we have noted, a strong movement against the early Christian church was gnosticism. This word for knowledge is used to label a diverse group of people.

Some scholars place the gnostic movement before the Christian experience. They point to religious forms that embrace the concept of escaping material existence for a heavenly or other-worldly level of special knowledge. Some people claim that the presentation of Christ is strongly influenced by this viewpoint. Indeed, a gnostic-redeemer myth is suggested as the basis for many aspects of the biblical picture of Jesus. But there is very scant documentation to support Jesus' being a gnostic.

There is no doubt that a strong counter-canon arose in Christianity's first five centuries. The church fathers use a great deal of space in the Bible protecting the canonical view of Jesus Christ.

It is understandable how the church struggled with the tension between the Son of God who is both fully human and fully God. In our own day, some believers seem to want only one aspect of their Lord. Indeed, the disciples were often torn in this tension. Do they want to stay in the moment of transfiguration or do they want the Lord who can be touched and loved? John provides the language and image forms that seem to draw the reader into "higher" and more imaginative understandings of God's love. Yet, John clearly portrays a Lord who is fully human and who must suffer for our sins. The book's "middle-of-the-road" stand explains why it was alternately blessed and cursed. Those who focus on theological extremes can't stand John's wholistic presentation of Jesus.

These verses offer precious information about Jesus' arrest. We do not experience the arrest on a mystical level. It's all too real and unjust. The author has added bits and pieces of reality that prepare us for the final drama of Jesus' passion.

VERSES 12-18: Jesus is taken to Annas. Caiaphas decides that it is more practical for Jesus to die than to upset the Roman establishment. Note the irony of Caiaphas' motive in verse 14. The high priest's counsel was fulfilled in a larger way than he could have imagined. It is easy to judge the politics of the legal forces in the story. But there were things they had to consider. The opponents of Jesus wanted him to be judged on a political charge instead of a religious disagreement.

Who is this mysterious disciple that goes with Peter? He is important. Does this indicate the popularity and spread of the Christian movement? The maid either knows that the stranger is a Christian ("also") or she recognizes Peter as a follower of Jesus. Peter denies Christ and sets the pattern for two later denials (verses 25-27).

VERSES 19-38a: The religious people take care not to defile themselves by not entering the praetorium. Yet they participate in the sinful act of condemning an innocent person.

The religious and civil authorities bounce Jesus back and forth. No one wants to be responsible for Jesus. The religious establishment fears the Roman authorities while Pilate diplomatically states a concern for the religious law. There is tension between an absolute morality and relative morality.

Pilate and Jesus have a misdirected dialogue, so frequent in the fourth Gospel. The Roman official simply doesn't realize what is happening before him. Note the situational irony of Pilate's question, "What is truth?" Pilate has no idea that Ultimate Truth stands right before him.

VERSES 38b-40: Pilate suggests the opponents of Jesus release him in accordance with a Passover custom. Instead, the crowd chooses to release Barabbas, a robber.

Creative Bible Study Ideas

SESSION BASED ON 18:1-11

The Son of God is delivered into the hands of his enemies. Does this garden setting remind us of the Garden of Eden? Jesus is returning to "the garden." What does that suggest?

Ask your students to close their eyes. Provide a guided journey into this passage. You might use a nature sound-effects record to provide the aural awareness of the outdoors (birds, insects, stream, wind, etc.) as you lead them across the rocky soil into a place of olive trees. Suggest the things they should "experience" in their imagination.

"Your sandaled feet feel the earth beneath you. Smell the Palestinian evening." Each person will fill in the sensual and mental picture in his or her own way. Take your time leading them into this passage.

Now describe the characters coming into the scene. You have Jesus, disciples, Peter, Judas, soldiers and a slave named Malchus. Place each of them at a different spot in the garden. Try to nudge your students into the minds of these characters.

Present the action for the scene. This can be done by reading the text. Ask each person to imagine playing a particular role in the story.

Come out of the imaginary journey into the Bible. Ask students to share how they felt about the dynamics of Jesus' arrest. Why did the different characters respond the ways they did? What puzzled or disturbed them the most?

Spend time with each of the characters in the story. The student who focused on that person can tell how he or she felt. Read the story again. Close by using a cup. Put juice in it and pass it around the group, but suggest that no one drinks from the cup. They should look at it, but let it pass by. Have everyone pray for the strength to drink from the cup of Jesus in our daily lives.

Someone in the group may want to share a problem or burden in his or her life. You will need to determine the group's level of Christian love. If your people are free to share, this can be a moving and healing time. Ask the members of the group to pray during the coming week for those who expressed burdens. The prayer can be offered each time they take a drink from a cup or glass. At the next session, the class members can talk about the trials of the previous week. Did knowing you were being prayed for make a difference? What was it like to support others by prayer? Did the communion cup take on a different meaning when you were reaching out to others?

SESSION BASED ON 18:4-11

1. Create several brief scenes capturing typical confrontational moments in the family, at work, in school, with loved ones, in a store, etc. Be sure that the conflict creates distance and tension between people.

2. Have the students act them out quickly. Be sure that everyone gets a chance to do these short role plays.

3. Discuss the role plays. Did they seem natural and typical? Was it easy or hard to directly and honestly face conflict? How do these moments compare with the clean, crisp, direct exchange that Jesus initiates?

4. Read the text.

5. Pass around a short sword or knife and ask each person to compare the actions of Jesus with those of Peter.

6. Ask them to share how Jesus guides Peter's behavior in this text. Would it be hard for them to do? What does Jesus' model contribute to our interactions with others?

7. Ask each person to focus on the teaching of this passage every time he or she uses a knife at work, home or school.

SESSION BASED ON 18:12-24

1. Create a list of forced choices between two undesirable alternatives.
2. Give copies to each student.
3. Ask each to make a decision about these difficult choices.
4. Read the text. Focus on verse 14.
5. Present the concept that Jesus applied an absolute morality concerning right and wrong while Caiaphas functioned under a sense of relative morals.
6. Ask students to go over the decisions they made in #3 and determine what kind of morality or ethical system they utilize.
7. Dig into verse 14. Is it true? What are possible meanings of the text (Jesus must die to give to others; a scapegoat is an easy way out of a political situation)? Can a decision have two different results for different reasons?

This discussion can easily enter into the lives of your students. There are many contemporary decisions that are complex and difficult. The church has been guilty of trying to provide easy answers to confusing questions. Don't feel that you have to neatly wrap up this discussion. The people in the garden would spend their lives struggling over how to be faithful to the Word in such moments. We cannot ask our students to do more than the text itself demands.

You might continue this lesson by looking again at the text in the next session. No biblical passage can be considered finished or completed. You might even live with one text throughout a six-week study session. The more deeply you crawl into the text, the more relevant it will be to your people and the more deeply it will speak to you!

SESSION BASED ON 18:15-18; 18:25-27

1. Create a campfire setting. If you study this passage in a cold season, give a candle to each person in the class. These candles will warm their hands. Hold the class in a dark room so that you can explore the environment of the passage. Peter is drawn to the fire and light while he turns his back on the Son of light.
2. Divide the class into three sections.
3. Read the first part of the text.
4. Assign a character in this story to each group: Peter,

the mysterious disciple, and the maid.

5. Have groups create profiles on their characters, using the text as the source of clues. Who was the mysterious disciple? What does this say about the spread of Jesus' teachings? Before they return with their results, have each group create a symbol that expresses as much as possible about the personalities of these persons. They can use newsprint and markers to draw this design.

6. Have each group present its character in a role play. The character could explain his or her feelings in a conversation with Jesus. Have someone play the role of Jesus.

7. You might want to share the session's creations with the whole church in worship.

SESSION BASED ON 18:19-24

1. Read the text.
2. Gather in a circle.
3. Play the telephone game. It is played like this: Whisper a two-sentence message to the person next to you. Then ask him or her to repeat it in the ear of the next person.
4. When the message has passed around the circle, ask the last person to repeat the message aloud. Then tell him or her the original statement.
5. Discuss the change in the message. How and why did it change?
6. Diagram the communication process: message ▶ receiver ▶ message ▶ receiver. At each point of receiving and sending, there is the possibility for transformation of the message.
7. Discuss how the Word underwent this process. Is it important to know the person who transmits the message in order to understand the message fully? What happens when we get the Good News from different media (means of communication)? Is Christianity's message different when it comes to us through television and records? Does this problem explain why God sent the Holy Spirit to us?
8. Play the telephone game once again. Start a comment about the last person in the circle.
9. When the comment arrives at the last person in the circle, stop the process.
10. Ask for the last statement of the comment to be spoken aloud.
11. Read the passage again.

12. Discuss whether the last person in the circle would want to be judged by the gossip of others. How can this be dangerous?

13. Ask students to intentionally work on the problem of gossip during the next week. Encourage them to stop the flow of gossip at school or work until the group meets again. What happens when the grapevine is stilled?

SESSION BASED ON 18:28-40

1. Bring a tasty-looking cake, a knife and plates to the class.

2. Read the passage.

3. Tell them about this delicious cake. Describe the ingredients and how good it will taste. Also mention that the person who cuts the cake cannot eat it. Who wants to cut it?

4. Ask them to compare how this situation is like that which the opponents of Jesus faced. (Everyone wanted Jesus dead but nobody wanted to be responsible for his death.)

5. Reflect together on the question of moral responsibility and guilt by distance. Is passing the buck really a way out of responsibility? The religious people claim they worry about Roman law while the Romans claim concern about the law of the Sanhedrin.

6. Have group members solve the cake-cutting problem. Make this treat a love feast in which everyone shares responsibility for making decisions.

Creative Speaking and Preaching Ideas

A CLUE FROM 18:1-11

The text dramatically tells the story of Jesus' arrest by the authorities. All sorts of characters are seen against the backdrop of his capture. This clue into the Son of God's impending passion is rich with possibilities for preaching.

Any of the characters could provide a first-person account of the scene in the sermon or homily: soldiers, Judas, Peter, Jesus and Malchus. Malchus might offer a particularly fresh perspective. His Semitic name was common among portions of the Arab community and means "king."

You might use a sword or dagger in your presentation. Perhaps the story could be told from the perspective of the dagger. This projection-monologue technique is an excellent way to enter into the passage.

John doesn't describe the healing of the slave as recorded in Luke. But you can safely assume the healing if you plan to use the first-person monologue approach. A slave who is called "king" is attacked by Peter but healed by the King of Kings. The King is willing to die for a slave. This story has the makings for a very rich presentation.

Don't be intimidated by this kind of presentation. Most preachers have never utilized this simplest of sermon forms. The model is not based on your acting ability. You simply step into the biblical character in order to give your listeners a chance to view the biblical message from the inside out.

You might carry a piece of cloth that has the markings of blood (poster paint). Wave it when you talk about the attack.

This model and most of the other suggestions for preaching in this series assume that the preacher is willing to present the Word in a skin-close relationship to his or her material. One can't use notes in this kind of living-scripture speaking and preaching.

A CLUE FROM 18:15-18; 18:25-27

Peter's denial of Jesus is our story. These passages are a fine opportunity to relate our experiences to the biblical story. The charcoal fire is the focal point for this betrayal. Peter seeks warmth while leaving Jesus out in the cold.

You might place the remains of a charcoal fire at the center of the worship area. Set the scene of the campfire. Tell how people are drawn to the source of light and warmth. You might wonder aloud about the stories the campfire would tell if it could speak.

A series of people should then come into the area and report how they were drawn to the fire for strength. These short scenes can run just a minute or so:

- A Nazi soldier: "I am a member of the German State Church. When the Fuhrer came to power in 1933, many of us in the church were glad that someone had finally come to put backbone back into German morals. We have learned to suppport the National Socialist reorganization of the church to serve Christian morals better. You know, Herr Hitler does not smoke!"
- An alcoholic or drug addict: "This whole world is a

bunch of garbage, ya know! I work myself to the bone to pay my bills, feed my family, educate my children. For what? It is so cold out there. I get my warmth from this (holds up drink)."
- A pew warmer: "I think it is nice to go to church. It is so holy. The stained-glass windows, the candles on the altar, the neat rows of pews with my own reserved seat give me a warm feeling. Nothing changes and it is so comfortable!"

These are the kind of vignettes you and your people can create. Explore the use of costumes and gestures. The characters should represent a variety of people who've let themselves be drawn to a destructive flame.

After a character finishes a vignette, he or she should sit with you around the fire. After all vignettes are done, take some of the charcoal (or coal) and pass it around the group with the blessing that God is the only source of light. He will protect them from the cold and burn away their failures and sins.

Turn to the congregation and ask the people to reflect on their inner raging fires. Bless them with the same assurance that you shared with the characters. Hold the charcoal over the heads of the congregation as you offer the closing benediction.

A CLUE FROM 18:28-40

Find a lawyer or judge in your church or community who would be glad to help your congregation experience the courtroom scene in this passage.

Stage this as if a judge were listening to a case and trying to find out what the accused did wrong. You can expand the scene by working in other sections of the fourth Gospel (Jesus' signs, etc.). The professional can also be cast as the person explaining the terms of the law. This narrator role suggests a model we developed a few years ago for a television show. We wrote a script from this passage that was presented in a "You Are There" format for television. A noted judge was utilized. The station was so pleased that they broadcast this media sermon at a prime evening time slot on Easter Sunday. We were amazed at the cooperation we got from actors, actresses, writers and other media people.

A CLUE FROM 18:38b-40

Barabbas has caught the eye of creative writers and artists throughout the ages. He is a curious character. His viewpoint could shed a lot of light on the unfolding situation. It takes a little imagination.

Utilize the robber's perspective to give people a fresh view of the trial of Jesus. You might offer the dramatic material without playing the role of Barabbas. Instead, take the role of a historian going over the file of Barabbas. Create a montage of pictures and words from the newspapers. Print this visual piece inside the bulletin. Include 60 or 70 items that reflect the pressures and promises Barabbas may have confronted after his rescue from the cross. The montage will invite the worshipers to look at a familiar passage with new spectacles of faith.

Ask them to share, based on thoughts conjured by the bulletin, some of the robber's pressures and promises after his undeserved pardon. After some sharing, put the congregation in the shoes of Barabbas. Lead them to the natural conclusion: Barabbas did not deserve pardon. And no one of us deserves pardon. But God gives us unconditional pardon. What does this say about the way we should treat others?

CHAPTER 19

PILATE SCOURGES JESUS; THE CROWD DEMANDS CRUCIFIXION

Then Pilate took Jesus and scourged him. ²And the soldiers plaited a crown of thorns, and put it on his head, and arrayed him in a purple robe; ³they came up to him saying, "Hail, King of the Jews!" and struck him with their hands. ⁴Pilate went out again, and said to them, "See, I am bringing him out to you, that you may know that I find no crime in him." ⁵So Jesus came out, wearing the crown of thorns and the purple robe. Pilate said to them, "Behold the man!" ⁶When the chief priests and the officers saw him, they cried out, "Crucify him, crucify him!" Pilate said to them, "Take him yourselves and crucify him, for I find no crime in him." ⁷The Jews answered him, "We have a law, and by that law he ought to die, because he has made himself the Son of God." ⁸When Pilate heard these words, he was the more afraid; ⁹he entered the praetorium again and said to Jesus, "Where are you from?" But Jesus gave no answer. ¹⁰Pilate therefore said to him, "You will not speak to me? Do you not know that I have power to release you, and power to crucify you?" ¹¹Jesus answered him, "You would have no power over me unless it had been given you from above; therefore he who delivered me to you has the greater sin."

12 Upon this Pilate sought to release him, but the Jews cried out, "If you release this man, you are not Caesar's friend; every one who makes himself a king sets himself against Caesar." ¹³When Pilate heard these words, he brought Jesus out and sat down on the judgment seat at a place called The Pavement, and in Hebrew, Gab'batha. ¹⁴Now it was the day of Preparation of the Passover; it was about the sixth hour. He said to the Jews, "Behold your King!" ¹⁵They cried out, "Away with him, away with him, crucify him!" Pilate said to them, "Shall I crucify your King?" The chief priests answered, "We have no king but Caesar." ¹⁶Then he handed him over to them to be crucified.

THE CRUCIFIXION AND DEATH OF JESUS

17 So they took Jesus, and he went out, bearing his own cross, to the place called the place of a skull, which is called in Hebrew Gol'gotha. ¹⁸There they crucified him, and with him two others, one on either side, and Jesus between them. ¹⁹Pilate also wrote a title and put it on the cross; it read, "Jesus of Nazareth, the King of the Jews." ²⁰Many of the Jews read this title, for the place where Jesus was crucified was near the city; and it was written in Hebrew, in Latin, and in Greek. ²¹The chief priests of the Jews then said to Pilate, "Do not write, 'The King of the Jews,' but, 'This man said, I am King of the Jews.'" ²²Pilate answered, "What I have written I have written."

23 When the soldiers had crucified Jesus they took his garments and made four parts, one for each soldier; also his tunic. But the tunic was without seam, woven from top to

bottom; ²⁴so they said to one another, "Let us not tear it, but cast lots for it to see whose it shall be." This was to fulfil the scripture,

"They parted my garments among them,
and for my clothing they cast lots."

25 So the soldiers did this. But standing by the cross of Jesus were his mother, and his mother's sister, Mary the wife of Clopas, and Mary Mag′dalene. ²⁶When Jesus saw his mother, and the disciple whom he loved standing near, he said to his mother, "Woman, behold your son!" ²⁷Then he said to the disciple, "Behold, your mother!" And from that hour the disciple took her to his own home.

28 After this Jesus, knowing that all was now finished, said (to fulfil the scripture), "I thirst." ²⁹A bowl full of vinegar stood there; so they put a sponge full of the vinegar on hyssop and held it to his mouth. ³⁰When Jesus had received the vinegar, he said, "It is finished"; and he bowed his head and gave up his spirit.

31 Since it was the day of Preparation, in order to prevent the bodies from remaining on the cross on the sabbath (for that sabbath was a high day), the Jews asked Pilate that their legs might be broken, and that they might be taken away. ³²So the soldiers came and broke the legs of the first, and of the other who had been crucified with him; ³³but when they came to Jesus and saw that he was already dead, they did not break his legs. ³⁴But one of the soldiers pierced his side with a spear, and at once there came out blood and water. ³⁵He who saw it has borne witness—his testimony is true, and he knows that he tells the truth—that you also may believe. ³⁶For these things took place that the scripture might be fulfilled, "Not a bone of him shall be broken." ³⁷And again another scripture says, "They shall look on him whom they have pierced."

JESUS' BODY LAID IN A TOMB

38 After this Joseph of Arimathe′a, who was a disciple of Jesus, but secretly, for fear of the Jews, asked Pilate that he might take away the body of Jesus, and Pilate gave him leave. So he came and took away his body. ³⁹Nicode′mus also, who had at first come to him by night, came bringing a mixture of myrrh and aloes, about a hundred pounds weight. ⁴⁰They took the body of Jesus, and bound it in linen cloths with the spices, as is the burial custom of the Jews. ⁴¹Now in the place where he was crucified there was a garden, and in the garden a new tomb where no one had ever been laid. ⁴²So because of the Jewish day of Preparation, as the tomb was close at hand, they laid Jesus there.

CHAPTER 19

Creative Commentary on the Scripture

VERSES 1-7: The passion of Christ is one of the most moving events in history. The innocent one is killed by the guilty ones. The powerful emotions in the passion invite us into reverent experiential communication. Mockery of Jesus (the crown of thorns and purple robe) is very suggestive to our task. The theme of thorns connects to many other motifs (rose of Sharon, the blooming desert, etc.). There is also a garden imagery (Eden, betrayal, burial, resurrection) running through the salvation history. This is a major event.

The masses who hailed Jesus at his entry into Jerusalem are now instruments of his condemnation. Public favor is a fickle companion. Those who earlier wanted to "see Jesus" can now "behold, the man."

VERSES 8-16: Pilate and the powers of the world are portrayed as prisoners to the very power they hold. Jesus proclaims the power to take up or lay down his life. In his choice to submit to crucifixion, he exercises a power that runs against the values of the world.

VERSES 17-22: Jesus bears the cross upon which he will suffer and die. Pilate provides the epitaph for Jesus. He is firm about this decision. Has he given in to evil on the major points, but balked at the minor points?

The place of the skull, the two other people crucified with Jesus, and the epitaph are rich invitations to an experiential presentation. This moment is the door from the old age to the new age. A mysterious place, shady characters and outdoor advertising forces us to explode with fresh ideas as we enter into the text.

VERSES 23-24: The soldiers play at the lottery while the Son of God suffers on the cross. A quote from Psalm 22:18

relates the Old Testament picture of suffering to Jesus. He is fully human as well as fully God. Once again, the author provides a strong anti-gnostic presentation of Jesus.

VERSES 25-27: Jesus creates a new concept of the family with this exchange between son and mother. The old boundary lines of biologically-defined kinship are extended. A new kind of security is provided for those within the faith community. Jesus' blood now flows in the veins of those who believe. The beloved disciple has a new mother and she has another son. Every blended, single-parented or divorced family can relate to what Jesus has done here!

VERSES 28-37: Jesus suffers to the painful end of his earthly life. The source of living water now thirsts. The Son of God suffers the death of a human.

The flow of water and blood counters those who denied the real human suffering of Jesus. It also has the theological hint that the new stream of living water and grace would pour forth from this moment on. The witness of John (verse 35) is passionately stated. Personal testimony has always been the key ingredient in making Christ known to others.

VERSES 38-42: Joseph of Arimathea is an important disciple who provides the garden for Jesus' conclusion of his ministry. Nicodemus returns to care for the body of his Lord. The spices, linen cloths and the garden are vital experiential entry points to this passage. This scene is easy to see, taste, smell, feel and hear.

Creative Bible Study Ideas

SESSION BASED ON 19:1-7

1. Construct two crowns, one of thorns and one of paper. Use any natural thorn-type material for the crown of thorns. You might find a child's paper crown at a fast-food restaurant.

2. Place the crowns in the middle of the circle of students.

3. Tell the students about the crown as a symbol of honor. In ancient sports events, the winner received a crown of laurel.

4. Pass the paper crown around the group.

5. Ask each person to wear the crown and share how it symbolizes something good about his or her life this past

week. There will be laughter and good-natured response to this childlike sharing.

6. Read the text.
7. Pass around the crown of thorns.
8. Ask each person to wear the crown when it comes to him or her.
9. Ask the student who is wearing the crown to share a failure or sin of another person that he or she is willing to bear symbolically at this moment.
10. Ask students to share the feelings they had when they took the role of Jesus in his humiliation.
11. Disassemble the crown.
12. Place a piece of the thorn material directly in the hand of each student. Look him or her in the eye and offer a one-line affirmation (e.g., "Christ died for your sins. Go in peace."). Take your time going around the circle. Make this a special moment for each person.
13. Your class might want to look at the flow of justice in our day. There is gross injustice for certain people and situations. They could interview lawyers, judges and prisoners, and report results at a future session. The fact that Jesus suffered unfairly means that we have a responsibility to minister to those in such situations.

SESSION BASED ON 19:1-11

Find a large piece of purple cloth. You need not buy it. Many seamstresses will be glad to help you. Use heavy material if possible; burlap may be a good choice. You will also need materials that can be used to create a banner. Ask people in your class to help find these materials. You may also seek out a couple people with sewing skills.

1. Gather the students.
2. Read the text.
3. Pass the piece of purple cloth around the group.
4. Ask each person to share some of the humble feelings conveyed through this cloth.
5. Pass the cloth around once again and share how the text brings Good News to us through this cloth.
6. Place a pile of cloth scraps on the table. You will need needles and thread or glue and scissors. Your sewing people can help those who do not know how to sew.
7. Invite the students to make a banner that expresses the message of this passage. The piece of purple cloth will be

the background.

8. Make arrangements to have the banner displayed in the worship area.

SESSION BASED ON 19:1-22

1. Read the text.
2. Place a large piece of wood before the students. It should be long and strong enough to resemble the crossbeam of a cross.
3. Give each student a piece of newsprint large enough to fit on the crossbeam.
4. Ask each person to list the sins that the cross carried for us.
5. Share the lists by having each student tack his or her inscription on the piece of wood. Each piece of paper is placed over the last one.
6. Repeat the exercise. But this time ask each student to write the epitaph for Jesus.
7. Share these epitaphs.
8. Have the students write their own epitaphs and compare them to the ones they wrote for Jesus.
9. Share these personal epitaphs and comparisons.

SESSION BASED ON 19:17-22

Christ on the cross is the turning point of human history. For the Christian, there is no moment that touches so deeply.

Create an experience that brings your people into the crucifixion in a new way. This model could also be a way for the class to provide a ministry to others in the church.

The text presents the moment of salvation as a public event. Taking this clue, your class can create an experiential learning and growth event for others.

Get permission to use a church room for a Sunday morning. Study the Gospels' accounts of Jesus' crucifixion. Then construct a full-sized cross fastened to a platform. Place a handle on each of the crossbeam's left and right sides.

In front of the platform, construct a large screen by using large bedsheets. Place two slide projectors behind the screens. This will give you a rear-projection screen. You will show slides that deal with the suffering of the world. These slides can be seen by a person standing at the cross with hands in the crossbeam handles.

Record on audio-cassette tape a special sound track that includes the reading of the crucifixion passages and perhaps the cries of the world. This can be played through a headset or through speakers in the room.

Invite the church members to this special room for a unique experience. Lead them in one at a time or build three crosses and have three people on them. Your people will enjoy the senses-filled multimedia environment. The room could be run a couple hours each Sunday during Lent.

You might have a debriefing room where people can be served refreshments and encouraged to share their feelings. Your students will learn a great deal in this experience. They'll learn basic multimedia skills as they create an authentic experience for others.

SESSION BASED ON 19:23-27

The story of the soldiers gambling for Jesus' tunic provides an opportunity for your students to gather also at the foot of the cross. Find a large cross in the church or perhaps somewhere outside the building. Take the class to this place.

Read the text as you sit beneath the cross. Bring a simple piece of white cloth that resembles a tunic. Separate students into clusters of three or four.

Using several pair of dice, clusters should gamble for the robe. Repeat the process while playing a recording of a collection of Jesus' sayings. You can use your audio-cassette recorder to produce this tape.

After a few minutes, stop and discuss how the students felt doing this insensitive thing while Jesus gave his life for the sins of the world. Probe ways that we mock Jesus in our daily lives.

Have someone stand at the cross with his or her arms outstretched. You might rotate your students to this position during the gambling portion of the class. You can now discuss how the world looked from Jesus' perspective.

SESSION BASED ON 19:25-27

The act of the cross changes human history and human relationships. Mary has lost a son and gained a son. The beloved disciple has gained a new mother.

1. Ask your adult students to bring pictures of their mother and their children. Those without children should

bring pictures of children who are special to them.
2. Spend some time going around the circle sharing comments about mothers as the pictures are shown.
3. Repeat the process with pictures of children.
4. Read the passage.
5. Ask students to reflect on what Jesus' comments say about family relationships. How has the blood of Christ made new ties of blood?
6. Close with prayer for the kinship of Christ that draws us together across time and bloodlines. Also include thanksgiving for those who gave us life and sustained us.
7. You might carry this biblical message closer to the experience of the congregation. The nature of the family has changed radically in recent years. In all congregations, there are blended, broken and extended families. Yet most churches have not really done anything to meet the needs of such families. How should worship, education, fellowship and mission change in light of the fact that the family's structure has changed? This passage suggests that we must be open to the kinship created by Christ. Ask your students to make some practical suggestions for helping families and present them to the church board or committee in charge of these matters.

SESSION BASED ON 19:28-30

1. Set a small bowl of vinegar in the center of the class circle.
2. Ask all the students to stand with their arms held straight out from their sides. Ask them to close their eyes and imagine that they are on the cross with Jesus.
3. Play a paraphrased account of the passion of Christ recorded on your audio-cassette recorder. Or, read the accounts. Take the script from John and the other Gospels. The story should run three to four minutes. The students should keep their eyes closed and arms outstretched while the story is read.
4. When you come to the end and Jesus is thirsty, go around and touch the lips of each person with a cotton ball dipped in the vinegar. Use a different cotton ball for each person.
5. Finish with the words of verse 30.
6. Ask students to open their eyes and let their arms drop to their sides.

7. Share how students feel after being on the cross. They will feel a great physical relief because their arms will be very tired from being outstretched. In fact, a warm sense of relaxation will fill their bodies. Start by debriefing with the physical feelings. Move from there to the emotional and theological relief Christ gave them in those few minutes. How did the vinegar taste?

8. Discuss the mission of Jesus to fulfill the scripture. Why was this important for him and for us?

9. Probe how the historical cross touches the lives of your students today. What difference does it make for what will happen today or next Friday night?

10. Ask students to create a Christopher ("Christ bearer") model for their daily lives. How do we walk in the step of the Christ every day? Encourage students to keep diaries for the next week and record what it is like to act in each moment as if they were carrying the cross of Jesus. A famous book (**In His Steps**, by Charles Sheldon) was written about a person who undertook such a task. Have students share experiences at the next session. They would also make a fantastic sermon.

SESSION BASED ON 19:31-37

In verse 35 the Gospel writer speaks in the first-person to add a personal testimony concerning the cross. You might utilize this clue and ask your students to write a journal account concerning the cross. Provide class members with a notebook that has a cover. Seat the people so that each person has some personal space. This can be done by scattering the chairs and facing them in different directions.

Present the passion account. Either play a recording of it or read it with soft music playing. Classical music provides a good atmosphere for reflection.

Ask each person to write a dialogue between himself or herself and Jesus on the cross, focusing on the actual words spoken. Tell students they will not have to read their compositions to the class unless they volunteer.

After a few minutes, discuss the experience. What was the most painful part of the dialogue with the suffering Jesus? What was the most pleasing? What did you discover in the conversation that had never occurred to you before?

SESSION BASED ON 19:38-42

1. Bring in long pieces of linen cloth. This material can be borrowed from people in the church.
2. Take the class to a setting that in some way resembles a tomb (basement room, etc.). You could even use a garden or storm shelter. Spread the linen cloth on the ground or floor to symbolize the body of Jesus.
3. Play instrumental music softly in the background.
4. Gather around the linen cloth.
5. Read the passage.
6. Explain that we are the body of Christ.
7. Ask students to roll up shirt sleeves if they are wearing long sleeves.
8. Rub aloe lotion on the hands and arms of the students. Ask them to imagine that they are the body of Jesus and are being prepared for the tomb. Be gentle and kind as you do this to each student.
9. Ask your students to share how they felt when they received the loving preparation for the grave. Ask them to smell the fragrance. What kinds of memories does it bring?
10. Challenge your students to a ministry of touch during the next week. Many older people are never touched or embraced. They live alone and have no one to hug. Ask each person to daily "reach out and touch someone" with the love of Christ. This can mean special handshakes and actual hugs. There are many people who need and deserve such a ministry and are waiting for someone to respond to them in this biblical manner.

Creative Speaking and Preaching Ideas

A CLUE FROM 19:1-42

The garden is an exciting motif emerging from this and the preceding chapters. Jesus is betrayed, buried and raised from the dead in the garden. One cannot help but be drawn into the garden motif of Genesis 3. In the garden we fell to sin and through the garden we discover our forgiveness in the resurrection of Jesus Christ!

With some simple adjustments your worship area can become a garden! We have used flowers and trees in worship as decorations for years. It is fitting that we use them to present the gospel message. Again, you will find all the help you need for making this transformation in your congregation. There are amateur and professional gardeners in every Christian community. Invite them to share in the task of creatively presenting the Word.

Perhaps the "garden" can be created in the whole room. We often "frame" the setting for worship by using only the "up front" area. But worship should involve the whole people of God. With the "up front" setting, the pastor is the sole star and bearer of the gospel. Biblically, it seems that every believer is called to participate in the work of worship.

It might be wise to place fruit trees, bushes and other interesting and natural-looking plants in every corner of the room. Don't limit worship floral arrangements to the funeral-home variety. Eden and the garden of the tomb had a natural, gritty quality to them.

Walk the congregation into the chapter with Jesus. Move around the room. Let the trees and flowers carry the flow of the story. The crown of thorns can be "plucked" from a bush.

Use this moving sermon as an intergenerational experience. Take the young people with you on this tour in the garden. I am not suggesting the usual "children's message." Your sermon is *the* sermon for young and old. The gospel can be understood, on some level, by everyone present! Briefly share the theological implications of the passion of Christ. Weave the experiential and the cognitive into the authentic fabric of the gospel.

Close with the anointing of the body of Jesus. Use the linen cloth to suggest the body. Anoint the children's hands with aloe lotion. You might even want to anoint the whole congregation. Perhaps the children could do this!

A CLUE FROM 19:1-7

The thorn is both experientially and theologically suggestive. It hints of the rose of Sharon (Song of Songs 2:1) and the desert blooming (Isaiah 35:1). Paul talks about the thorn in the flesh.

Draw upon your naturalists for help with the thorns. They will help you find a thorny plant that grows in your area. Explore the motif of the thorn with its pain and beauty. Pass out pieces of the thorn material.

Use the thorn as a medium for prayer (petition: self-needs; intercession: needs of others; thanksgiving; confession; pardon; adoration; etc.).

Ask the people to share how the crown of thorns touches something in their lives. You might move from the pain to the beauty of thorns by introducing some roses. If they are not available in quantity, pass two roses through the pews. Ask each person to smell a rose and think about the blessings that Christ has created from the despair of the cross. The rose can become the symbol of the victory over death and sin.

A CLUE FROM 19:17-42

Take your people to the cross. This passage underscored the reality of God in humanity. Christ pays the price for our sins with his blood, sweat and pain. Ask everyone to raise his or her arms out to the sides. When the arms are raised, present the passion in about three or four minutes. Ask them to hold out their arms while you do this.

When you have completed the reading, people may relax their arms. Say the words of Jesus, "It is finished" (verse 30). Now focus on the physical experience of the people. Most people have not used these arm muscles for a long time. Urge them to rub their arms and appreciate how good it feels to be done with those few straining minutes.

Focus on the relief that Christ brings to us through his pain. Ask the worshipers to share the kinds of feelings they had during the physical strain. For some (the athletic-type younger people) it will have been very easy, but for others (the older with certain physical disorders) it was almost impossible.

A CLUE FROM 19:25-27

The concept of family is being scrambled by the trends of the culture. We have multiple marriages, blended families, dislocated families and even avoidance of marriage. Most ministers fall into the trap of assuming that family structure has been transformed elsewhere but not in the congregation around him or her. The broken family, however, *is* very much a part of contemporary Christian lives.

This text offers an exciting clue to the meaning of the cross for those searching for a "family" lifestyle. Maybe our use of the term "family" is limited. Many old people are alone and forgotten. The young singles in search of work often find themselves far from a biological family.

Jesus changes our thinking about the genetic family with the new blood ties of the cross. Through the cross we have all become kin! We have given lip service to this desire, but the cross makes us literally the family of God.

Ask the worshipers to look at their hands. Guide them as they observe their lines, scars and other particular qualities. Encourage them to imagine that their mother is looking at her children's hands. What would she notice that would worry her, please her, make her sad?

Ask them to imagine they are Mary, looking at the hands of Jesus on the cross. Read again the exchange between Mary and Jesus in which he creates the new kinship. You can conclude by asking people to join hands as kin in Christ. Let the closing hymn be "We Are the Family of God."

A CLUE FROM 19:28-37

Sensual clues to the Good News abound in this text. One way to take people to the cross is to crawl into the moment of Christ's suffering. Dip the bottom corner of the bulletins in vinegar. When you present the passage, ask the worshipers to taste the corner. Explore the experience as Jesus' life draws to an end.

A CLUE FROM 19:28-37

Ask everyone to stand while you read the passage. Lead them through a series of body gestures that duplicate the positions of Jesus.

As they stand with their arms stretched out, ask them to rise on their toes for a few seconds. This will give their legs a sense of the cross. You might ask each person to place a hand on his or her side. With a little pressure, they can be aware of the moment when the soldiers pierced Jesus' side with a spear.

Have the worshipers sit down and reflect on Jesus' crucifixion. John gives his account (verse 35). What would we have written? Encourage people to share their stories at the cross.

THE RESURRECTION

Now on the first day of the week Mary Mag'dalene came to the tomb early, while it was still dark, and saw that the stone had been taken away from the tomb. ²So she ran, and went to Simon Peter and the other disciple, the one whom Jesus loved, and said to them, "They have taken the Lord out of the tomb, and we do not know where they have laid him." ³Peter then came out with the other disciple, and they went toward the tomb. ⁴They both ran, but the other disciple outran Peter and reached the tomb first; ⁵and stooping to look in, he saw the linen cloths lying there, but he did not go in. ⁶Then Simon Peter came, following him, and went into the tomb; he saw the linen cloths lying, ⁷and the napkin, which had been on his head, not lying with the linen cloths but rolled up in a place by itself. ⁸Then the other disciple, who reached the tomb first, also went in, and he saw and believed; ⁹for as yet they did not know the scripture, that he must rise from the dead. ¹⁰Then the disciples went back to their homes.

"WOMAN, WHY ARE YOU WEEPING?"

11 But Mary stood weeping outside the tomb, and as she wept she stooped to look into the tomb; ¹²and she saw two angels in white, sitting where the body of Jesus had lain, one at the head and one at the feet. ¹³They said to her, "Woman, why are you weeping?" She said to them, "Because they have taken away my Lord, and I do not know where they have laid him." ¹⁴Saying this, she turned round and saw Jesus standing, but she did not know that it was Jesus. ¹⁵Jesus said to her, "Woman, why are you weeping? Whom do you seek?" Supposing him to be the gardener, she said to him, "Sir, if you have carried him away, tell me where you have laid him, and I will take him away." ¹⁶Jesus said to her, "Mary." She turned and said to him in Hebrew, "Rab-bo'ni!" (which means Teacher). ¹⁷Jesus said to her, "Do not hold me, for I have not yet ascended to the Father; but go to my brethren and say to them, I am ascending to my Father and your Father, to my God and your God." ¹⁸Mary Mag'dalene went and said to the disciples, "I have seen the Lord"; and she told them that he had said these things to her.

JESUS APPEARS TO THE DISCIPLES

19 On the evening of that day, the first day of the week, the doors being shut where the disciples were, for fear of the Jews, Jesus came and stood among them and said to them, "Peace be with you." ²⁰When he had said this, he showed them his hands and his side. Then the disciples were glad when they saw the Lord. ²¹Jesus said to them again, "Peace be with you. As the Father has sent me, even so I send you." ²²And when he had said this, he breathed on them, and said to them, "Receive the Holy Spirit. ²³If you forgive the sins of any, they are forgiven; if you retain the sins of any, they are retained."

THOMAS FINALLY BELIEVES

24 Now Thomas, one of the twelve, called the Twin, was not with them when Jesus came. ²⁵So the other disciples told him, "We have seen the Lord." But he said to them, "Unless I see in his hands the print of the nails, and place my finger in the mark of the nails, and place my hand in his side, I will not believe."

26 Eight days later, his disciples were again in the house, and Thomas was with them. The doors were shut, but Jesus came and stood among them, and said, "Peace be with you." ²⁷Then he said to Thomas, "Put your finger here, and see my hands; and put out your hand, and place it in my side; do not be faithless, but believing." ²⁸Thomas answered him, "My Lord and my God!" ²⁹Jesus said to him, "Have you believed because you have seen me? Blessed are those who have not seen and yet believe."

30 Now Jesus did many other signs in the presence of the disciples, which are not written in this book; ³¹but these are written that you may believe that Jesus is the Christ, the Son of God, and that believing you may have life in his name.

CHAPTER 20

Creative Commentary on the Scripture

VERSES 1-10: The Garden of Eden is again recalled. This is the setting for the most creative of God's acts: the resurrection of Jesus. There is mystery in the darkness. But light is about to come through the Son of light.

The writer of the fourth Gospel underscores the special role played by women in the life, death and resurrection of Jesus. Mary Magdalene's response to the empty tomb is despair and fear. She is a messenger of this news to the males of the church.

Either Peter should take up jogging or he is hesitant to see what has happened. The beloved disciple arrives first. His conclusion after seeing the linen and the empty tomb is belief. The men return to their homes.

VERSES 11-18: Mary Magdalene remains and weeps. She has been to the tomb before the others, but she must look once again. She, like Moses at the burning bush, must turn aside to see this strange wonder again. During her response to God's wonder, she has a further revelation. Two strangers in the tomb ask her about the source of her grief. Mary tells of her love and concern for her Lord. It is at this point that Jesus appears to her, yet she does not recognize the resurrected Christ. He calls Mary by name and her eyes are opened!

She addresses him as teacher and wants to cover him. Jesus bides her to hold off touching him because he has not yet ascended to the Father. Mary now knows the ecstasy of experienced faith. I am moved to tears as I write these notes on this text. There is such power in Christ's return for us! When have we last enabled others as students and worshipers to emotionally and intellectually experience the power of the Bible?

VERSES 19-23: Fear grips the disciples. They wonder about their fate. They have not yet been filled with the Holy Spirit. It is important to remember that the continuous mention of the "Jews" here has nothing to do with the Jewish people who live in our time. The opponents of Jesus were his own people who were resistant to his message. Jesus is a Jew. People within and without the Christian community have irresponsibly used the fourth Gospel to justify racism and hatred. The Jews did not attack and kill Jesus. Each person who turns from him and sins—in every age—is the opponent of Christ.

Jesus gives the greeting of "peace" to the disciples. He shows them his wounds that they might experience the miracle. They are commissioned and endowed with the Holy Spirit. He breathes on them. There is an echo of Genesis 2:7. They are now truly living beings.

VERSES 24-31: Thomas is called the "Twin." This interesting nickname appealed to gnostic people who believed that external life was dirty and only the secret particle of light was pure. This kind of thinking saw Jesus and Christ as two different entities: Jesus died upon the cross while Christ (the gnostic spirit) laughed. Thomas, however, is seen as the most earthy of all. We cannot draw any particular conclusion from his nickname. He doesn't want speculation. Let him touch and see.

Jesus gives Thomas a chance to touch him and confirm his faith. We, who will come later, are blessed for believing although we did not participate in the earthly ministry of Jesus.

The book seems to end here. Most scholars believe that chapter 21 is a later addition.

Creative Bible Study Ideas

SESSION BASED ON 20:1-10

The opened tomb in the dark garden suggests that the best way into this passage is through a similar environment. Have an early morning Bible study for adults and/or young people who can jog together in a traveling experience.

Many people are now practicing the discipline of intentional walking or jogging. The gospel calls us into a complete encounter with Jesus Christ. There is no reason why you should not crawl into a passage by jogging at dawn on

Easter. God wants more than our minds.

You can stop at several points and focus on a portion of the passion story. Direct the group's meditation for the next mile or so. Then stop and share reflections while you all stretch (to keep from getting too cool). Finally, jog into a cemetery or other gardenlike environment, preferably a place that has a cave or tomb. Let the women go first and return with the news that someone has taken Jesus' body.

Follow the flow of the story. Be sure to check out the location for such a class beforehand. You can even conclude by stopping at a fast-food restaurant for fish (chapter 21) or some other breakfast meal.

SESSION BASED ON 20:1-10

The movement of the passage triggers the design for your study. Have your students move spacially through the text. You can do this right in your classroom. However, it would be better to move through the church building.

Get to know the story well so that you can tell it in an expanded form. Give the students shifting roles or all the same character. There is a style of group drama in which the leader describes the role and scene and makes dialogue suggestions. The actors chosen for the parts then create the scene. It is easy to do.

Place the items mentioned (rolled-away rock, linen cloth, etc.) in the places you will be at in that part of the story. This kind of in-house movement can be a slow-paced or in-place jog that does not require special shoes.

Spend time debriefing. Is Mary suffering from paranoia? She assumes that the tomb has been robbed. What is significant about the fact that Peter is the second one to arrive at the tomb yet he is first among the disciples?

SESSION BASED ON 20:1-10

1. Read the text.
2. Pass a good-sized stone around the group of students.
3. Ask each one to share what the stone symbolized for Mary Magdalene. Ask them to make the comment as though they were Mary.
4. Read the text again. Use a different translation this time.
5. Pass the stone around again.
6. Ask each student to share what the stone symbolized

for Peter. Have them say it as though they were Peter.

7. Read the text yet another time using another translation.

8. Pass the stone around again.

9. Encourage the students to share what the stone symbolized to the beloved disciple. Have them respond as though they were he.

10. Read the text again. You might try still another translation.

11. Pass the stone around once more.

12. Ask the students to share what the stone means to them.

SESSION BASED ON 20:1-10

1. Take the class to a room that is bare and has a cave-like quality (basement closet, etc.).

2. When they enter, have them gather around pieces of linen cloth. Place a napkin near the linen pile.

3. Light the room with a candle. This will give it an early morning darkness suggested by the text.

4. Read the text.

5. Tell them that these cloths had been on the body of Jesus but that he is not there.

6. Pass the napkin around the group.

7. Ask each person to share the thoughts that Peter, the beloved disciple and Mary Magdalene may have had.

8. Ask them to role play a situation in which they are one of the characters in the story. The setting is with the other disciples. The characters must explain to others what has happened. The rest of the class reacts with the skepticism of nonbelievers. The characters must defend their positions.

9. Talk about the kinds of feelings that keep us from sharing the risen Lord with others at school, work, etc.

10. Pass the napkin around once again as a sharing prayer. As the napkin comes to a person, invite him or her to add a few lines to the group prayer.

11. Cut the cloth into strips and give a piece to each person.

12. Ask each student to carry it as a wrist tie or in a pocket during the next week. It is a reminder that Christ has risen and he walks with us. You might develop this further by asking the people in the group to pray for each other at a certain time each day. Why not work out a schedule for this?

The linen cloth can be the reminder for this act of mutual care.

SESSION BASED ON 20:1-18

This passage bristles with Mary's ordinary emotional response to an extraordinary moment in human history. Jesus has a special appreciation for women. They play an important role in this Gospel.

Help your class enter into the many sides of Mary Magdalene at the tomb. She expresses fear (verse 2), sadness (verses 11-15), awe (verse 16) and ecstasy (verse 18).

You might show the reflections of these responses by using a mirror. Read the part of the text which shows one of her emotional states. Pass the mirror around. Ask each person to look into the mirror and describe Mary's feelings in first person. Repeat this process for each of her four emotions.

Spend some time talking about how students felt while trying to understand Mary's emotions. To what feeling could they most easily relate? If you were in the garden with Mary, what moment would move you the most?

Pass the mirror around the circle again and ask students to share when, but not why, they last shed a tear of sorrow. What happened to make the situation better? How did they find comfort? Focus on the feelings and how the emotion was changed.

SESSION BASED ON 20:19-23

1. After the students have gathered, someone enters the room with a sheet over his or her head.
2. Ask the students to share whether they are frightened by this person. Explore reasons why this hidden character is not an object of fear.
3. Read the text.
4. Discuss the emotional state of the disciples. Why were they afraid? What helped them change their minds?
5. If a stranger claimed he or she were the Messiah, how would you know whether the person was telling the truth?
6. Close by going to each person and blowing gently on his or her head. Ask the Holy Spirit to be with each person.

SESSION BASED ON 20:24-31

The Gospel writer has given the final scene a setting that

would please most playwrights or film producers. This might be the perfect passage to find expression in a videotape production. You can borrow video-cassette equipment from people in the congregation, your local school, library or car dealer.

The goal of this presentation is to create a television production. The student will need to probe and digest the content in order to find a focus for the actual production. You are not concerned about final results. Place the highest value on how the people who create the show will learn and grow.

Divide your group into units of three to five people. Select someone as the director/producer. Read the story and/or display a copy of the story on newsprint. Ask each group to develop a theme in a particular style: historical, present and future. Let them write the script and design the production. They can find costumes and props around the church. Take turns doing the actual productions. Each production should not run more than two minutes.

You might design a payoff for the group by scheduling places where the productions can be shared with larger audiences. You can make such arrangements with other church school teachers. It will only mean a three- or four-minute interruption of their classes. Use a cart on wheels to move the equipment from room to room.

Creative Speaking and Preaching Ideas

A CLUE FROM 20:1-18

Place a large rock in the middle of the worship center. At the sermon time, go stand by it. Ask the congregation to imagine that they are in the garden at the time of Jesus' resurrection.

Ask the ushers to distribute a small stone to each worshiper. (You might have someone help gather them beforehand. Ask a lapidary [a stone polisher] in the congregation to be your support on this matter. In fact, the simplest stones can be polished to real beauty.)

Ask the worshipers to reflect on the stone they hold. If that stone had been at the tomb on that dark morning, what would it have to tell us? You can then present the story as if you were an observer at the tomb. Close the story with the stone "looking" at the congregation. It can make some very direct comments. It is funny how much energy develops by speaking in the voice of another.

The story unfolds with the complete range of human emotions. This material begs to be creatively expressed. Let the stone describe the characters as persons caught in the crosswinds of the past and future. God transforms their humanity before our eyes.

Invite your people to share what their resurrection stones say about the problems of today. Have them share their thoughts after experiencing the model of your reflection with the large stone.

In the benediction or closing prayer, ask each person to hold the stone over his or her head (as you are doing). Pray that God may bless each of us with the joy of the empty tomb: "May the resurrection stone be a memorial to what God has done for us in Jesus Christ."

A CLUE FROM 20:1-18

This text is racing with action. There is movement of the spirit and the body (Jesus' and others). Overcome the physical rigidity that infects most preaching moments. The context demands action!

You might place a large stone as the visual focal point in the worship center. As you read the text, have the characters move into the center and mime the actions of the message. You can draw upon adults and young people of your congregation to do these mimes.

Have the people portray Mary, Peter and the beloved disciple as they sit beside the stone. Walk down from the pulpit and do an "Our Town" style of narration that enables a person to wander through life scenes and make comments. As you talk about each of the early church people, he or she can come alive to mime his or her part.

A CLUE FROM 20:1-10

Accept the invitation of this passage and climb into the minds and spirits of Peter and the beloved disciple. You can do this in a fresh way by putting your whole message on cassette tape! Record the stream of conscious thoughts of both men in advance.

When you play the tape in worship, become the two persons and walk through the scene. Simply mime or move through the actions of the characters. Indicate role changes by putting on different head coverings.

You don't have to be an actor to give the content a dramatic presentation. The closer you get to the people inside the Gospel, the better you will be able to breathe life into them in your sermon.

A CLUE FROM 20:11-18

This moving encounter contrasts the missing body and the living actions of bodies moving and believing. The text is perfect for liturgical dance. This mode of expression in worship may be unfamiliar to your setting. Some of your people may associate anything called "dance" with the devil. Perhaps worship "movement" is a better description for expressing the love of Christ within the community of faith.

Gather several adults and young people. Take them into this passage and its characters. Develop some simple mime movements that act out the words of the text. Just try this communication form with this story. It is powerful!

You might use several pieces of linen cloth as props. The person presenting Mary's story can use the cloth as a handkerchief. When you come to verse 17, she can drape the cloth across the person playing Jesus.

She can run into the congregation as you read the words of Mary that Jesus has risen. If you think that there are people who might be offended by seeing adults or young adults in an art form analogous to dance, use children for the mime. The honesty and authenticity of this expression will break into the lives of even the frozen persons.

Now step down to the pew level and ask the congregation: "How has the Holy Spirit moved you through this story by giving you insight into the gospel message?" Accept their comments without debate or comment. You might also invite the people who offered mimes to join in the responses.

A CLUE FROM 20:19-23

After you have read this text, ask the congregation to imagine being with Jesus in this passage. Let their imaginations permit them to see the scene from the perspective of our Lord. Tell them that you will become a companion with the disciples.

Start a first-person monologue as a disciple. Talk about being frightened. When Jesus appears in the passage, ask the congregation to say his speech. Practice it with them. Lead them in the verses.

When you come to verse 22, ask people to undertake this Jesus ministry with a neighbor. Ask them to hold the hand of the person next to them as they gently blow on it and say "Receive the Holy Spirit."

Once your people have entered into the spirit of this text, ask them to struggle with verse 23. Does it apply to our relationships in the church community (penance) or to those outside the faith community?

Close by reading the text again. The benediction can be the blowing of breath on the hands of neighbors once again.

A CLUE FROM 20:24-31

This portion of the chapter also beckons us to a dramatic presentation. Jesus returns for those of us who have difficulty believing what we have not seen, tasted, touched, smelled or heard.

Turn the whole worship room into the hide-out of the disciples. Plant persons who are in the roles of the disciples throughout the pews. You can play the role of Thomas. Enter the area. Have the other disciples stand where they are and tell you about Jesus' return. Give your famous challenge to them and Jesus. Pause for 30 seconds. Continue with the rest of the story (eight days later). Another person can play the role of Jesus.

Ask everyone to cover his or her eyes with both hands as you repeat the blessing of Jesus (verse 29). Then lead the closing prayer for all of us who have come later and yet craved to touch and see Jesus.

You might also want to include the "yes, buts" of so many people who yearn for the physical presence of Jesus and have not had the kinds of experiences they desire. The closing blessing will then have even more power.

CHAPTER 21

THE NET FULL OF FISH

After this Jesus revealed himself again to the disciples by the Sea of Tibe′ri-as; and he revealed himself in this way. ²Simon Peter, Thomas called the Twin, Nathan′a-el of Cana in Galilee, the sons of Zeb′edee, and two others of his disciples were together. ³Simon Peter said to them, "I am going fishing." They said to him, "We will go with you." They went out and got into the boat; but that night they caught nothing.

4 Just as day was breaking, Jesus stood on the beach; yet the disciples did not know that it was Jesus. ⁵Jesus said to them, "Children, have you any fish?" They answered him, "No." ⁶He said to them, "Cast the net on the right side of the boat, and you will find some." So they cast it, and now they were not able to haul it in, for the quantity of fish. ⁷That disciple whom Jesus loved said to Peter, "It is the Lord!" When Simon Peter heard that it was the Lord, he put on his clothes, for he was stripped for work, and sprang into the sea. ⁸But the other disciples came in the boat, dragging the net full of fish, for they were not far from the land, but about a hundred yards[m] off.

9 When they got out on land, they saw a charcoal fire there, with fish lying on it, and bread. ¹⁰Jesus said to them, "Bring some of the fish that you have just caught." ¹¹So Simon Peter went aboard and hauled the net ashore, full of large fish, a hundred and fifty-three of them; and although there were so many, the net was not torn. ¹²Jesus said to them, "Come and have breakfast." Now none of the disciples dared ask him, "Who are you?" They knew it was the Lord. ¹³Jesus came and took the bread and gave it to them, and so with the fish. ¹⁴This was now the third time that Jesus was revealed to the disciples after he was raised from the dead.

"FOLLOW ME"

15 When they had finished breakfast, Jesus said to Simon Peter, "Simon, son of John, do you love me more than these?" He said to him, "Yes, Lord; you know that I love you." He said to him, "Feed my lambs." ¹⁶A second time he said to him, "Simon, son of John, do you love me?" He said to him, "Yes, Lord; you know that I love you." He said to him, "Tend my sheep." ¹⁷He said to him the third time, "Simon, son of John, do you love me?" Peter was grieved because he said to him the third time, "Do you love me?" And he said to him, "Lord, you know everything; you know that I love you." Jesus said to him, "Feed my sheep. ¹⁸Truly, truly, I say to you, when you were young, you girded yourself and walked where you would; but when you are old, you will stretch out your hands, and another will gird you and carry you where you do not wish to go." ¹⁹(This he said to show by what death he was to glorify God.) And after this he said to him, "Follow me."

20 Peter turned and saw following them the disciple whom Jesus loved,

---
m Greek *two hundred cubits*

who had lain close to his breast at the supper and had said, "Lord, who is it that is going to betray you?" ²¹When Peter saw him, he said to Jesus, "Lord, what about this man?" ²²Jesus said to him, "If it is my will that he remain until I come, what is that to you? Follow me!" ²³The saying spread abroad among the brethren that this disciple was not to die; yet Jesus did not say to him that he was not to die, but, "If it is my will that he remain until I come, what is that to you?"

24 This is the disciple who is bearing witness to these things, and who has written these things; and we know that his testimony is true.

25 But there are also many other things which Jesus did; were every one of them to be written, I suppose that the world itself could not contain the books that would be written.

CHAPTER 21

Creative Commentary on the Scripture

This chapter is included in all of the manuscripts we have of the fourth Gospel. Yet most scholars believe the chapter is a postscript added after the rest of the book was written. It may have been added to reach a different audience than that of the previous 20 chapters.

VERSES 1-14: The fishing expedition starts out with no success. The disciples are depicted as fishermen. Jesus appears to them on the beach, but they don't recognize him. This is his third appearance to the disciples according to this passage and yet it seems as if it were the first.

We once again note the strong anti-gnostic quality to the text. The physical and social features of the passage are not at all consistent with what one would expect from a sect of believers who felt that Jesus' human form was a mere disguise.

The meal, the forgiveness of Peter and the destiny of the beloved disciple are almost housekeeping matters for a church that will go forth into the world to change the spiritual and human condition of believers. The historical quality to this and the many other "media events" of the fourth Gospel calls for an experiential presentation of the message. When you think about the way we have traditionally taught and proclaimed the gospel, it is a wonder that more are not following a speculative Christian faith.

The fact that many people from the historical faith have been captured by sect groups bears witness to our failure to follow the lead of the fourth Gospel. These groups promise secret or special knowledge and abandonment from the world where people hunger and thirst without the historical Christ. It is easy to understand why the early church was so concerned with the danger of gnosticism. The fourth Gospel played an important role in presenting the total Christ, who was both human and divine.

"Children" is an interesting greeting. There is an intimacy about this salutation. The fishing advice proves quite beneficial. The beloved disciple recognizes Jesus.

Jesus has a fire awaiting the preparation of the fish fry. The description of the catch has given church interpreters nightmares. The almost allegorical use of the 153 fish in the passage has encouraged all kinds of numerical schemes to explain the deep meaning. While several explanations are intriguing, there is no way we can reclaim the author's intent.

Around this beach breakfast the disciples recognize Jesus The meal has eucharistic overtones. The hospitality meal has often been a time of divine revelation.

VERSES 15-19: Jesus and Peter engage in a dialogue about love. But Jesus is using one term and Peter is using another. In the last exchange, Jesus changes to the one Peter has been using. There is a scholarly tradition that assumes the three Greek words for love carried separate meanings. This concept breaks down in the fourth Gospel and elsewhere when Jesus uses at least two of the words interchangeably.

Jesus commissions Peter to his role of leadership. He also seems to reveal Peter's cost of this discipleship.

VERSES 20-25: There is a discussion about the beloved disciple. This echoes a problem experienced by the early church: Some people believed Christ would return before the disciples died. This chapter answers that problem. Those in the early church who thought that the beloved disciple was Lazarus are given an explanation why he died.

The final word suggests that there was much more that Jesus said and did but was not recorded. This anticipated the flow of non-canonical literature about Jesus that found a willing audience in the ancient world.

Creative Bible Study Ideas

SESSION BASED ON 21:1-14

The fish fry on the beach is a post-resurrection celebration that sends the disciples off to their mission. This passage provides the perfect learning/fellowship model for youth and others.

Imagine a post-Easter congregational gathering that re-enacts this beach event! The invitation to the love feast could be a piece of fishing net. If weather or setting permits, go to a beach or lake shore for the study experience.

Even the charcoal fire with fish and bread provide the form and content of your dinner and study. When the students have gathered to eat, suggest that there is a stranger in their midst. Ask them how we would know the Christ if he were here. Share these probes. What are the marks of the Son of God in a normal setting?

Give each person a small fish cookie or bread roll. These can be baked by your creative cooks. Ask them to eat them in order that they might be prepared to be fishermen for God.

SESSION BASED ON 21:1-25

1. Bring in several items and place them before the class: a dish of sand, a piece of fishing net, a piece of charcoal, a loaf of bread and fish-shaped cookies.

2. Pass one item around the group.

3. Encourage the students to share anything that this object can reveal to us about Jesus Christ.

4. Repeat the process for each item while someone records the ideas on newsprint.

5. Play the sounds of the sea from a sound-effects record. You can find one in a public library.

6. Read the passage.

7. Eat bread or the fish cookies.

8. Ask students to share what Jesus tried to teach the disciples at this breakfast.

9. Talk about discipleship and mission outreach.

10. Give each person a small piece of fishing net as a symbol of our role in gathering in and feeding others.

11. Assign each student the task of reaching out to someone in a special way during the next week. Perhaps the students can invite a different person to lunch each day during the week. If the student is in school, he or she might invite this person to sit at the same table. It is in the hospitality of the meal that the love of Christ is known. These luncheon stories can be shared at the next session.

SESSION BASED ON 21:1-25

This chapter appears in all the ancient manuscripts we

have of the fourth Gospel. However, students of the New Testament generally agree that it is a postscript to the original book. The Gospel of John seems to conclude at the end of chapter 20. The flow of the material, the style interpretation (allegorical) and the areas of interest (role of Peter) indicate a different purpose from the fourth Gospel proper.

This intriguing situation suggests a means to teach the Bible. Present chapter 21 as a mystery. Tell them that some people claim that it is different from the rest of the fourth Gospel.

Ask them to solve the problem through research. Any good Bible commentary will give you the conclusions of scholars. However, it will be best if you permit students to do their own research with the primary document.

Divide the class into two or three working groups. Give them one of these predetermined viewpoints: (a) it is added; (b) it is a part of the original; and (c) we can't know for sure. Each group must develop support from the material to affirm its viewpoint.

This kind of study enables students to come close to the material. Don't push the class to reach a particular conclusion.

Let the teams present evidence for their viewpoints. Then have the class decide which is the best position. If they can't or don't want to decide, permit this stalemate as an acceptable conclusion.

Shift to the content of the book. What section or portion of the book spoke to the students? If they cluster around a particular section, focus on the study of it. What is it saying or teaching? How does it fit into other parts of the gospel story? How does it relate to the Old Testament? What does the text say to the lives of the students? Does its teaching in some way affect how one lives and thinks?

You might suggest that students produce a creative sermon from the passage. Lead them through the process suggested in the introduction to this series.

SESSION BASED ON 21:4-14

1. Spread out recent newspapers on the floor of the classroom.

2. Place an old fishing net over the newspapers. Anchor the net with bricks or some other items at the corners.

3. Read the story while playing the sounds of the ocean in the background.

4. Ask the students to close their eyes and imagine that they are standing in the water pulling in the fishing net. It is very heavy and they must be careful not to break it.

5. Ask the students to kneel on the net and look at what has been caught. They will see bits and pieces of the news showing through the holes in the net.

6. Encourage them to tear out pieces of news stories that in some way strain and threaten people in the church.

7. Have students share what the net has caught.

8. Write the stories on newsprint.

9. Lift the fishing net from the floor.

10. Have students stand in a circle so that everyone is holding onto part of the fishing net.

11. Read the text once again.

12. Cut a section of the net for each student.

13. Give each person a piece as a symbol of the strength we have in holding our faith together.

SESSION BASED ON 21:15-19

1. Bring a number of popular magazines to the class.

2. Ask the students to tear out ads that mention or reflect on love.

3. Share what the students have found out about love from the ads.

4. Write the definitions of love that emerge from them.

5. If this is a youth class, you might ask students to bring in examples of love themes from pop music and play them on a record player or cassette deck.

6. Read the love dialogue in verses 15-19.

7. Explain that Jesus is using one word for love (agape) and Peter is using another (philos). Scholars differ about the meaning of the passage. However, it does seem clear that Jesus is gently prodding the person who denied him into a deeper understanding of the meaning of love.

8. Have the students take turns reading the dialogue with different inflections on "love."

9. Write out the students' suggestions for the meaning of this word in this context. Note that verses 18-19 refer to Peter's death. It will result from his love for the gospel. This is tough love.

10. Discuss how Christlike love differs from the pop love.

11. Using the ads collected earlier, translate the cheap view of love into Christian love. How would these promises and situations be changed with this love?

12. Invite each student to map out a campaign of Christian love for someone in his or her family. How can we share the kind of love Jesus gives? Focus on one person in the family and deliver this gift of love with sensitivity and care. Have the students share their experiences at a later session.

SESSION BASED ON 21:24-25

This epilogue adds the author's final note. This suggests that Jesus did other things that have not been included in the records of his life and work.

1. Read the text.
2. Ask the students to suggest areas of concern in their lives about which the teachings of Jesus could have been more direct.
3. Write these on newsprint.
4. Ask the students to review the key teachings of Jesus. You may want to suggest passages where such a review could be easily undertaken.
5. Ask them to imagine that they were in the spirit of Christ and had to write the sayings which were not recorded. What would Jesus say to the issues you have listed on the paper? Of course they don't know what Jesus would say. Yet, this experience will draw them into the spirit of Jesus and help them to bring their lives in line with their faith.
6. Ask the students to write new stories about Jesus.
7. Share these new tales about Jesus.
8. Discuss how they would help people in the church.

Creative Speaking and Preaching Ideas

A CLUE FROM 21:1-14

The fishing net is a helpful image when presenting a sermon. Explore the kinds of fishing nets available in your area. If you are lucky, you might be able to find a rugged one. If you live near the sea, collect seashells or seaweed as well.

The net was used by the fishermen of New Testament times. In fact, there were even gladiator events that featured the net. For many Christians, the net became the symbol of evangelism (Matthew 4:19 and parallels).

Place the net on the altar or communion table at the base of the cross or over the cross. You might even combine the net with seashells. Have ushers use offering plates to distribute the shells to the congregation.

Suggest that God calls us to cast our nets into the sea of our culture. Each person caught in the net of the gospel is special.

Ask each worshiper to reflect on his or her shell. Who are some of the people who need to be gathered into the net of the faith? Perhaps some of your people will call out others who have this need.

Have several young people come up and stretch the net. How strong is it? Share the tensions which have always raged within the faith community. You might collect the shells in the net. How much can the net of faith hold in terms of controversy? Have people offer suggestions about the strains in the net of faith. You may be worried about disagreements within your faith community. Don't feel that you have to do battle over such a discussion. You are an instrument of the gospel. Transform the energy into love.

A CLUE FROM 21:9-14

This text has strong eucharistic overtones. It provides a perfect setting for a communion or love feast celebration. You might take the congregation to the beach for breakfast.

Have a simulated charcoal fire set for the center of the worship area. Hold a fishing net as you talk to the worshipers. Tell them that this old net could tell a marvelous story. Speak for the net. Relate what has happened this strange night.

At some point, talk about the many fish that have been trapped. Have ushers pass out the offering plates that have netting placed over them with small fish-shaped cookies on the netting.

Ask each person to take a fish. Encourage people to share their thoughts about the gifts God has given to nourish us. This may be pushing the interpretation in the direction of allegory. However, this type of understanding seems to be encouraged by the text. After they have shared their ideas, invite people to partake of the fish.

A CLUE FROM 21:15-25

This is an excellent text to help explore the implications of calling or vocation. This can apply to church officers, to Christians in their vocations of daily witness and to membership in the church community.

Create a sermon with a structure following the form of the passage. This dialogue almost has the quality of a litany. Jesus asks a question and Peter responds. Then Jesus calls him to service. This refrain is repeated.

You might create a series of carefully crafted (not necessarily written) stories. These vignettes can be drawn from interviews you have conducted with people. They can focus on the ways that your people respond to their call as Christians. The process of talking with your people about the subject of your preaching before the sermon will enrich worship incredibly and assure the worshipers' interest.

After each story segment, lead the congregation through a litany created from recasting the dialogue between Jesus and Peter.

You might ask the people to tell their own stories. They can stand and share a brief account of their work and service. You might want to take your clue from Jesus and conduct a *terse* exchange with each person. This will help give the congregation a sense of vocation in everyday life.

At the end of each exchange, lead the congregation in the litany. It can be printed in the bulletin and triggered by the words, "Jesus says to us: Do you love me?"

Close the sermon experience by summarizing Jesus' warning that discipleship is costly. Have the ushers pass out small red cinnamon candy hearts to worshipers. Ask them to taste this item as a reminder of the love Christ has for us.

A CLUE FROM 21:25

This editorial note provides an interesting clue for your sermon. If Jesus had a ministry of one to three years, he must have said more than was recorded in the Gospels. It is true that we have enough of his life and ministry to base our life of faith. Yet, perhaps the clue of this note can help our people appreciate more fully what we do know about our calling.

Work with a group of people in preparing for this sermon. Search through the four Gospels and the rest of the New Testament to find the material on the life of Jesus. Create a list of moments from his life. You will be looking for the "many . . . things which Jesus did."

Also gather several apocryphal or hidden works concerning Jesus. This material was written much later than the New Testament and was not accepted into the official listing of the inspired books of the Bible. There are several books of this material. Work through these with your group and collect non-canonical stories about Jesus.

Write summaries of the stories about Jesus from both the Bible and other literature and print them on slips of paper. You may want a calligrapher in the congregation to letter the events on parchment-type paper. Print enough so that each person in the worshiping congregation will have a slip.

Open the sermon time with a white robe in your hands. Tell the worshipers that our Lord has been raised from the dead! Suggest that it is time to reflect on his life. How can we tell others about who he was and is? Speculate that this robe saw all of his ministry and has much to tell.

Have ushers pass out the slips of paper, using the offering plates. Talk about the scraps of stories that have been recorded by people who knew Jesus.

Ask people to suggest stories to be included in our message about Jesus. They can look at the ones they have received. Use an overhead projector to write down the suggestions. After someone gives a story, you can dialogue with him or her and bring out the features of the particular story.

Once you have received many contributions, raise the question of how to choose the ones to keep. This will be a rich discussion.

Close with the imperative of the fourth Gospel that we tell the story of Jesus to others. Say something like: "The robe can't really speak. We can't include stories that the witness of the church found unacceptable. (Pick up the Bible.) However, we do have the marvelous story and stories of salvation to be shared."

I realize this model from the fourth Gospel may sound complex. It assumes that you approach preaching as the work of the whole people of God. However, I assure you that the co-leadership of your people in proclaiming the Word will be the most enriching spiritual experience you will have in your ministry. This modest model suggests that a dozen or more people be deeply involved in this one part of worship. At a time when the young (and the old) are staying away from worship or sleeping during liturgy, it is imperative that worship be the work of the people. God, through the Holy Spirit, works as the people of faith gather in communion around the Word.

Glossary

Circle: The setting of a learning experience is very important. The birth of the church (Acts 2) first bubbled forth in a context in which the people of God were gathered in one place. The Greek of the passage suggests that they were physically close together! Intimacy is so important to those seeking to hear the Word of God. This most often unfolds when people are physically gathered together. This means that your circle will have to be formed intentionally. A group of people who are only marginally comfortable with each other will be scattered in their seating as a class or congregation. Draw your people into a circle by having some reason for close proximity. For example, a prayer circle may be naturally created by holding hands. If your students are young and very sensitive to touch, you may want to use a gathering game such as "electricity." This simple game asks the participants to hold hands around a circle. One person squeezes the hand of a person next to him or her. Someone is chosen to stand in the middle and identify the place where the electricity is at a given moment as it moves around the circle. When it is found, the person in the center changes places with the person caught holding the electric current. The strange thing about this game is that there is usually total silence while it is being played.

Clowning: Until the work of Floyd Shaffer and others, we often thought of the clown as a simple entertainer. Theological clowns, however, have discovered a new world of creative possibility for teaching and preaching. The clown is seen as an image for Christ. He or she surrenders self (through white face paint), and lifts up the discipleship qualities and shares these

GLOSSARY 307

with others. Floyd suggests that liturgy be used as the content for a clown experience. There is often a radical transformation in the lives of those who become clowns. They discover the capacity to give love and receive love in a special way. Floyd and I developed a kit that will be helpful: "The Complete Floyd Shaffer Clown Ministry Workshop Kit," available from P.O. Box 12811, Pittsburgh, PA 15241.

Commentaries: The Bible has always attracted commentators. Indeed, perhaps the Bible itself can be seen as a commentary on the life, death and resurrection of Jesus. There are many fine commentaries available. These are important because they witness how the Word of God has worked in the lives of other sisters and brothers in the history of the faith. This testimony protects us from letting our subjective concerns blind us to the eternal message. Always start with the text. First crawl into the passage, book and whole body of the Bible. Then go to the wealth of commentaries. You will find your personal plunge into the passage even richer. I have found these commentaries on the Gospel of John very helpful: American Bible Society: **A Translator's Handbook on The Gospel of John**; Raymond E. Brown: **The Gospel According to John**; Rudolph Bultmann: **The Gospel of John: A Commentary.**

Dancing: See **Liturgical Dancing.**

Debriefing: A role play, mime, creative act (e.g., collages) must be clarified for maximum educational value. Debriefing is a process to help your people understand what has happened, why it happened and how the experience has meaning in their day-to-day living. Ask the people to tell what has happened, what made a point, what new things they've thought about, etc. If a session has been confusing or difficult, debriefing will usually "save" at least some of it.

Exegesis: This term is used in biblical studies to describe the process of "digging out" the meaning of a text. It suggests that we receive its content with an open mind. Exegesis does not encourage projection of personal biases into biblical passages. This process always risks a distortion of the Word as seen through our subjective "lens." Yet, such a task is set before each person of faith.

Gnosticism: See page 23.

Lining Out: See page 60.

Litany: The traditional use of litany has been spoken responses between clergy and worshipers from a prayer book. That is not our use here. We encourage you to use the litany model for lively interactions between people. For example, a living litany can interplay mimed responses to various prayer requests.

Liturgical Dancing: There are over 30 references to dancing in the Bible, none of them with any negative connotation. The use of liturgical dance (dance expression of a faith concept) can be a powerful medium for expressing the Bible. If your tradition allows for liturgical dancing, the best place to start learning it is through your denominational national or regional office. They can provide you with plenty of resources for learning and using this medium. And, check with local ballet dance groups. They may be able to help you.

Mime: People have always known that universal communication can take place between people of different cultures, languages and ages through body language. A complex message can be told with a roll of a shoulder, a flip of the hand or a tilt of the head. Mime is the use of such simple gestures to tell a story. It is an enacted parable. It is very easy for people to learn this kind of communication. You will find particular enjoyment when several people mime a scene as a team.

Morality Plays: The Middle Ages have left the modern person many interesting legacies. One is the communication of the faith to those who could not read. The stories and messages of scripture were presented in the form of plays. These plays were often presented in the open market and in special celebrations. Some of the plays featured characters presenting simple characteristics of life rather than real-life characters. Comedy and other crowd-pleasing techniques were employed to capture attention. It is quite easy to design such works with your people. The popularity of television advertising and common television formats have made allegorical and stereotypical characterization familiar to most modern people. See page 60 for an example of a morality play.

Passing Around: Many of the texts in the Bible suggest an object that can be used to probe the message. It is amazing to look through a concordance to the Bible and note the media objects that are associated with the most moving passages. Indeed, one of the most impressive symbols of the covenant passages in the Old Testament is a stone, set up so that the people remembered their promises to God. In fact, God became flesh (to be touched) in order that we might understand the most deeply spiritual and intellectual moments of human existence. We, therefore, feel that the Bible compels us to draw upon the senses in our faith journey. Don't be afraid to let your people focus their thinking on a stone or a piece of clay. People will always exceed your expectations! We are artifact-gathering, symbol-creating creatures. There is no biblical faith apart from objects of that faith.

Press Conference: There is nothing mysterious about having a press-conference setting in study or worship. The main thing to remember is that a press conference is a dialogue. The interviewers and interviewees exchange questions for answers. You can do this several ways: Set up a long table and a few chairs in the worship center. Set up a microphone in the center or ask people to speak loud enough for all to hear. Or, ask worshipers to raise hands and ask questions.

Readers' Theater: This simple technique asks that the leader select a literary story, a television script or any other written source. The material can be quickly structured with a pencil into a script. Narrative passages become parts for a narrator. Dialogue in a story becomes parts for different readers. Suddenly you have a play in which many of your people can participate! You might stage the readers by arranging stools in a semi-circle with special lighting. Biblical material adapts particularly well to readers' theater.

Role Playing: Psychologists, acting schools and primary Sunday school classes have all used this popular communication technique. The leader needs only to prepare a number of situations that focus on a confrontation between several characters in an ethical and emotional issue. Write out on paper slips the roles or perspectives of each person in the vignette. Give volunteers a slip and ask them to engage each other publicly in the scene you described. As they present the story, they simply speak to each other out of the perspective of the character they are playing. Afterward, debrief with the audience and the actors how they felt about the situations. Did they solve the problem? Why or why not? How could it be done differently? You might have other people play the same scene again. Or, have the actors change roles and do the vignette again.

For further information on creative art forms and media, consult **The Youth Group How-to Book, The Basic Encyclopedia for Youth Ministry** and **Hard Times Catalog for Youth Ministry**. These resources are available from Christian bookstores or Group Books, P.O. Box 481, Loveland, CO 80539.

The Holy Spirit at Work: The Contributors to The Bible Creative

The Holy Spirit draws me to the Word of God. And the Holy Spirit's work in the Bible is through the community of faith. Each member of the faith community, past and present, is chosen by God to celebrate the message of salvation within the fellowship of the faith community.

My own faith journey has celebrated the reality of the Holy Spirit within the faith community. Indeed, **The Bible Creative** is a witness that the Holy Spirit works through a community rather than an individual. **The Bible Creative** is not a solo effort. It is the result of the Holy Spirit's work in my life through incredibly diverse experiences with thousands of unique people. I stand before the Word of God as part of a family that extends back thousands of years. As Joseph Haroutunian first taught me in seminary, I am called not as an individual, but as a person before God. And each person has meaning only in relationship to other persons.

So many people have guided and helped me on my 20-year journey to **The Bible Creative**. Some of the more influential people in my life have been scholars in the academic world, especially in my graduate studies in early church history and New Testament. Floyd Filson, Paul Davies, Norman Perrin and Robert M. Grant have been kind mentors. Each one represents different thrusts in the academic community. Yet their influence has been profound. They jostled my comfortable faith system and pushed me to explore new vistas of possibilities. They also encouraged a healthy skepticism toward "experts" that I carry to this day. For example, it was a chilling experience to sit in Robert Grant's office while he picked my paper apart, line by line, challenging me to prove that my footnotes were more than a loose string of experts'

Schooley, Floyd Shaffer, David Shaheen, Henry Simon, Wesley Taylor, Frank Trotta, William Wakeland.

Dale Goldsmith has been a great help in this project. This New Testament scholar and former squash partner is able to combine the best in scholarship with a deep appreciation for creative biblical proclamation. His terse criticism of this volume has been a great aid in drawing together the worlds of scholarship and creative communication.

My own special relationship with the Gospel of John comes from the years I have spent teaching lay people to read the Greek New Testament. It is a moving moment for the student when he or she is able to read John 3:16 from the Greek for the first time. There are often tears when the student stands before the Word in a new and very special way.

Alfaretta Mason and I started reading Greek together several years ago. This scholar/churchwoman, in her eighth decade, has been the moderator of the largest presbytery of the United Presbyterian Church. She is also one of the keenest exegetes I have known. Alfaretta and I provided our contributors with a working model for drawing out creative ideas for teaching, speaking and preaching. I took their clues from the text and created the form for this series.

If you are interested in contributing to a volume of **The Bible Creative**, please write me at: P.O. Box 12811, Pittsburgh, PA 15241.

guesses. "Don't trust the opinions of even the most lauded scholar to do your thinking for you, including mine," he said.

I battled through reading examinations in seven languages and found hours of joy and frustration in unpointed Hebrew and scraps of Greek papyri. Yet academic pursuits found new and delightful challenges when I combined them with the simple, but demanding, vigors of experiential communication.

My life has also seen many exciting challenges outside of academic towers. It has been my joy to teach New Testament Greek and exegesis at McCormick Theological Seminary, work as a chaplain in the children's hospital, pastor a suburban church, direct several youth groups, serve as chaplain of a small college and direct radio and television production for a Catholic/Protestant agency. I've authored over a dozen books, taught Greek to lay people, done theological clowning, written films, produced nationally syndicated radio programs, edited media newsletters and hosted radio talk shows. These years found me marching for civil rights with Martin Luther King, Jr., interviewing over 350 rock stars, leading scores of workshops and retreats, praying with dying cancer patients and seriously studying karate.

But the most moving and meaningful part of my journey to **The Bible Creative** has been the "cottage ministry" with my wife and co-worker, Marilyn. From our home we have enabled and encouraged thousands of diverse brothers and sisters around the world to share their creative ministries with others. These gentle people are members of our "recycle" community. They are the co-creators of **The Bible Creative**. They are people who so love the gospel and people that they will risk of themselves in order to bring the two together in an authentic and creative relationship.

The contributors to this volume include David H. Barnes, Jim Bell, Roger Boekenhauer, James Boos, Henk Bossers, Steve Brewer, Don Chichester, Ron Clark, Ronald Creager, Fred Dickerson, Fred Doscher, Darrell Faires, Sr., Bud Frimoth, Lenore Frimoth, Paul Graves, Dan Griggs, Paul Gysan, Larry Hauder, Raymond Heist, Skip Herbert, Jack High, Dave Holmes, Charles Holsinger, James Huffstutler, Gary Jenkins, Toni Johnson, Russ Jolly, David Keller, Jean Lersch, Phil Lersch, Al Lustie, Mardie MacDonald, E. Jane Mall, Ray Mendenhall, Tim Morrison, Bonnie Munson, Lynn Potter, John Rawlinson, Henry Sawatzky, Christopher